Therapeutic Practice in Sc

This book is an indispensible guide to providing therapy services for children and adolescents in primary and secondary schools settings. The contributors have extensive experience in the field and carefully examine every aspect of the work, ranging from developing an understanding of the school context in all its complexity, through to what to say and do in challenging therapy sessions and in meetings with school staff or parents and carers.

Therapeutic Practice in Schools opens with an overview of key psychoanalytic concepts informing therapy practice. This is followed by a detailed exploration of the hopes and anxieties raised by providing therapy in schools, the factors that either enable or impede the therapist's work and how to manage expectations as well as measure outcomes. The practical aspects of delivering therapy sessions are also covered, from the initial assessment phase through recognising and working with anxieties, defences, transference and countertransference to working with endings. An awareness of the impact of social identity, gender, race and culture on both the therapist and client is woven throughout the book and is also discussed in depth in a dedicated chapter.

The manual offers a comprehensive yet highly readable guide to the complex world of school-based therapy. It provides practical examples of how therapists translate theory into everyday language that can be understood by their young clients, ensuring that trainees starting a placement in schools, as well as therapists beginning work in the educational setting for the first time, are enabled to take up their role with confidence.

Lyn French is an art therapist, counsellor and psychoanalytic psychotherapist. As a Director of A Space for Creative Learning and Support, Hackney, East London, she supervises trainee and qualified therapists and manages school-based services. She also teaches on the MSc in counselling and psychotherapy with children and adolescents at Birkbeck College, University of London.

Reva Klein is a psychodynamic psychotherapist working with children and adolescents and an adult psychoanalytic psychotherapist. She works as a counsellor with children, adolescents and school staff at A Space for Creative Learning and Support, Hackney, East London.

Therapeutic Practice in Schools

Working with the child within: a clinical workbook for counsellors, psychotherapists and arts therapists

Edited by Lyn French and Reva Klein

Routledge
Taylor & Francis Group
LONDON AND NEW YORK

First published 2012
by Routledge
27 Church Road, Hove, East Sussex BN3 2FA

Simultaneously published in the USA and Canada
by Routledge
711 Third Avenue, New York NY 10017

Routledge is an imprint of the Taylor & Francis Group, an Informa business

© 2012 selection and editorial matter, Lyn French and Reva Klein; individual chapters, the contributors

The right of the editors to be identified as the authors of the editorial material, and of the authors for their individual chapters, has been asserted in accordance with sections 77 and 78 of the Copyright, Designs and Patents Act 1988.

All rights reserved. No part of this book may be reprinted or reproduced or utilised in any form or by any electronic, mechanical, or other means, now known or hereafter invented, including photocopying and recording, or in any information storage or retrieval system, without permission in writing from the publishers.

Trademark notice: Product or corporate names may be trademarks or registered trademarks, and are used only for identification and explanation without intent to infringe.

British Library Cataloguing in Publication Data
A catalogue record for this book is available from the British Library

Library of Congress Cataloging in Publication Data
Therapeutic practice in schools : working with the child within : a clinical workbook for counsellors, psychotherapists, and arts therapists / edited by Lyn French and Reva Klein.
    p.; cm.
  Includes bibliographical references and index.
   ISBN 978-0-415-59790-6 (hbk. : alk. paper)—
 ISBN 978-0-415-59791-3 (pbk. : alk. paper)—
 ISBN 978-0-203-80615-9 (ebk) 1. Child psychotherapy. 2. Counseling in secondary education.
I. French, Lyn, 1958– II. Klein, Reva, 1951–
  [DNLM: 1. Psychotherapy—methods. 2. Adolescent.
3. Child. 4. Counseling—methods. 5. Schools. WS 350.2]
   RJ504.T474 2011
   618.92'8914—dc22
                                                                2011005714

ISBN: 978-0-415-59790-6 (hbk)
ISBN: 978-0-415-59791-3 (pbk)
ISBN: 978-0-203-80615-9 (ebk)

Typeset in Times New Roman
by RefineCatch Limited, Bungay, Suffolk

Paperback cover design by Aubergine Design
Cover image © Neeta Madahar **Sky, Seeds and Me**, 2005
Courtesy of the artist and The Institute of International Visual Arts (**iniva**)

Printed and bound in Great Britain by TJ International, Padstow, Cornwall

Contents

Contributors viii
Foreword xi
Acknowledgements xiii
List of abbreviations xiv

Introduction 1
LYN FRENCH AND REVA KLEIN

PART I
Key psychoanalytic concepts as applied to work with children and adolescents 5

1 **Theoretical framework** 7
   SUE KEGERREIS

2 **Recognising defences, resistance and anxieties** 19
   DAVID TREVATT

3 **Transference and counter-transference** 28
   HILARY ANN SALINGER

4 **Observing and interpreting** 36
   JENNY DOVER

PART II
Working in schools: the context 51

5 **The symbolic function of a school-based therapy service** 53
   LYN FRENCH

6	Working in the primary school setting REVA KLEIN	60
7	Working in the secondary school setting STEFANIA PUTZU-WILLIAMS	67

PART III
Practical approaches to the work **77**

8	Preparing the room CAMILLA WALDBURG	79
9	The referral process CAMILLA WALDBURG	90
10	The assessment process STEFANIA PUTZU-WILLIAMS	99
11	Meeting with parents or carers REVA KLEIN	113
12	Meeting with teachers and other school staff ANGIE DORAN	124
13	Informing the child or young person about the first session LYN FRENCH	131
14	The first session REVA KLEIN	142
15	Working with difference AKIN OJUMU	152
16	Managing the therapeutic frame REVA KLEIN	164
17	Working with school staff ANGIE DORAN	170

18	The ending process LYN FRENCH	187

PART IV
Monitoring and evaluation   199

19	Writing case notes STEFANIA PUTZU-WILLIAMS	201
20	Identifying the impact of therapy services in schools LYN FRENCH	207
	Afterword LYN FRENCH AND REVA KLEIN	230
	Index	233

Contributors

Angie Doran works as a counsellor in both secondary and primary schools for A Space for Creative Learning and Support. She is also the lead researcher on a joint PhD research project set up by A Space with University of Essex (Centre for Psychoanalytic Studies) focusing on how assessment and evaluation are conducted in school-based therapy services. She received an MSc in Psychodynamic Counselling with Children and Adolescents from Birkbeck College, University of London.

Jenny Dover is a senior educational psychotherapist who has worked in CAMHS in inner London for 24 years since training as an educational psychotherapist at the Tavistock Clinic. She also teaches on the MA at the Caspari Foundation and, as well as contributing to a range of journals, co-authored with Gillian Salmon, *Reaching and Teaching Through Educational Psychotherapy*, published in 2007 (John Wiley).

Lyn French is an art therapist, counsellor and psychoanalytic psychotherapist. She was one of the original team members contracted in 1997 to set up A Space for Creative Learning and Support, a partnership between Alex Sainsbury (Sainsbury Family Charitable Trusts), the Social Science Research Unit (Institute of Education, University of London) and Hackney Education. She has been the Director since 2000 and continues to oversee service delivery across Hackney schools as well as designing research and publishing projects. A Space is running a research project with the University of Essex (Centre for Psychoanalytic Studies), which she is leading on behalf of A Space. A long-term partnership with the Institute of International Visual Arts (iniva) brings artists into A Space to work in collaboration with art therapists. Out of this work, Lyn co-designed two sets of emotional learning cards with iniva, which are sold internationally: *What do you feel?* and *Who are you? Where are you going?* She is a sessional lecturer on the Birkbeck College MSc Course in Counselling with Children and Adolescents.

Sue Kegerreis is Senior Lecturer at the Centre for Psychoanalytic Studies at the University of Essex, where she is Programme Lead for the Foundation Degree Therapeutic Communication and Therapeutic Organisations. She trained as a teacher, as a child and adolescent psychotherapist at the Tavistock Clinic and later as an adult psychoanalytic psychotherapist with the Lincoln. She has practised in a range of settings: hospital, CAMHS and privately and worked for many years as a school counsellor, as well as teaching on many courses, both clinical and applied. She has published widely in professional journals and her book *Psychodynamic Counselling with Children and Adolescents* was published in 2010 (Palgrave Macmillan). She originated and was course director of the MSc Psychodynamic Counselling with Children and Adolescents at Birkbeck College.

Reva Klein is working as a counsellor with children, adolescents and school staff at A Space. A freelance journalist for over thirty years, Reva is the author of three books on education, *Defying Disaffection* (Trentham, 1999), *Citizens by Right* (Save the Children, 2001) and *We Want our Say* (Trentham, 2003), and co-author of *Reluctant Refuge: The Story of Asylum in Britain* (British Library, 2008). She twice won the Commission for Racial Equality's Race in the Media Award for her writing in the *Times Educational Supplement*, for which she was a regular contributor and columnist. She was shortlisted for the NASEN award for her first book, *Defying Disaffection*. She founded and edited *The International Journal on School Disaffection*, an Anglo-American publication now in its ninth year. She sat on the Secondary School Reform Committee of UNESCO in the late 1990s and taught journalism at Goldsmiths College for 15 years.

Akin Ojumu is a school counsellor at A Space working with children and adolescents. He is training as a Child and Adolescent Psychotherapist with the BAP. Prior to this, he completed the MSc in Child and Adolescent Counselling at Birkbeck College while working as an arts editor on the *Observer*. Akin has a long history in journalism and has published many articles, including one on the role of black fathers ('As a Father, Why I Fear for my Son', *Observer*, 20 July 2008). He continues to write and publish as a freelance journalist while working at A Space and training in child psychotherapy.

Stefania Putzu-Williams completed her first degree in psychology at Rome University before receiving an MA in Psychoanalytic Observational Studies at the Tavistock Clinic and University College London and an MSc in Psychodynamic Counselling at Birkbeck College. After writing a thesis on child abuse in the UK, she began specialising in the care of children and young people and has worked therapeutically since 1989. From in-depth experience including residential assessment of high-risk families prior to Family Court decisions, she has developed expertise as a counsellor in community and school-based projects (since 2003 within CAMHS), and for the past three years also as a counsellor at Bacon's College in Southwark. She is developing a framework for school counsellors.

Hilary Ann Salinger works as a child and adolescent psychotherapist in the South London and Maudesley NHS Trust and Lewisham CAMHS. She is also senior tutor on the MSc in Psychodynamic Counselling and Psychotherapy with Children and Adolescents at the School of Psychosocial Studies, Birkbeck College. She previously worked as a teacher and head teacher at a school for children with emotional and behavioural difficulties before training at the Tavistock Clinic as a psychoanalytic psychotherapist. She also supervises and teaches staff working in government mental health provision for children and young people in Cape Town, South Africa.

David Trevatt is a consultant child and adolescent psychotherapist and co-director of Open Door, a centre for young people aged 12 to 24 and their parents in Haringey, North London. He is also clinical manager of Hear and Now, an adolescent counselling service in the North East London Foundation Trust of the NHS and Clinical Consultant to A Space. He trained at the Tavistock Clinic and previously worked as a social worker and probation officer in different settings, including several CAMHS teams. He is engaged in research on the Open Door brief approach to working with parents of adolescents, which will be published as a manual for professionals in the near future.

Camilla Waldburg has been the Development Officer for support services at A Space since 2001 and is also working as a clinical practitioner within the reclaim social work model in the London Borough of Hackney. Following on from a degree in psychology, she trained in play therapy at Roehampton University and has developed the play therapy service at A Space, where she now supervises trainees. She has a postgraduate diploma in systemic practice with families and couples and is working towards an MSc in systemic psychotherapy with families and couples. In parallel, she is developing the family consultation service at A Space.

Foreword

Schools are special places filled with all kinds of possibilities. The potential of children is at stake and teachers work hard to cultivate children's minds to equip them to take their place in the world ahead of them. This is no easy undertaking and all concerned struggle to get things right. But, even on a bad day, something new becomes possible for most.

Teaching is the main name of the game in a school – and when all goes well, that's enough. But inevitably difficulties arise along the way. Children vary a great deal in their capabilities and talents and in the experiences they bring to school from their homes and neighbourhoods. Teachers then have to face the challenge of meeting the often quite bewildering needs of their pupils. All teachers, no matter how well their schools are run, can well do with support in helping them carry out their basic tasks.

Psychotherapy for children is one such form of support. There are many different psychotherapies, but the kind of psychotherapy developed in this book is essentially psychodynamic and exploratory. In many ways, it is an activity that does not sit comfortably with that of teaching – it is more reflective than instructional or directive. And yet it joins teaching in its fundamental purpose of enabling children to learn and develop. This book shows how.

It throws light on the great care taken in psychotherapy to help children make sense of their difficulties. Unlike many psychotherapists, who are accustomed to practising in settled clinical settings, the psychotherapists in this book work in the lively and busy atmosphere of schools. They take their place alongside teachers, fitting in as best they can with the 'myriad intricacies' of timetables, curricula and other teaching preoccupations.

Explaining what psychotherapists do is not always straightforward. Most people and many teachers have only a hazy idea of what goes on and, all too readily, are inclined to conclude that whatever it may be cannot be too difficult – just sitting and talking, or, in the case of children, just playing. This, of course, is far from the case and the book spells out why. As its subtitle indicates, the task of the whole enterprise of psychotherapy is to enter 'the child within' in order to free the child to relate and learn with his or her peers. This, to put it mildly, is complicated and requires a particular discipline.

The theoretical foundation for this discipline is psychoanalysis with its sure appreciation of the power of the unconscious and the force of anxiety and fantasy in affecting relationships and attitudes. The psychotherapy explained in this book is a working psychoanalysis. It is not fanciful. And it makes demands on psychotherapists to conduct themselves in ways that foster the developing process of children as they discover things about themselves. To do this properly, these professionals need to be observant, open minded and consistent. They need to be able to play and at the same time be receptive to the child's communications. Their sensitivity to the meanings of a child's communications is crucial. So too is their self-awareness, which must ensure that they do not intrude unnecessarily into the child's world or react impulsively or over-defensively to the ways a child might express his or her feelings

This book will be of unique value to anyone seriously interested in understanding children. It will be especially valuable to practitioners and trainees working psychotherapeutically with children. The contributors to this book clearly know their business and write with clarity about what they do and what they think can be most helpful. Numerous case examples, vignettes, forms of words and questions for learning demonstrate clearly how psychotherapy can help both children and schools.

Peter Wilson
Founder, Young Minds
and Clinical Advisor for The Place 2 Be

Acknowledgements

We are indebted to A Space for Creative Learning and Support, a project set up in 1997 by Alex Sainsbury in partnership with the Social Science Research Unit at the Institute of Education, University of London and Hackney Education for providing the context for this book. A Space has expanded significantly since then, offering therapeutic services and specialist projects to primary and secondary schools across Hackney.

We would also like to thank all the trainee therapists from postgraduate courses at Birkbeck College (University of London), Roehampton Institute (University of Surrey) and University of Hertfordshire, who have taken up placements at A Space with enthusiasm, dedication and a wish to learn more. As well, we would like to acknowledge the many teachers and school staff who have welcomed and supported therapists working with their pupils; and of course we are grateful to the children and young people who have had the courage, willingness and motivation to use school-based therapy services.

Numerous individuals have made publishing this book possible. In particular, we would like to acknowledge the significant contributions of Alex and Elinor Sainsbury of The Glass-House Trust (a Sainsbury Family Charitable Trust) and Nicola Baboneau, the Chair of A Space.

Abbreviations

ADHD	Attention Deficit Hyperactivity Disorder
BAP	British Association of Psychotherapists
BBC	British Broadcasting Corporation
CAMHS	Child and Adolescent Mental Health Services
CP	child protection
GCSE	General Certificate of Secondary Education
iniva	Institute of International Visual Arts
INSET	IN-SErvice Training (for teachers)
IQ	intelligence quotient
LSA	learning support assistant
NASEN	National Association for Special Education Needs
NHS	National Health Service
NSPCC	National Society for the Prevention of Cruelty to Children
PSHE	Personal, Social, Health and Economic (education)
SENCo	Special Education Needs Coordinator
UNESCO	United Nations Educational, Scientific and Cultural Organization

Introduction

Lyn French and Reva Klein

All therapists working in the education sector have had to go through the experience of starting their first school-based role either as a qualified therapist new to the educational setting or else on placement as a trainee psychotherapist, counsellor, creative therapist (art, drama and music therapists) or play therapist. Writing and editing this book offered us the opportunity to look back on our first experiences of engaging in the complex and multifaceted business of working in primary and secondary schools. We remember very clearly how daunting the prospect was. We recall wondering how we could be taken seriously as professionals by head teachers, governors, staff and parents or carers – never mind pupils – when we ourselves were not only finding our feet as therapists but were also new to the school setting. Additionally, we've both had school-based posts where we were launching the service as sole practitioners linked to an external agency, with no co-workers on-site to check things out with or with whom to share impressions, anxieties and successes.

It is useful and even, perhaps, essential, to navigate one's way through 'start-up' anxieties in order to test out and build one's internal resources. By providing a detailed description of the tasks involved in taking up the role and suggesting guidelines for practice, we do not aim to do away with these anxieties. Instead, we think of it in a similar vein to that of a new mother who can use parenting manuals to help her reflect on her role and on what might be demanded of her without detracting from the complex and rich experience of interacting with her newborn. So too, we hope, will this book provide support for the trainee or qualified psychotherapist, counsellor or creative therapist new to working in schools, without detracting from the uniqueness of each new relationship entered into with clients and with the organisations in which they find themselves.

We all, no matter what our age, carry with us memories of our own school experiences – conscious and repressed, positive and negative. The mere whiff of chalk or chlorine can be enormously evocative, hurtling us, rather like Proust and his madeleines, back to our primary school classroom on a warm spring day or a less than joyous school swimming lesson in the local pool. Many decades on, Sunday nights can still induce a sinking feeling at the memory of hastily finished homework and packing schoolbags in preparation for a new week.

As well as memories, we all – whether parents/carers, school staff, policy makers or therapists – will have conscious and unconscious assumptions, fantasies, associations and beliefs about what schools 'should be' or 'should aspire to be', often formed in reaction to our own experiences. For some, school days will have been the best years of their lives, while for others they will have been precisely the opposite. For some, the fact that we work in schools will reflect a desire for reparation: for ourselves and for children present and future.

Working in schools is rewarding, compelling, frustrating, challenging and so much more than working in a room with a child. It is about being aware of the desires, fears, anxieties, hopes, fantasies and projections that emanate from every person in the organisation: from the lunchtime supervisors to office staff to caretaker to support staff to teachers to senior management and to all the children who are not being referred for therapy as well as those who are. It is about developing an awareness of how we as therapists are perceived and interacted with in our everyday work. It is about developing an understanding of the conscious and unconscious forces at work in how the organisation functions. It is, in a nutshell, an endlessly fascinating microcosm in which to work.

Many school practitioners deliver a range of services in addition to individual work with children or adolescents, such as psycho-educational groups for selected pupils or, in whole-class settings, parent/carer support groups, and work discussion groups or consultation sessions for school staff. Qualified therapists may also give policy advice to management, contribute to safeguarding or child protection procedures and protocols, offer training sessions for staff, run peer support or buddy schemes for pupils, speak about emotional well-being at assemblies, and so forth. However, this book limits itself to a detailed exploration of the therapist's defining role: that of offering one-to-one sessions on a weekly basis to referred pupils. This reflects the fact that our work with children and adolescents involves not only learning a therapeutic language but also making it accessible to younger clients. The practice-based chapters to follow cover all the related tasks including liaising with staff and parents/carers, informing the child or young person, conducting the initial assessment, thinking about the first session, working with difference and working through endings. Uniquely, most of these chapters includes vignettes that illustrate the kind of language one might use when talking to a teacher, parent/carer or young person. There are opportunities as well for readers to try to formulate their own response before looking at the suggested replies provided by chapter authors.

As therapists, the relationship we establish with our client is our primary tool. How clients perceive and interact with us provides vital information about their internal world and attachment patterns. A key developmental task for us all is learning to identify, contain and work with the primitive and everyday anxieties that are inevitably aroused by the very process of forming and sustaining relationships. This applies not only to our work with our clients but also to forming partnerships with the schools in which we provide services.

Whether or not a school therapist is taking up a role in a long-established service or introducing a new provision, acknowledging the anxieties inherent in the task and trying to understand the unconscious forces at play is necessary. Fortunately, it is also tremendously stimulating. All therapeutic work triggers a range of anxieties. Most notably, at the start of our professional training it is likely that we will wonder whether or not we have sufficient internal resources to provide clients with a 'good enough' experience. Working with children and adolescents is particularly anxiety-provoking, as they are among society's most vulnerable groups.

In addition, schools generate their own particular anxieties and institutional dynamics that need to be mindfully navigated. Schools may start by viewing their therapy service through the unconscious filter of a positive transference or, conversely, one that is more negative in quality. This will inevitably continue to shift over time in subtle or obvious ways, depending on the dominant preoccupations of the school at any given period.

All schools work under numerous – and often seemingly relentless – pressures arising from different sources. Teachers may bring to the job their own deeply felt commitment to make a difference and to enable pupils to fulfil their potential. This can be transformed from a motivating belief into a driving pressure to succeed when it is accompanied by, for example, an unconscious urge such as wishing to make up for what they feel they themselves missed out on or, conversely, had more than their fair share of. Head teachers will want their school to be one that everyone is proud of. A healthy need to achieve can become stressful when unconscious rivalry and competition enter the frame, perhaps fed by a government agenda that is seen to push targets ever higher. Rather than being stimulated by the challenge, school staff can feel persecuted by what may be experienced as over-ambitious demands and an unrealistic timeline.

Trainees placed in schools or therapists choosing to work in the educational sector are entering a complex field. The authors contributing to this book, each with extensive experience of working in the educational context, draw from their own learning experiences and from their work in schools, translating complicated realities and sophisticated analytic concepts into accessible language that clarifies rather than simplifies.

As will be evident, some of the themes covered move across more than one chapter. We hope that rather than being repetitive, revisiting some of the key ideas demonstrates how useful it is to review our practice from different perspectives and to think about how the external environment in which we work can shift along a spectrum, at times enabling, at others impeding therapeutic processes. As therapists, our work is enriched through the use of supervision, case discussion seminars and sounding things out with professional peers. These chapters reflect these processes, providing a range of voices and viewpoints, each offering its own 'take' on themes that necessarily overlap.

The expectation that public services will be both monitored and evidence-based has been filtering through to the field of psychoanalytically informed therapies. One of our aims is to show that the need to be more rigorous in how we think about our practice and its outcomes *can* sit comfortably alongside the actual work we do with children and young people. In fact, writing reports, liaising with other professionals and creating a structure for evaluating our service will enhance and sharpen our thinking about what goes on in the consulting room rather than detract from or distract us from our central tasks.

By offering a framework and practical guidance designed to enable therapists to fulfil their roles as professionals working within schools, we aim to demystify aspects of our work. At the same time we have set out to illuminate the transference and many layers of meaning that staff, parents and our clients themselves bring to their understanding of who we are and what we do. It is only by defining more clearly the boundary and scope of our practice, as well as the complex context in which we work, that we can become better equipped to take up the authority invested in our role appropriately and sensitively.

If there's nothing simple about working as therapists in schools, we have at least tried to simplify the terminology somewhat. The terms 'therapist' and 'therapy' are used throughout, rather than 'counsellor' and 'counselling', in order to cover the spectrum of trainees and professionals being addressed. Only when it aids understanding will the therapist or therapy be referred to by a specific discipline (e.g. art therapist or play therapist). Children and adolescents are assigned male gender for simplification and both are referred to as *children* unless the meaning of the text depends on differentiating between the two. Therapists are assigned a feminine gender, again for simplification, although this also reflects the general gender imbalance of school-based therapists. 'Parents and carers' are used in headings and subheadings but abbreviated in the body of the text to 'parents' for brevity's sake.

The book is divided into four main sections. Part I covers key psychoanalytic concepts as they apply to work with children and adolescents. Through exploring the context of both the primary and secondary school sectors, Part II sets the scene for discussing school-based services. Part III comprises the 'tool kit', outlining in some detail practical approaches to the work. Part IV offers nuts and bolts guidance on record keeping, writing case notes and evaluating the service we provide. Throughout, study questions, study guides and vignettes are provided to aid learning, reflection and reviewing of one's practice in general. The tools we suggest are not exhaustive: they are best viewed as a starting point for thinking about how the school therapist might approach the work. A key task for all trainees is to learn the language of therapy. This book sets out the 'vocabulary' and 'basic grammar' required to take up the role of school therapist with integrity, compassion and the desire to learn more.

Part I

Key psychoanalytic concepts as applied to work with children and adolescents

Chapter 1

Theoretical framework

Sue Kegerreis

Why do we need theory?

All school therapists need theoretical underpinning for their work. This sounds like an obvious and unnecessary statement, but it needs to be given thought. It could be argued that the key elements in a good school therapist are the capacity to connect well with children and to offer a well-intentioned, supportive presence. Some might fear that too much theory could get between the child and us. It is true that all of us can use theory as something to hide behind, or as a way of avoiding our own vulnerability and anxiety in encounters with our clients. There is a danger that we might impose our theories on the children, seeing them as embodiments of what we have learned about, rather than as the unique and necessarily puzzling individuals they are. We might see what we expect to see and 'understand' what we expect to find. Most importantly, if the theory is in the front of our minds and too much the focus of our interest, then we could avoid a real meeting with the child; the encounter is then rendered at best sterile and at worst provocative or unhelpful.

However, we all have theories, about how the children's difficulties began, or about how we could intervene in a helpful way. We cannot operate at all if we have no underlying idea about what is wrong or what might make a difference. Even without any training or specific orientation, there will be theories in our intellectual arsenal. Moreover, our capacity to connect with the emotional reality of the child and thereafter to offer helpful interventions will be affected by the quality of the theories we are using. Theory is a means to make our perceptions clearer, our connections more meaningful and a way of enabling us to get closer to the child in all his complexity.

What is even more powerful is the role theory can have in making us more resilient, as it makes the children we work with more comprehensible to us. It enables us to better manage their impact on us and to continue working with them when things get difficult. Theory can give us tools to decipher what is going on, to process how the children affect us, and to use all the experiences they give us to enable us to become more finely tuned to them, equipping us to offer them something usable and useful. It can stop us prematurely foreclosing on our ability to offer something to them and it can stop us from simply reacting or even retaliating because we do not understand.

This says something about how theory needs to be situated; it needs to sit at the back of our mind rather than in the front, allowing us to be fully present in each session, but there as a resource to call on to inform our thinking and help us steer ourselves and our work more accurately.

What is particular about the psychodynamic perspective?

Psychodynamic therapy in schools has its theoretical roots in psychoanalytic child psychotherapy, which itself is an adaptation of psychoanalysis. There are many ways of trying to describe the core elements of this approach, so although the ideas I have chosen to illustrate it here are indeed central, they constitute only one possible constellation of key concepts. I will focus on **the unconscious, the importance of early experience** and the **use of the relationship in the therapy room**. These will provide a foundation for the potential exploration of more complex and subtle thinking in the vast and ever-growing literature. Psychoanalysis is the rootstock for the theory, but grafted onto it are many other layers of understanding as psychodynamic practitioners explore their field and extend their thinking through learning from their clients.

The unconscious

The first and most fundamental principle behind all psychoanalytic and psychodynamic thinking is that all human beings have an unconscious, which is hugely influential in shaping our perceptions, our relationships and our responses to experience. We are able to make conscious choices, of course, but are heavily influenced in everything we do, say and feel by elements of which we have no conscious awareness. We are only intermittently and partially in touch with all that motivates us; what is more, we are only intermittently and partially aware of our true feelings at any given time.

This has many levels. On a level relatively close to consciousness, we may be aware of one kind of thought or feeling, but are breathtakingly capable of deceiving ourselves about what we think and feel, in ways that can seriously lead us astray. We may hide with contempt or critical responses the fact that we are envious or scared; we can hide our need for others in spurious superiority; or we can get angry when we are feeling loss or hurt deep down. We can pretend that we don't want something when really we fear it is out of reach or we are not worthy of it. Brearley has spoken eloquently on this kind of self-deception (2010). We can simplify what we see and feel, as in idealising someone or seeing them as simply bad, in order to avoid conflict and ambivalence.

At a deeper level, our perceptions, relationships and choices are fundamentally affected in an ongoing way by patterns that have been established in our minds.

We do not see things as they are, whatever that may mean; our vision is distorted by a complex amalgam of what we have made of our experiences and our emotional state then and now. We can be compelled, despite our best conscious intentions, to repeat patterns. We may find ourselves in similar relationships with partners: being disappointed in the same ways or being abused or neglected just like before; or we might repeatedly find ourselves, for example, overburdened and taken for granted at home or in work, find ourselves with a contemptuous boss, or outshone by a colleague. These are not just unhappy coincidences; they are the result of unconscious dynamics that lead us to seek out and create repetitions of emotionally familiar situations in which we construct well-known, even if hated, situations and relationships.

Or we may deceive ourselves about where a feeling belongs. For example, when Jan (17) is anxious about her boyfriend's loyalty and becomes jealous and intrusive she may be hiding from herself the awareness that *she* is having doubts about *him* or fantasies about another relationship. When Kemal (14) is feeling hostile and critical of those around him, what he may experience consciously is that people are being hostile and critical towards him. This may of course be grounded in reality; but even if not, he may experience this because he is attributing to others a feeling or quality that is being disowned in himself. One of the clearest examples of this dynamic (in psychoanalytic terms known as **projection**) was humorously portrayed in the late 1990s BBC sitcom *The Royle Family*. Denise was always palming off the care of her child onto others out of supreme laziness. Yet her brother Anthony, who was far more conscientious and helpful both to himself and others, was the one labelled lazy a great deal of the time. In fact Denise would complain indignantly if he hesitated for a moment when asked to look after little Dave – 'Anthony, he's your only nephew!' – missing entirely any awareness of her *own* laziness and neglect of her only son. By projecting her laziness onto Anthony, she attributed to him what she failed to notice or do anything about in respect to herself.

As mentioned, patterns of relating have been laid down by our previous experiences and get repeated. Mariam (13), who has been rejected at home, finds herself over and over again acting in such a way as to make it likely she will continue to be rejected, despite the fact that this is the last thing she apparently wants. Milo (10), who has felt it was his job to keep his mum going, will find himself repeatedly in that supportive role at school or with other adults, despite his wish to be with adults who do not require this of him. Our unconscious manifests itself in all aspects of our lives, from the largest-scale of our experiences – the jobs we are in, the roles we play, the partnerships we establish or fail to establish – to the smallest: the pictures we draw, the tunes we hum absent-mindedly, the books or films we like and dislike, what we forget, how we dress and the way we fiddle with our pens.

What this means is that the unconscious roots of our characters and behaviours are not only immediate responses to the present, but in many cases can be tracked back to their origins in our earlier experiences. This takes us on to the second of the key ideas I am putting forward as a fundamental theoretical foundation.

The importance of early experience

This second related key idea is the fundamental importance of early experiences. What is most powerfully at work in our unconscious is laid down in our first days, weeks and months. Certainly the first three years of life are crucial in creating templates that then have the power to give shape to all that comes later, for both good and ill (Karr-Morse and Wiley 1999; J. Klein 1987; M. Klein 1959). Our characters are forged out of the unique combination of what we bring in ourselves (of which more later) and the environment into which we are born and that surrounds us as we start out in life. Good experiences later in life can repair early damage just as trauma can challenge those who have had a good start, but the early foundations have great power to affect how we experience and behave throughout our lives.

Babies are born only partly 'made' – the key ingredients are there but there is a long way to go before they take the shape they will have for the rest of their lives. Recent neurological research has brought new awareness of the unique plasticity of the human brain and of the way in which our long dependency period in early childhood provides us with experiences that radically affect the neurological and hormonal systems that govern our cognitive and emotional responses to the world (Schore 2002, 2003; Gerhardt 2004; Music 2010). We may each be born with differences in our capacity to manage frustration or to engage readily with the outside world as well as in such physical factors as our ease of digestion or of gaining physical control of our bodies. But major elements – such as our capacity to regulate our own emotional responses or our ability to resist being overwhelmed by stress and anxiety – have their origins in how we are treated and the extent to which we are helped to manage the vicissitudes of being very small and helpless.

We start out with our genetic heritage but are also much affected by our pre-birth environment and experiences (Piontelli 1992) and the actual events of our birth (Waddell 2002). Furthermore the circumstances of our conception, the experience our parents had of the pregnancy and of the process of delivery have considerable impact on how we are welcomed into the world, even before we have had a chance to bring our own contribution into the mix. Once we are born, an utterly unique process of interaction begins; each of us will have our own impact on those caring for us and the emotional environment in which we find ourselves. The complex tapestry of relationships that surrounds us, that shapes, colours and flavours our personal world, has an enormous influence on how we experience and relate to what life brings, both to our significant others and, underlying and behind all of this, to ourselves. This consists of more than just how we are treated: each family in subtle ways creates its unique emotional repertoire and atmosphere.

It needs to be stressed that this is a two-way process as, in the other direction, each of us has our own impact on those caring for us. It is never the case that a 'blank page' of an infant is passively imprinted on by his parents and family. Some babies can by their temperament and nature bring out the best in their mothers, helping them find the strength in themselves and building their self-esteem. Others can bring out the worst, tapping into their mothers' anxieties and undermining their capacity to feel nurturing and capable. Each nursing couple is different and a mother who could do well with one baby might not do so well with another.

A mother who is secure in herself and well supported will react in a particular way if paired with a baby who has an uncomfortable start and cannot easily cope with being outside in the world. She will, most of the time, be able to remain patient when he is hard to comfort or difficult to feed, gently helping him develop resources to cope with his new and alien environment, offering a calm and understanding response to his anxieties without experiencing him too much as a judgement or a punishment. She will be able to tune in to his feelings and give his experiences meaning. In contrast, a mother who is insecure and unhappy for whatever reason may easily be tipped into a vicious circle of persecutory feelings, experiencing herself as hopeless in the face of the baby's difficulties and therefore rapidly running out of resources to cope with his physical demands – let alone connect with his feelings or offer him helpful meaning-making.

The same mother, if blessed with a baby who is ready to meet the world and is endowed with a lust for life, ease of digestion and a forgiving temperament, may find that he brings out the best in her and puts in motion some major reparative emotional dynamics, reassuring her of her creativity and goodness. But even the most well-adjusted and generously supported mother may find herself unable to cope with a particularly difficult or rejecting baby.

Beyond these very early dynamics, the family of each child creates a unique environment that will for ever shape him in a multitude of ways, exerting its force on his character and relationships and open up an emotional repertoire that is particular to them. The family will greatly affect the child's capacity to be in touch with reality, to face and manage pain and difficulty in his life, to be curious and to learn, to love, to play, to be creative and to have a constructive part in his own and others' lives. If he has attuned, attentive parents who can relate to his individual self and give him a sense of security, of being valued and of having a viable future, he indeed will have been dealt a good hand. If life goes relatively smoothly, with few significant losses or major disruptions, he has a chance of establishing internal stability and a self-esteem not threatened by the experience of being left or mistreated.

Many, of course, do not get these inestimable gifts and have to find a way of dealing with the world despite traumatic disruptions with their ensuing insecurities, anxieties about their own capacity to contribute to the world or to have fulfilling relationships. They are often increasingly trapped in patterns of relating that owe more to their need to defend themselves against vulnerability. They create barriers to development, learning and intimacy, provoking hostility in others and setting in motion vicious circles that stack the odds against their managing to make the most of their abilities and the resources around them.

By the time children get to school, many of these key patterns have become strongly established. Their capacity to make good use of education has been deeply affected by how they feel about being a vulnerable child, which has direct links to the vulnerability involved in being a learner. Their ability to relate constructively to teachers has been laid down by the experiences they have had so far of being dependent on adults (Youell 2006; Salzberger-Wittenberg 1983). Furthermore other elements vital to their capacity to function well in school will already have been either enhanced or jeopardised by the way they have been helped in their early years or bombarded with unmanageable impingements. They will have evolved a particular relationship with their own minds, for example, in their capacity to be curious, to entertain and play with thoughts, to be in touch with or intolerant of their inner processes. Their ability to know about and manage their own feelings will already be profoundly shaped by their experiences, as will their capacity to manage setbacks and frustrations.

So when a child is referred to the psychodynamic therapist, this theoretical background is there to help. The therapist is attuned to pick up how this child is functioning, to discern what early experiences he brings with him into the school setting and how these have affected the unconscious underpinnings of the child's behaviour and relationships. Out of these experiences the child will have established an inner world, a set of characteristic 'shapes' to how he copes and relates, and a set of templates based on established inner figures he is likely to use to make sense of all new relationships. He will have an array of mostly unconscious strategies for managing anxiety and threat, for defending himself against the outside world and from being fully in touch with his internal reality. New people, including teachers and peers, will be experienced in a way that is distorted by the relationships the child is bringing into school in his mind, both consciously and unconsciously; the need to keep himself safe from unmanageable anxiety and pain is likely to get in the way of his being able to learn that *this* time adults may be different.

The use of the relationship in the room

We have not yet heard about the third key element in psychodynamic thinking – because this one depends entirely on what has gone before. Because of the psychodynamic therapist's understanding of the unconscious roots of all that we are, and because she knows that the child is bringing an inner world based on the meaning that his early experiences have had for him and on their legacy, she is then poised to use this in a way that is unique to psychodynamic work – that is, to use the relationship in the therapy room as her key tool.

The psychodynamic approach, using these theoretical ideas, emphasises that what uniquely comes to life in the relationship with the therapist constitutes a most precious window into the child's unconscious and into his templates for relationships. We observe how the child experiences us, how he uses us or is perhaps unable to connect with us. We work with how he brings alive this inner world in his work with us, giving us direct access to the issues likely to be getting in his way in life and in school. As a vital corollary of this, it follows that simply trying to teach the child to manage his difficulties differently, or trying to train him to respond in more helpful ways, is not very likely to help; such an approach will bring conscious and surface changes, rather than tackling the early and unconscious roots of the difficulties. A psychodynamic orientation implies that for change to become established it needs to result from a shift in the child's inner world – a change in how he perceives and relates to the outside world which emanates from a change in his capacity to relate both to his own feelings and to the people he encounters.

A psychodynamic therapist uses the way the child plays, draws, talks and behaves in sessions as evidence of the unconscious dynamics shaping his way of being in the world. We use the way he perceives, responds to and manages himself in relation to us as the key to understanding his way of relating to others. We use how he impinges on us, such as how he provokes, excites or placates us, and how he makes us feel and act, as windows into both his internal and interpersonal emotional dynamics.

Projection and transference

This brings us on to some of the terminology used in psychodynamic thinking. We have looked at how we often hide from ourselves what we are feeling. It can be too painful and threatening to become aware of difficult feelings, and in order to defend ourselves against too much anxiety we can use an array of mechanisms to evade or disguise what is going on inside. One way of dealing with a difficult feeling is to attribute it to someone else, as was indicated in the example of the jealous girlfriend. So Gary (14) feels that his classmate is being aggressive and cruel, which is a way of not having to acknowledge his own aggression and cruelty. He can see someone else is being a bully, and even be angry about this, without noticing that at home he is bullying his mother badly. This mechanism is called **projection**. It is easy to understand if we think of the link with the cinematic use of the word projection; that is, it is a *putting out* of a feeling *onto* the other, something that is sent out and then seen on the screen. We can do this at a distance. We need never meet that person and can do this in very general terms; for example, attributing certain characteristics to whole nations or groups of people. Those most vehement in their condemnation and vilification of, for example, paedophiles, may not be managing their own parenting terribly well, or those who are less secure in their sexuality may be the most intolerant of homosexuals. We are often fiercest in our hatred of something that is not far from our own denied impulses.

This leads on to another way the term **projection** is used – when twinned with **splitting**. This is a term used to describe the difficulty of managing the fact that we have mixed feelings about someone or something. Having mixed feelings *is* very difficult and the more insecure and vulnerable we are, the harder it is to cope with the painful experience of ambivalence. In order to avoid dealing with both loving and hating someone, with having angry or disappointed feelings about someone we also care about and need, we often employ splitting so that these contrasting feelings can be kept separated from each other. Thus one teacher is wonderful and another dreadful, or mother is utterly kind and father is utterly hateful. One friend is idealised and my enemy is denigrated and therefore safe to hate. One religion or political movement or country or football team, and so on, is seen as right or good and the others all wrong and bad. Feelings are parcelled up into far neater packages than reality is ever likely to allow. One aspect is projected in one direction and the other somewhere else, and it is difficult to take back these projections and acknowledge that good and bad coexist, in all people and all other entities large and small.

The way the therapist is experienced by the child in the room will be full of information about these mechanisms; we will be on the lookout for what is being projected onto us through our perception of how he is experiencing us. However, as the relationship develops, the projections will be rooted in more than just the elements the child does not wish to acknowledge in himself. They will, as described earlier, be shaped by the inner templates laid down by earlier experiences. The psychodynamic term for this is **transference**. The child brings all his unconscious expectations of relationships into the room, and sees, feels, hears and understands us in a way distorted by the particular 'lenses' with which he has been endowed from earlier relationships. These inner patterns and shapes are shown to us through the child's interactions with us, revealing the nature of the figures within and the distortions created by their influence. We must, of course, honestly allow for the reality of who we really are and how we really do deal with them; but having attended to this, we can make sense of what they make of us as privileged communication about their inner world.

To sum up, **transference** is the way the child experiences us, influenced by what is already established inside *him* rather than simply by how we are, and **projection** is the mechanism by which a transference is created.

Projective identification and counter-transference

There is more, however, that is there to be observed in the relationship itself. Transference can be observed, and projections noticed, without these directly affecting the way we feel about ourselves or our relating to the child. However, there is a further, more powerful and more primitive level at which the relationship will be working. The child not only perceives us in a particular way, depending on his transference to us, but also creates a set of feelings and responses in us, that is unique to him. This is **projective identification**. He will, unconsciously of course, set about creating a familiar kind of relationship with us, exerting pressure on us to become more like some aspect of or figure in his inner world. There are two main versions of this kind of mechanism: one is to do with the people in his inner world (in psychoanalytic terminology his **objects**), and the other to do with elements in himself.

An example of the first is if a child has been rejected many times, then it is probable that he will repeatedly do things likely to turn us into another rejecting adult. He will relate to us in such a way as to elicit from us the same feelings and responses with which important people in his life have presented him. We will become aware of this when we recognise our responses to the client as being somewhat out of character, feeling judgemental perhaps, or depressed, defeated or punitive. We will, if we are not on our guard, play a part he has scripted for us from his inner drama, a role similar to someone he has already experienced. Children who have often been neglected or forgotten can make us careless or forgetful; children who have felt cruelly treated can call forth something cruel in us. If we stop to watch carefully how we feel and conduct ourselves with this child, which differs from the way we are with others, if we attend carefully to our responses and keep questioning how we are playing our part in the relationship, we can get a picture of what kind of person this child is making us into.

There is a second kind of projective identification, when elements of the child's own feelings are given over to us. For example, it could be that he is despairing of ever being able to control his own life. He might then set about making us feel out of control and impotent. If he is always on edge as to what is going to happen next in his life, he may set about making us feel exactly that by constantly shocking and surprising us, making us aware that at any moment something terrible could happen. If he feels deep down inside humiliated and despised, he may act in a way that makes us feel humiliated and despised. Thus he communicates to us the deepest and most difficult levels of his own world, not by talking about, drawing or enacting them while playing, but by evoking and giving them to us to process and manage.

He is letting us know how he feels deep inside in the only way he can, which is by stirring those feelings in us, partly to be rid of the feelings, like dumping on us the awfulness he cannot cope with. However, it can also be done with the unconscious hope that we will be able to make sense of the feelings, process them, manage them and be able to offer him some new capacity to make room for them himself. Even if he has no hope that we can do this, our capacity to process these feelings can create conditions for them to become less toxic and gradually make it possible for something different to happen. Eventually, if we can cope with what he cannot cope with, he will have a chance of becoming able to deal with it himself.

Using these ideas has powerful implications for practice. In discussing the **transference** we have noted the need to register how the child is experiencing us. In our present discussion of these other mechanisms there is a stress on how we need to monitor how the child is making us feel. We use this as a communication from a deep level of his own experience, whether it comes from feelings too unbearable for the child to experience or process, or from figures in his inner world. What we are monitoring is our **counter-transference**: the responses we detect in ourselves that are caused by the action on us of the child's unconscious communications and transference.

A caveat is needed at this point. We can confidently call our feelings or reactions 'counter-transference' only if they are what a particular child calls forth in us. We need to be clear that they are not a general trait of ours nor is it caused by factors in our own lives that are affecting us. To do this work we have to know ourselves very well and be able to disentangle what belongs to us and what is coming from the child. If I find myself feeling impatient and critical with a child, I need to know and be honest with myself about whether, for example I have been up too late the night before, or am feeling disaffected with the work for reasons of my own and/or am angry or resentful about my role in some way. I also need to work out whether I myself have a transference to this child. Am I responding to this child in a way that is distorted by my own projections – for example, if he reminds me of my brother with whom I was rivalrous and judgemental, or is it because he is being clumsy or ineffectual in a way that reminds me of aspects of myself that I am trying not to know about but am responding to?

Only if these do not apply can I wonder whether there is an important communication from the child himself that is making me feel the way I do. This is different to projection in that the feelings have not been put *on* to me, leaving me (perhaps) aware of them but unaffected, but *in* to me. What is he unconsciously trying to provoke in me? Why might he be exerting pressure on me to be just another person who tells him off or puts him down? Is he disowning a more assertive and critical part of himself that he cannot manage, and/or is he making me play a part in his inner drama that is all too familiar? If he is making me feel useless and foolish, is this because these are feelings he knows all too well and desperately needs me to feel and process for him? Is he making me feel persecuted and believing that he is too much for me because he always feels he is too much for others and believes *they* can only feel persecuted by him rather than being able to detect the vulnerable and needy child underneath?

We now have quite a set of theoretical tools:

- We know that the child is operating in a way that gives us a whole array of windows into his unconscious: through what he does and how he does it, through his play, his art and his verbal and non-verbal behaviour.
- We know that the child is coming to us having already built up an inner world based on his earliest experiences, with his early relationships and emotional world colouring his ways of relating to himself and to others.
- We know that the child is perceiving us and relating to us in a way that is shaped by these inner templates, so that he will be bringing into the room his transference to us and will be experiencing us in a way that is unique to him.
- We know that the child will evoke in us some feelings and responses that are not primarily created out of our own personal lives. They are responses to what he is emotionally bringing into the relationship, calling forth in us emotions and behaviours that can give us vital clues as to the figures in his inner world and the feelings he cannot manage to process himself.

Armed with these theoretical ideas, the psychodynamic therapist is able to use the clues the child gives us in order to tune in as accurately as possible to all his emotional communications. We are able to discern the emotional world he brings into the room with him and begin to make sense of it with him.

However, going back to where this chapter began, what use should we make of the theory when with a child? All this theorising is all very well, but how is it going to affect what actually happens when we meet the child? One of the most vital uses of this theoretical armoury is to help us stay with, and attentive to, the child even if he makes this difficult. It enables us to stay curious and to try to make sense of what is happening, to hold on to the conviction that what he presents us with *does* make sense, *does* have a logic to it. Even – indeed especially – if it is destructive and/or self-destructive it is still communicating something with real and important meaning.

In my opinion it is often this curiosity and the determination to find meaning that are far more important than whether the meaning we are piecing together is 'accurate'. The emotional connection created for the child by having an adult in the room who is attentive and thoughtful, who thinks rather than reacting instinctively to his impact on us, is perhaps the key element of the work. The role of the theory is less for us to be 'right' about the child than to put us in this questioning, meaning-seeking position, tuning in to the child's emotional world and being able to bear, process and maybe even put into words the features of the child's emotional landscape as we begin to discern them. Each of us would most likely put together a different set of meanings to what a child does or how he relates, but if we are each trying hard to understand, with honesty and perceptive inquiry, it may be that it is this rather than our correctness that makes us able to help the child.

Above all, the theory invests us with resilience and patience, enlivening our interest in the child, however he presents and whatever he faces us with. This gives the child a renewed chance to have an experience that perhaps he missed out on earlier in his life, one that will allow him to come to understand more fully who he is, to encounter and make sense of his feelings, to learn to defend himself less destructively from what is inside him – all this in the presence of someone who is focused squarely on his development and emotional reality, neither pursuing her own agenda nor using him to help her deal with her own needs or emotional turmoil.

Conclusion

Theory is therefore essential, but we need to be careful how we employ our theoretical tools, to make sure we use them to connect as closely as possible with the child's own emotional world and to make it safer for the child to encounter his own feelings more fully and with less need to distort experience or hide from himself. That way, changes can take place in the child's inner world and he can become less dominated by unconscious mechanisms and less driven to repeat the patterns established in his beginnings. He can become more open to the real world, more able to use his own resources and those of the people trying to teach, help and nurture him.

Study questions

- What unconscious roles have you taken up in your workplace or your relationships?
- What unconscious wishes or needs might you be fulfilling by choosing to work in the therapy field?
- Many authors, past and present, have contributed to psychoanalytic literature. Whose writing do you relate most to? What in particular resonates?

References

Brearley, M. (2010) Love and Its Distortions: Exaltation and Cynicism. Annual Freud Memorial Lecture, University of Essex.
Gerhardt, S. (2004) *Why Love Matters*. London: Routledge.
Karr-Morse, R. and Wiley, S. (1999) *Ghosts in the Nursery*. New York: Atlantic Monthly.
Klein, J. (1987) *Our Need for Others and Its Roots in Infancy*. London: Tavistock.
Klein, M. (1959) Our Adult World and Its Roots in Infancy. In *The Writings of Melanie Klein*, vol. 3, 247–263. London: Hogarth.
Music, G. (2010) *Nurturing Natures*. London: Jessica Kingsley.
Piontelli, A. (1992) *Twins, from Fetus to Child: An Observational and Psychoanalytic Study*. London: Routledge.
Salzberger-Wittenberg et al. (1983) *The Emotional Experience of Teaching and Learning*. London: Routledge and Kegan Paul.
Schore, A. (2002) Dysregulation of the Right Brain: A Fundamental Mechanism of Traumatic Attachment and the Psychopathogenesis of Posttraumatic Stress Disorder. *Australian and New Zealand Journal of Psychiatry*, 36, 9–30.
Schore, A. (2003) *Affect Dysregulation and Disorders of the Self*. New York: W. W. Norton.
Waddell, M. (2002) *Inside Lives*. London: Tavistock.
Youell, B. (2006) *The Learning Relationship*. London: Karnac.

Chapter 2

Recognising defences, resistance and anxieties

David Trevatt

The importance of being defended

It is natural for all individuals to have the capability to defend against perceived threat or attack from outside. We need skin and an immune system to withstand intrusion from physical attacks or internal infection. In a similar way the mind needs to develop ways to defend itself against anxieties and perceived threats from hostile sources, whether real or 'imagined'. Adults are usually thought to have well-reinforced defences, which have been developed and strengthened over many years. But what about children?

Defences were first recognised by Freud in his early psychoanalytic work. The idea became highly significant in therapeutic treatment when it became clear that there were those who looked for psychological help but were not always able to use it. The roots of defences are thought to begin in very early infancy. (Melanie Klein [1932] and Anna Freud [1936] found that defences were at work much earlier than Freud had originally thought.) Close observations of babies and young children show the workings of defensive behaviour. These enable them to cope with anxiety states arising from the presence or absence of various phenomena such as hunger, danger, fear, abandonment, and so on. Children of school age, from early years through to adolescence, can also be seen to have developed their own various methods of dealing with anxiety. For example, a child who is considered to be in need or difficulty may deny that there is a problem; or if there is a problem, then it is not *theirs*. It is not uncommon for young people to report that they are being 'picked on', either by other children or by teachers or parents. If there is a disagreement or a fight with another child, they may say that someone else started it, implying that they have been unfairly targeted and identified as the perpetrator or instigator. In such cases it is difficult to feel that the child or adolescent is fully in the therapy room, and, moreover, for the right reasons.

The reason for the referral may be at variance with the child's view of the problem; so the problem remains 'out there' with the adults or the institution and no responsibility is accepted by the child for his own behaviour. One might say that there is a *projection* at work in such cases: it is *not me* but rather some other person or thing that is to blame. Projection can be a common method of defence to ward off the presumed accusation for which the child feels blamed and made to feel responsible.

Resistance in the therapy room

Some young people may anticipate and experience us as a blaming figure, an ally of the school who is seen as being there to make the child confess and be changed from bad to good. But even if this is an accurate representation of what the child feels and how we are seen, it may not be overtly acknowledged. To do so would be to have a very direct communication that might have unpleasant consequences. The child's sense of self, his *ego*, needs to be protected; and while he may wish for relief from feelings of guilt or wrongdoing, he may fear that this is not possible or the price to pay may be damaging to the ego. He may have fears that the sense of shame and guilt could not be managed and lived with. In such a circumstance the therapist is likely to encounter *resistance*.

Freud recognized that resistance occurred in order to avoid conflict and the anxieties arising from it. Furthermore, resistance arises from two sources: (1) from the mind trying to *repress* internal unconscious thoughts and feelings, and (2) from external sources, when, for example, the therapist may be trying to encourage someone to make contact with repressed material that is a source of conflict and anxiety for the client.

Here is an example of a child struggling with internal conflicts:

> An eight-year-old girl named Petra was referred for therapeutic help because of her very low mood. She was very guarded about talking to a therapist but was able to let the therapist know that she was troubled by some things that she could not name or talk about. In spite of this internal conflict she attended her sessions regularly, but could not bring herself to say what it was that worried her. Her therapist recognized the girl's willingness to come to the sessions as well as her fear of communicating something that she seemed to believe could have far-reaching consequences. He did not push her to reveal whatever it was but let her know he was there to listen, to think and to talk about whatever she felt able to bring to the sessions.
>
> Gradually Petra built up trust in her therapist's patient attention. She used modelling clay to depict her feelings and gradually revealed her fears that monsters both within her and on the outside were threatening to destroy her. Her therapist wondered if there were real external threats to her safety and made appropriate discreet enquiries to satisfy himself she was not in danger. However, there were the other real threats to consider, the feelings Petra had that she was both the source of something monstrous as well as the victim of her fearful fantasy. She felt unable to control or eradicate these beliefs without feeling that she would perish in the process.

This example is not untypical of many young people who have difficulties that, for reasons that remain largely unknown, cannot be formulated. Petra, like many others in similar situations, feels isolated, alone and as if no one understands her. Her terrifying fantasy cannot be put into words because she would feel she would then be punished in a part of her mind by something, from somewhere, for revealing the identity of her fears. Wilfred Bion (1967) referred to this as 'nameless dread': something so terrible that it cannot be thought about or identified and yet exists in the mind in a very real way. Bion's formulation came from his own horrific experiences of war. But he applied it to the experiences of the mind that are difficult if not impossible to communicate, either because they are so terrible, or, in the case of young children, because there is not the capacity to put the terror into words.

We need to be aware of the difficulties young people coming to therapy may face, particularly those who are unused to talking about themselves, their feelings and their circumstances. It is important to be patient, allowing children to test the therapeutic space they have come to. They may well be suspicious of us and have all sorts of unasked and inchoate questions about who we are, what we are there for and what will be done with any information that might emerge from the therapeutic process.

It is important for us to be interested in the child's verbal and non-verbal communications but also to be contained in our manner. To come across as too interested may feel excessive for the guarded child, too much for him to bear.

Seeing what's in front of us

How does a child understand the reason for therapy? Sometimes there will be adults in the child's life who believe that therapy would be of some help, whether they are parents, teachers or other professionals. But the child, as in the case of Petra, may feel more conflicted. What does the therapist want to find out and what would be the consequences of revealing feelings or the facts of certain events? Will someone – parent, relative or friend – get into trouble?

Defences are a natural and essential construct of the mind. Children become aware of the uncertainties in the world outside the family and develop ways to protect themselves from unwanted feelings or the perceived threats that may be experienced from others. Defences can be elaborate and complicated; understanding them and how they are present may take a long time. They can be veiled and disguised, so that the child may deny that they *are* defences.

In the therapeutic encounter it is important to be aware of the necessity of defences and to recognize the reasons for them. We can anticipate that there will be defences that prevent the child from communicating certain feelings or information. We also need to bear in mind that defences can be strengthened and reinforced by attempts to dismantle them. Therefore we should try to be aware of what it is that we see in front of us and work with it – as difficult as that invariably is – rather than to weaken defences or penetrate them. If this does not happen, it is possible that the child will shut down, refuse to keep coming to therapy or turn the session into a neutralized play space.

We as therapists can be keen to help and to feel that some progress is being made in our work with a child. However, we should moderate and manage our enthusiasm and be circumspect in our approach and delivery of questions, formulations and interpretations. Bion's advice to eschew memory and desire is a helpful reminder that we should control and contain our ambitions to be successful (desire) and that we should also allow the child to begin each session in the present rather than automatically to link it to the previous session (memory).

The child who is open

There are some children who do not appear to have very robust defences nor much resistance to engaging in therapy. They may, on the contrary, be very open and accepting of the therapeutic contact. This may be because they are secure in themselves and in talking with adults; or it may be that they are desperate for adult attention or that they do not have successfully developed defences to protect themselves from real or imagined dangers. A child who is open and friendly may be just so, or they may idealise the therapist and the therapy as their ally and sanctuary. The child may use the strategy of denying that problems exist or that there is anything to hide or defend in an effort to convince the therapist that everything is fine and there is no need to look any further for difficulties.

But 'fine' can be a convenient façade. We know this from our own experience: how we automatically reply that we are 'fine' when asked how we are. When the therapist asks the child how he is, he too is quite likely to say he is 'fine' even when, as with all of us, it can be very far from the truth. So it is better not to ask the question when the answer is possibly misleading and even untrue. The child may think that if he says things are not 'fine', it may lead to unwelcome enquiry from the therapist.

The impact of children's previous experiences of professionals

Some children have had experience of professional services and can be highly suspicious of what professional adults want and what their role is. Children in care can have had extremely difficult experiences in their family of origin as well as in the care system. They can be very hard to reach because of feelings of mistrust or being let down through previous adult unreliability. Such children may have had very complicated or very poor experiences of relationships with family members and with professional workers who come and go in their lives. Some very deprived children use therapy to explore their inner fantasies as well as some of their external realities in quite bizarre and worrying ways. They may relate to the therapist as an ally with deep expressions of attachment, which are followed closely by great hostility combined with extreme fight and flight behaviour. This may seem to express some of their confused experiences as well as the threat they fear of allowing themselves to feel closer to their therapist. Letting down their defences in a new therapeutic relationship means exposing their neediness and the vulnerability they experience from realizing how much they have missed in their lives – thoughts that they have tried to put out of their minds in order to survive.

The long road to gaining children's trust

It takes time for children to build up trust in unknown adults. They can be highly curious about our real lives, who we are, who is in our family and what sorts of things we like to do. It can also be very hard for us to resist giving some factual response to seemingly innocuous questions. It may feel almost as if we are being cruel not to share the simplest facts about our life and interests. Some children react in a retaliatory manner, refusing to tell us anything if we refuse to give the child anything. It is worth commenting to the child that he may feel ignored or excluded, but that we are here to think about *him* and *his* needs and not to engage in a friendship of peers. There are many other ways in which our mind and feelings can be engaged and explored. For instance, knowing how to play and valuing play for all its symbolic possibilities: using play, whether with animal or human figures, games or drawing can be a very good way to build a relationship and to get to know what someone is really like. But there will be some children who will be highly suspicious of what we might see or read into the activity. And we need to be prepared for the challenges that games bring to us. How do *we* cope with losing a game? Do we reveal something of our personality beneath the professional role?

The particular challenges of adolescents

When working with adolescents, there are more factors to take into consideration. It is problematic to generalize but adolescents can be more resistant to therapy than younger children. They have reached an age when they may decide for themselves whether they choose to engage in therapy and can refuse to attend. They can be self-conscious and sensitive to criticism, whether real or imagined. They can, too, be easily embarrassed and less able to tolerate silences and being alone with a therapist. Typical adolescent attitudes (which are not universal) include the following:

- superficially appearing detached, aloof and unaffected by anything and anyone;
- easily feeling misunderstood;
- becoming less confident and articulate, which can happen when adolescent brain development switches off some acquired abilities while other processes are enabled.

Adolescents also have a whole new range of emotions and capacities to learn to manage that they may not wish to have close attention drawn to.

Working with trauma and grief

Another group of children who may have very robust defences are those who have been bereaved or traumatized through their experiences, whether in the form of abuse, war or the death of a close family member. Defences may become strengthened by trauma in a rigid, inflexible manner so that almost nothing is let in or out.

Extreme experiences can take a very long time to heal. There may be a feeling that nothing and no one can help or make anything better because the world is a hostile place populated with dangerous or unfriendly people. If a parent has died, it may not only be impossible to understand how this could happen, but painful feelings can be shut off and locked away in the remotest part of the mind where they can be least thought about and consequently be least hurtful. In such circumstances the therapeutic endeavour may be perceived as a threat because it serves to put the child in touch with feelings he is trying to forget.

Of course, adults can act in similar ways. It is a fundamental principle in human psychology that we try our utmost to avoid pain and distress. So why is it a good idea to bring painful feelings, memories and thoughts into full consciousness? It can feel to us that in our attempt to help, we are asking the child to talk about something that is painful or sensitive. It is as if we are forcing the child to re-experience the trauma, to relive what he is desperately trying to put behind him.

We know that unprocessed grief or unresolved trauma can continue to cause difficulties for many years. This is known from the victims of abuse who received no help or recognition for their troubles. However, there is a common belief in therapeutic work that it can be better for the mind to be allowed to forget until it feels like the right time to open up troubling experiences. Some years ago the opposite belief was commonly held: that it was important to help the mind through therapy to process experience by articulating the traumatic experiences.

There can be fierce resistance to the therapist's efforts to encourage the child to 'open up' and reveal the details of disturbing events. The child may not feel strong enough or ready enough to cope with what lies beneath and it may be tactically better to leave well alone, for the moment; otherwise there is a danger that the trauma is relived and the defensive wall reinforced.

The aim of therapy is to provide something useful to the child so that he can benefit from the attention and understanding we bring to the therapeutic space. Exactly what the child takes or how he makes use of the therapy is something we should pay close attention to.

Patience and the therapist

One way to comment on defence when we see it in front of us is by saying something that acknowledges the need or wish to keep the therapist at bay and out of the child's mind. While the therapist is apparently there to help the child, the experience of having an adult's attention may be unfamiliar and too much to bear. The child's reaction is to see the therapist's presence as a hostile intrusion – as nosey and inquisitive. The therapist needs to be able to bear this reaction and not accept it as if it were true or overreact to justify himself and thereby become defensive of his own position. The child's reaction is what it is, and this is what the therapist has to understand. Why it is this way is something that may unfold in the course of the therapy. The belief that the therapist is someone to be wary of is a natural phenomenon, like stranger danger. Children are often warned by parents not to talk to strangers because of the risks that may be present with unknown persons. Just because the therapist has been given permission by the school and the parents to see the child does not mean that all defences are raised or dropped.

Defences can be so reinforced that they keep out helpful influences as well as potentially harmful ones. A child who has been let down by adults, whether a parent who might have left the home or others who have been unreliable, does not easily allow himself to be exposed to this disappointment again.

While the child may wish to have a relationship with the therapist or to communicate something important, he may find that his defensive organisation prevents this happening. The therapist has to adopt a circumspect attitude, allowing himself to wonder and not to know but at the same time not giving up. The psychoanalyst Donald Meltzer (1967) suggested that the therapist needs to tiptoe up to pain rather than confront it head on. A 'head on' approach is likely to encounter defences that will repel the therapeutic endeavour. The therapist needs to be very careful in how and when he decides to say something about his perception of the problems the child may have. Finding the right way to talk about or interpret the child's feelings is a skill that takes considerable practice and perhaps many attempts to get the words right at a time when the child may be receptive to them.

Denial

But what reasons can there be for this resistance? Like adults, children can be very wary of sympathy, experiencing it as humiliation or as weakening their sense of self-esteem. One way to deal with the unwanted effects of problematic experience is to deny it to oneself as well as to others. If the experience can be projected out or sealed off within the mind, it can appear to have gone or even never to have existed. Like the taunts of peers that identify a weakness or an embarrassing and humiliating aspect of oneself, it is a common reaction to behave as though it never happened. This allows the child to feel and behave as if there is no difference between himself and the others, mediating the fear of being seen as different and not normal. Take the example of a child who is aware of the existence of a learning difficulty that makes him feel embarrassed. It is natural to pretend that it is not there and to behave as 'normally' as possible. Physical disability that is overt can be troubling for young people who may have grown up with the limitations that it imposes and who feel sensitive to their difference being exposed and ridiculed by others. The therapist may wish to give reassurance and acceptance of difference while bearing in mind that children who have different needs and requirements do not want attention drawn to it, let alone sympathy.

Some children who are identified as having emotional problems and are brought to therapy by concerned adults may be quite worried by the implications of this arrangement. Whether it is concerned parents, teachers or social workers, the fact that an adult who knows them is encouraging them to spend time in a room with a therapist may feel quite strange and perhaps unwelcome. Like other more grown-up people, children want to feel competent and able to get on with their lives and do not like the suggestion, however tacit or covert, that they are not managing. They want to be 'normal' and like everyone else. But coming to therapy can feel terribly exposing and demeaning, especially when there are some problems caused by a trauma or other difficulty in the child's life. These children can go to elaborate lengths to hide their vulnerabilities, deny their difficulties and defy the therapist's attempts to reach and help them.

Some children keep the therapist at a distance by turning the therapy session into a well-defended play time, never allowing the therapist to make any progress towards achieving a therapeutic outcome. It can then become a battle for who has the most resilience and whether the therapist has enough patience and ability to think about what is happening in the room at that moment in time. Some children will interact with their therapist and be very controlling of him, ordering him about, telling him what to do. They will tell him not to speak if it seems he is about to say something therapist-like about what is occurring between them: that nothing much appears to be happening; or perhaps that the same thing seems to be happening again and again, but that it's not a productive something. These are defences that are very firmly in place and it is as if the child is saying he is not to be questioned or tampered with by the therapist under any circumstances.

Seeing ourselves through the child's eyes

Therapy is not for everyone. Most adults are able to decide if and when they seek therapy for themselves. However, even then many adults will pass through therapy encountering the therapist in different ways as a helpful and at times unhelpful presence, someone who could help them as well as potentially do them great harm.

In the case of children there is a different situation. The child is unlikely to seek therapy or know much about it. He may be disposed towards the process and the therapist or he may not. The presence or absence of choice is a significant element. Children are likely to accept what they may feel they have little choice in, if the decision has all but been made by the adults around them.

> Much of our understanding of the transference comes from our understanding of how our clients act on us to feel things for many varied reasons; how they try to draw us into their defensive systems; how they unconsciously act out with us in the transference, trying to get us to act out with them; how they convey aspects of their inner world built up from infancy – elaborated in childhood and adulthood, experiences often beyond the use of words which we can only capture through the feelings aroused in us, through our counter-transference, used in the broad sense of the word.
>
> (Joseph 1985: 157)

Following this line of thought, in order to understand our clients' internal worlds and the nature of their object relationships, defences, and so on, we have to experience them in the counter-transference. In doing so, we can temporarily inhabit their world. Some measure of being pulled in is inevitable and at times even necessary or desirable.

Conclusion

Defences can be thought of as necessary for attacks that are anticipated – consciously or unconsciously – from external sources or from the inside, such as a defence against psychosis or being overwhelmed with fears of disintegration. Defences are not only important: they are vital for all of us – children and adults – in order to function in a complex society where there are many real dangers and uncertainties.

The child may erect a mental brick wall to keep out the therapist. Any attempt to penetrate such a defence by means of an interpretation aimed to show our understanding of his feelings could be perceived as a destructive attack on his defensive organization, a structure that exists in order to resist understanding. The therapist needs not only to have an understanding of the child's resistance but to show an understanding that it is appropriate for the child to distrust and be unsure of him initially. Trust may grow from confidence gained when the child begins to know the therapist in the course of the treatment.

Study questions

- What do your first observations of the child tell you about the possible defensive anxieties he may have?
- How would you try to communicate your understanding of any anxieties the child may have about being there?
- How might you try to allay any fears the child may have about who you are and what you do?
- How would you deal with a child who seems unwilling or unable to communicate?
- Would you comment on the child's resistance to talking about something or engaging in an activity and, if so, in what way?
- What would you do if your attempts to inform and reassure a child about therapy appeared to have no effect?

References

Bion, W. R. (1967) *Second Thoughts*. London: Heinemann.
Freud, A. F. (1936) 'The Ego and the Mechanisms of Defense', in *The Writings of Anna Freud*, vol. 2. London: Karnac.
Freud, S. (1894) 'The Neuro-Psychoses of Defence', in S. Freud, *Standard Edition*, vol. 3. London: Karnac.
Joseph, B. (1985) 'Transference: The Total Situation', in *Melanie Klein Today*, vol. 2. London: Routledge.
Klein, M. (1932) 'The Psychoanalysis of Children', in *The Writings of Melanie Klein*, vol. 2. London: Karnac.
Meltzer, D. (1967) *The Psycho-Analytic Process*. London: Karnac.

Chapter 3

Transference and counter-transference

Hilary Ann Salinger

Throughout our lives, patterns of relating that have been established in early infancy between a baby and its primary caregiver remain active in all aspects of our interactions. When a child or young person enters a room for therapy, he brings a history of experience and a learned pattern of relating to others. His expectations of the therapeutic relationship and perceptions of what the therapist says or does are heavily influenced by what has gone on before.

Because these patterns determine what happens in the therapy room, they can help us understand the child's earliest struggles with frustration, discomfort, loneliness and abandonment – struggles common to all human infants – and they can show us how the child has overcome them. We call this *infantile transference* and our understanding of it is crucial if we are to help a child make the internal changes that will help to improve his life.

Understanding enactments

The lasting impact of early struggles as well as other potential developmental hiccups such as the arrival of siblings or the impact of family breakdown are acted out in the client's relationship to the sessions and the therapist herself, thereby providing insight into his inner, unverbalised world. Take this example of a seven-year-old whose repressed rage and sadness had been held in check until he felt sufficiently safe in the therapy to express himself:

> In every session, Timmie chose to take a family of dolls and subject them to sustained attacks, alternating between grinding wet sand into them and then aggressively washing them in as hot water as he could tolerate on his hands. Whilst playing he seemed calm and composed. His therapist remarked:
>
> > 'Watching you play with the dolls each week makes me think about babies in wet, uncomfortable nappies. When we're babies we have to wait to have our nappies changed, don't we?'

This allowed him to recall that, due to the arrival of a sibling, his own care had been neglected, and he talked about having had 'pink and green diarrhoea'. Once this recollection was talked about, he became quite angry towards the therapist as if she, on behalf of his mother, carried some responsibility for his early painful experiences. Timmie then made pots of 'secretly' poisoned ice cream in the sand and insisted the therapist ate it. Her response was:

> 'I believe you want to trick me into eating the poison so you could kill off this therapist who reminds you of those uncomfortable nappies and then you can begin again with a new therapist.'

Timmie also insisted over a number of weeks that he was invisible. He would play hide and seek but leave footprints around the room by wetting his feet to help his therapist 'find' him. She had to articulate this search and used the opportunity for a transference interpretation:

> 'I believe that Timmie is here but I cannot see him. I would so like to be able to find him and look at him. I must keep looking. . . . Sometimes little children can feel as if no one can see or hear them when they cry because they are hungry or need their mummy. But they can't move or talk or make people see them. I think that must feel very lonely.'

Sometimes there are obvious and understandable signs of learned patterns as, for instance, with an intimidated child who is quiet and withdrawn and avoids any activity that he believes might antagonise the therapist. At other times the child will make her feel that they are actors who have been given a carefully written script to perform. The script will create a role for each party, determined by the workings of the child's internal world and specifically his expectation of who he is in the mind of the therapist.

> Josh (15) was a school non-attender who attended therapy weekly but otherwise never left his room. He talked throughout his sessions about his opinions about life, philosophy, science fiction, computer games, not paying much attention to whether his therapist was following his train of thought or not. He conveyed his contempt for teachers and school in the pseudo-independent therapy he provided, apparently without the need of any participation of his therapist. With tolerance, the gradual building of trust and a non-judgemental approach he was able to look at his anxieties about the real world and his defences against it.

Working with the transference

The relationship on offer to each child entering therapy is ostensibly with someone new. But identifying, exploring and understanding how the client transfers the past onto the present experience in the room is an essential and informative part of the therapy process. It allows us to delve into aspects of the child's experience that may never before have been articulated and for which there has been no previous explanation. How he has processed events in his life or organised defences against their emotional impact is frequently beyond his present capacity to explain – or perhaps even to be aware of. As therapists, our task is to make ourselves available to be recruited into the child's drama and, at the same time, to remain aware of how this is happening and how the feelings are being communicated as events unfold in the room.

> Fatima (10) had been abused by her father over a number of years and had testified against him in court. She expressed her fury and guilt in therapy sessions through elaborate puppet shows delivered from behind a wall of chairs, allowing her to hide, which was something she had not been able to do in court. In the shows the narrative frequently involved either seductive children who had to be resisted and punished or alternatively overpowering and threatening adults from whom there seemed to be no protection.

The therapist's role here was one of an audience, offering non-judgemental comment – rather like a Greek chorus – along with an articulation of the emotional content of the tales. The following are excerpts from her commentary:

> 'These puppets seem to be frightening and dangerous but at the same time are frightened of grown-ups themselves.'

> 'It looks as if there are no kind grown-ups who can keep children safe from the giants and monsters in your stories.'

> 'The children seem to be punished even when they are telling the truth. That doesn't seem very fair.'

The uses of negative transference

Hopefully, children and young people enter the therapy space anticipating a relationship of trust, genuine concern and confidentiality. From this a therapeutic relationship can develop that is robust and positive. Alongside the positive transference, though, something more destructive and negative will coexist. It will contain less acceptable, and therefore less knowable, feelings of anger, rejection, envy and hopelessness; for example, children will frequently express anger towards the evidence of other therapy clients by attacking the cupboard where their individual boxes are kept or the space they believe others occupy in the therapist's mind, with insistent requests for information.

> Talulah (12) came to therapy at the end of the school day and was well aware that others came at other times. During school, she even conversed with those

students about the therapist and her fantasies about her (therapist's) life outside the school. During sessions, most commonly when her therapist made an interpretation – that is, that she showed evidence that she was thinking independently of her client – Talulah would ask a barrage of questions about her marital status, her children, her home and lose her temper when the therapist failed to give her the information she thought she desired. The therapist tried to continue to think with Talulah about her jealousy and the anguish at not monopolising her therapist's thinking space. The following are possible ways she might have addressed this with the girl:

> 'It is painful to realize that this very important person who understands you a bit has to be shared with other children and young people. I think to manage this pain you feel you need to know everything about me, maybe to control me so I can't see anyone else.'

Or

> 'It feels impossible at the moment to trust that I can hold you in my mind from one session to another, or over the breaks in sessions. I think your worry may be that if you don't control me, I might let you go.'

Unexplored and unchallenged, such negative transference will sabotage the help and support that the client wants. It can feel very cruel and withholding not to disclose seemingly unimportant information about yourself, but revealing personal information will inevitably obstruct the necessary projections for the young person for whom the aim is to be a canvas for their transference communications.

Counter-transference as a powerful tool

Transference, then, is what the child conveys about the internal figures that inhabit his emotional and mental life through the relationship he establishes with the adult in front of him. However, the therapist herself will have her own reaction to the material conveyed: perhaps hopelessness, boredom or powerful desires to rescue the client or even retaliate against him after a provocation. Sometimes these feelings will be determined by her own unconscious needs and determinants and the way the child's pain resonates with her own. At other times it will be a reaction to emotional currents the child has found overwhelming and unmanageable and lacks the strength to own. Like a screaming infant, the child needs his terrifying feelings received and processed by someone more resilient. The capacity to remain open to the painful and distressing counter-transference communications and to retain the reflective space to understand it for the child will enable the therapist to hand something back in a form the child can think about, revealing the possibility of breaking patterns of relating that have created problems for some time.

Rebecca (15) hints at risk-taking behaviours but holds back from anything specific that might enable her therapist to accurately assess the real level of risk the young woman is exposed to. This leaves her therapist in a state of high anxiety after each session and demoralised about her capacity to protect Rebecca, though she is functioning reasonably well outside the sessions. Later it transpires that Rebecca's mother suffered from prolonged post-natal depression. Through reflection and discussion in supervision the therapist was able to make a connection between this information and her counter-transference responses. It became evident that Rebecca believes she has to work hard at maintaining a place in her therapist's mind just as she did to enliven her mother in her earliest experience of a relationship. Once she begins to trust that her therapist can hold her in mind without the crises, she can allow herself to feel held and hopefully will be better able to keep herself safe.

Melinda (11) had been referred to the therapist because she seemed withdrawn and passive. She had disclosed a historical incident of sexual abuse by a family friend and it had been reported, investigated, but then dropped by the police and social services. In the first session she was composed, making intense unblinking eye contact and talking of the incident in measured language and without emotion throughout. She sat still on the chair and did not explore any of the materials available. That night the therapist had disturbing nightmares about being abused herself, surrounded by polite, but agonisingly unconcerned, adults. From this counter-transference experience the therapist was able to reflect on the unsayable aspects of Melinda's account and, later, to communicate to Melinda that she was aware of the possible range of emotions that she had perhaps not been able to process before this, as the case had been dismissed.

In order for the therapist to use herself in such ways, it is essential that she can step back and distinguish the feelings personal to her and those that belong to the child or young person in front of her. To do this requires self-knowledge, personal therapy and supervision.

Conclusion

We all transfer aspects of our past relationships onto our current ones. An obvious example is those times when we experience someone in authority just as we experienced our parents when we were children. We may then react to that person in a way that is similar to how we used to react to our mother or father. Even when we know about transference and are on the lookout for it, it will still come into play, as it is an internal process that is often unconsciously triggered. As therapists we can make use of it in our sessions with children and adolescents. This chapter has illustrated how helpful it is if the therapist can observe her client's spoken and non-verbal reactions to her and think about who she might be in that particular moment for that particular child. The therapist's capacity to react in a way that is different from what the child expects will be an important feature of the therapeutic encounter.

This chapter has also discussed why the therapist carefully tracks her own feeling responses to the child, noticing, for example, when she is lost for words, overcome by sadness, feeling cut-off or shut out, filled with uncertainty or confusion, unexpectedly angry, and so on. These feelings, the counter-transference, are vital unconscious communications from the client to the therapist. It may be that they are pre-verbal or have never been articulated. The therapist takes them in, much as a mother takes in and holds in mind her infant's distress, reflecting on and trying to understand the underlying meaning. Both transference and counter-transference are essential tools used by the therapist to contain and process the kind of felt-experience that cannot easily be translated into words.

Study questions

Vignette 1

For part of his session Mario (7) insisted that his therapist repeat exactly, in language, tone and tune, snippets of lullabies in his native tongue. Each week he demanded she imitate him and sing the songs to him, after which he could settle to playing.

- Who do you think Mario needs the therapist to sound like at these moments?
- What purpose was the transference to his therapist serving for him?

Vignette 2

Amelia (9) always arrived at therapy immaculately attired in pretty dresses. Once alone with her therapist, she threw herself across the chairs and kicked her legs in the air exposing her underwear and talking from an upside down position. She devised game after game, which resulted in her ending up in this way. When asked about this, she became aggressive and hurled toys at the therapist.

- When in the room alone, who might the therapist represent for Amelia?
- Was her transference towards her therapist a positive or a negative one?
- How can the therapist be reassuring towards her during each phase of the interaction?

Vignette 3

Peter (8) is a cooperative and smiling child who seems eager to please his therapist and follows every suggestion without hesitation or question. But being with him feels like being with a ghost who wears a mask; his cooperation feels seductive and uncomfortable and his therapist finds him difficult to like. He has a history of severe early neglect and adoption when he was aged four.

- What relationships are being explored in the transference to Peter's therapist?
- What does Peter's behaviour suggest about his adoptive relationships?
- What does his therapist's counter-transference tell you about his early attachments?

Vignette 4

Levi (5) played in the sand whilst his mother related her difficulties in feeling strong enough to provide for his needs. He frequently interrupted the conversation by asking the therapist to find things in the sand that he had buried. After a few times the therapist declined and suggested he ask his mummy, which he did. She found the half-hidden toy and shared the delight of discovering it with him. Levi then went to the couch and lay down sucking his thumb.

- What do Levi's approaches to the therapist convey to her about his worries about his mother?
- Do you think Levi is able to believe that there is help for him?

Vignette 5

Michael (11) was predictably angry and made a terrible mess in the therapy room each session, emptying the contents of his box over his head and refusing to clear up at the close. His therapist decided to end the session five minutes early so that he had time to clear up before leaving. Each week, on his journey home, the therapist found he drove very erratically and was anxious about his ability to remain safe on the road. He resolved to take a walk and to find recovery time after the sessions.

- What can you deduce about Michael's internal world by the counter-transference response of his therapist?
- What was the therapist conveying to Michael by taking the time to clear up in the session and to recover himself afterwards?

Vignette 6

Leanne (14) had been abandoned at the age of 6 by her mother, who had left Leanne's father for another woman. Her grandmother had died a year previously. The end of the first term of therapy arrived, resulting in a break of three weeks between sessions. At the start of the new term Leanne missed two sessions without explanation and, after numerous communications through members of school staff, arrived 20 minutes late for the next.

- Why did Leanne feel the need to 'punish' her therapist?
- What did the break in therapy represent for Leanne?
- What role did the therapist's actions to find her again mean for the therapy relationship?

Chapter 4

Observing and interpreting

Jenny Dover

Introduction

Fundamental to our work with a troubled child is our becoming familiar with his inner world – in particular the ideas and feelings associated with the area of difficulty. We do this through very close attention to what we see, what we hear, the way a child relates to us and also to the feelings evoked in us. Interpreting involves making sense of our observations and then finding appropriate ways of conveying our understanding to the child. As I shall describe later, we can convey our thoughts through both words and actions.

Bion (1962a, 1962b) said that the capacity to think arises out of an experience of being thought about. Through the mechanism of projective identification, an infant lets his mother know about his feeling state. A mother receives these communications, makes sense of them and conveys her understanding to the infant. For instance, she may soothe the child who is frightened or feed him when hungry. When she can accurately reflect on his psychological experience in this way, her responses validate the child's perceptions and he gains a sense of self, of agency and a belief in his capacity to anticipate events correctly.

Similarly, in therapy a child has a sense of someone who 'feels' his state, can bear it and will help him make sense of it. He also experiences an adult who is predictable and reliable. The therapist uses her knowledge of emotional development coupled with close observation to meet the child at the psychic place where he is located. She engages him in an interaction in which symbolic communication between them takes place. Winnicott (1971a: 47) called this 'the potential space'.

Being truly open to a child's projections and his powerful feelings can be challenging. Our capacity for emotional understanding and our capacity to provide containment are dependent not only on our ego strengths but also on how well *we* are contained in our working environment. Staying with painful or anxiety-provoking feelings rather than offering reassurance can be challenging for a trainee who is accustomed to taking a positive stance. Ultimately, though, it is more reassuring to a child to have his worries named and faced; otherwise he may feel that the reality of the situation is unbearable to the therapist as well as to him.

Comments such as 'Perhaps it's hard to believe you will manage your temper or be admired or become a reader . . .' are useful because they both acknowledge the despairing feelings and, at the same time, express hopefulness.

Early observations and setting the tone for the therapy

Getting to know a child or young person is an exciting and significant process. Despite detailed referral information, there can be surprising new insights into a child's views of the world and relationships. The therapist must put aside previous assumptions and remain flexible in her thinking, taking the lead from the child, their evolving relationship and the unfolding process in the room. Because of the heightened anxiety and, at the same time, the hopefulness that children bring to a new relationship, they will convey important information in the early sessions, so that everything – including body language, behaviour, words and creations – is significant.

The therapist sets the tone for a deep level of communication from the start by demonstrating her receptiveness. The impact of being alone with an unfamiliar adult can be profound for some vulnerable children.

> Lisa, an 11-year-old in foster care, was so anxious in her first session that she struggled to find words to express her thoughts. Having commented on how hard it might feel to be in a room with a new person, her therapist initiated a shared drawing activity giving her an opportunity for non-verbal communication. Lisa was then able to express her distrust of the therapist by drawing a picture of her with devil's horns. She arrived very early for her second session and had to wait in the corridor. When it was time for the session to begin, she dragged her heels and lingered at the water fountain. Her therapist was aware of her own impatient feelings as she waited for Lisa to follow her to the room. Once there she commented that perhaps Lisa was letting her know how hard it was to be kept waiting all week for her session.

> Tom (14) presented very differently to Lisa, expressing his hopefulness about finding a receptive adult by immediately producing a story that revealed his anxieties about his destructiveness. He called it 'The boy who spoilt everything and broke up the world'. His therapist said that perhaps it was hard for him to believe that she would keep things safe and manage his angry feelings.

In gathering information about a child or young person it is useful to establish why he thinks he is coming for sessions. What does he understand by therapy/counselling? Who is it that is worried about him? What is his 'story' about himself and his difficulties? It is common for children with long-standing histories of educational failure and emotional difficulties to wonder whether they are bad or even mad. Insecurely attached children tend to lack a coherent narrative of their own experience. Jeremy Holmes (2001) said that therapy involves both making and breaking stories that clients have created about themselves in the world – and it can be, at times, about retelling stories in a healing light.

Sensitive interpretation

A child initially learns about himself through his carer's mind. Winnicott (1971a) suggested that the baby looking into his mother's eyes sees himself reflected there and – when all goes well – it will be an accurate reflection of his personality. However, some of our young clients may never have had a parent who wondered about them at all. Others may have experienced a parent who attributed false thoughts and feelings to them. The way in which we understand a child and interpret what we see in the therapy room is informed by theoretical concepts around emotional development and our own very personal responses. The child's capacity to hear our comments is something we need to gauge very carefully.

> Lisa was able after a lengthy time in therapy to make a statement about her neglectful, abusive mother, letting her therapist know how hurt she was. But before the therapist could respond, Lisa stopped her ears with her fingers so that she would not hear. Her therapist understood that Lisa could not yet trust her to respond in a way that felt bearable.

A therapist has to be sensitively aware of timing and frequency of her comments – so that she is not experienced as intrusive or investigative. Gentle linking and understanding of possible connections may be all the child can bear. Winnicott (1990) warned that mistimed interpretations outside the ripeness of the material are indoctrination and may produce compliance. He also noted that premature interpretations may rob a child of finding out things for himself. Taking the lead from the child is, in other words, the best approach. A related methodology comes from Barbara Dockar-Drysdale (1993), who adapted to children rather than providing interpretations.

Martha Harris (1987) pointed out that although we do not always manage to respond with the right degree of understanding, the capacity to continue to try to understand is in itself of value, because we are presenting to the child a thinking object with which to identify. One therapist, shown a drawing that was clearly significant, helped the child enormously by simply acknowledging that although she didn't yet entirely understand its meaning, she knew it was important.

Sometimes simply getting alongside a child without being very active – particularly if he has missed out on positive early containment – is what is needed. Winnicott (1971a) proposed that a child needs to play alone in the presence of his mother if a true sense of self is to emerge. She must be sufficiently unobtrusive in order for the child to forget her and to be able to focus on the self-exploration that lies at the root of solitary play.

Winnicott (1971a) said that there were three conditions for the evolution of symbolic functioning in the transitional space between infant and caregiver:

- a sense of safety associated with experiencing the inner world;
- an opportunity for the infant deliberately to limit concern with external events;
- an opportunity to generate spontaneous creative gestures.

Providing such an experience in the therapy room is illustrated by the following example:

> Matthew, a very avoidant child in foster care, made good use of the safe space experienced with his therapist when he allowed her to write out a story he dictated to her over several terms. Matthew had been unable to talk directly about his abusive father who had sent him and his two brothers into the streets to forage for food and punished them severely if they failed. His story was about three princes who were sent by the wicked king to hunt for treasure in dangerous forests. If they returned empty-handed, the princes would be beaten. For Matthew, the experience of retelling his experiences through metaphor in the safety of the room with an unobtrusive adult was very helpful. Only later in the work did the therapist gently offer some thoughts about the feelings and dilemmas faced by the princes. Staying in the metaphor in this way respected the defences of this very vulnerable boy.

Avoiding direct questions that require 'yes' or 'no' answers facilitates the expression of feelings and thoughts in words, allowing communication to flow. Reflecting back a child's comments – or 'wondering how it feels' – encourages further communication. Sometimes too, in order to strengthen the child's sense of belonging to a world of individuals with diverse personalities, a phrase such as 'I wonder if you are a person who . . .' is helpful. 'Normalising' and 'generalising' can be useful – particularly with avoidant children. For example, one might say, 'Some children prefer doing things themselves without asking for help.' Some comments may be phrased in such a way that no response is expected: 'I notice that when we discuss your dad, you seem upset.'

It can also be helpful to remember that relentlessly focusing on difficulties is distorting. Talking with him about incidents in which he manages adversity by posing questions such as 'How did you manage to keep your temper or say no to the gang?' will offer him a perspective of himself as someone perhaps more resilient and resourceful than he is used to thinking of himself.

Of course, words can sometimes be the least important aspect of communication. Our willingness to pay attention, our attitude, our gestures and non-verbal signs – all can be highly useful in conveying understanding and connecting with a child. Dale (1992) said that the kind of silent communication in which another person feels understood and 'held' in someone's thoughts, where experiences of an intimate nature are shared and acknowledged, is when we get it right. This is what we call a 'transforming experience'.

A therapist may not always respond to a child's communications in words but may instead choose an activity or story that resonates with the child's dilemma or preoccupation. The choice of activity or reading material in response to a feeling or preoccupation that the child is communicating can be a powerful comment-in-action. Here are some examples:

- A child suffering bereavement benefited from hearing *Amos and Boris*, a story with a theme about separation and loss.
- The story of *Hansel and Gretel* helped a child to process some of her fears around kidnap and abandonment and allowed her to express hateful feelings towards the bad mother in the person of the witch.
- Playing 'hangman' with a very hostile child allowed him to express anger indirectly.
- An adolescent made good use of a book by Michael Morpurgo, *Kensuke's Kingdom*, to work through feelings about split loyalties towards his foster family and family of origin.

Self-observation

A therapist meeting a child will have views and feelings arising from her own history and circumstances. She needs to be conscious of the way this impacts on her responses and perceptions. Self-awareness supports the capacity to see the child clearly and objectively. One therapist felt particularly enraged by a 'contemptuous' boy. When she was helped in supervision to link this with her feelings towards her father who had treated her with scorn and derision, she regained a capacity to reflect objectively on his behaviour.

We need to ask ourselves, 'What particular responses does this child elicit in me?' These may include compassion, anxiety, irritation, fury and confusion. We may feel highly protective towards one child, didactic and punitive towards another. Attention to the counter-transference can helpfully inform us about feelings with which the children may be struggling and also about early experiences with carers. One therapist noted that the boy she was assessing made her feel first hopeful and then let down. Later she discovered that the child's foster placements kept breaking down. He was unconsciously but vividly letting her know about his own experience

For a therapist in training, managing a temporary sense of uncertainty, ignorance and feelings of being deskilled can be a useful reminder of her young client's experiences and of the enormous difficulties insecure children have in acknowledging helplessness and facing new challenges.

Observing the transference

Children bring their 'internal working model' (Bowlby 1969) of significant early relationships into the therapy room and expect a response that echoes this. Paying attention to how the child expects us to respond and behave gives important information about his past experience. In order to be clear about this, we need to keep a low profile and avoid imparting personal information that might influence his views.

Matthew, for example, had no expectations that his therapist might be someone who noticed his feelings, understood him or would find a way of communicating with him. Lisa continued for a long time to expect her therapist to abandon or forget her. Leroy believed his therapist would be overwhelmed by his difficult behaviour. The adult must resist the pull to mimic the child's earlier experience and consistently challenge these expectations by responding in a different way to the one expected. She may make comments such as 'Perhaps you think I can't bear to hear how upset, angry or despairing you feel.' Or 'I notice you expect me to help you do the puzzle before you try to do it yourself.'

Sometimes a surprisingly different reaction from a significant adult can be very powerful:

> When transfer to secondary school loomed, Lisa became increasingly difficult to contain in class and was aggressive towards her therapist. The latter responded by offering a second weekly session. Lisa was stunned by this unexpected response, which redefined her angry behaviour as distress, and this proved to be a turning point in the work.

Although she does not always share her observations about the transference with a child directly, the therapist will use them to avoid replicating unhelpful interactions. For example:

- resisting a child's attempts to make her do all the thinking and choosing for him;
- noticing and flagging up small indicators of dissent and negative feelings in a child who is overtly compliant and who idealizes her;
- challenging a child's omnipotence by creating firm boundaries.

It makes it easier for us to bear powerful negative feelings from the child, such as rejection, hostility or lack of engagement, if we can hold in mind that the interaction between a child and us is dominated by the transference. This awareness allows us to reflect on the meaning of difficult behaviour.

Observing attachment patterns

In observing the way a child relates to her, the therapist may also keep in mind the patterns of attachment in children identified by Ainsworth and Wittig (1969). As a rule, the children seen in therapy are 'anxiously attached' and fall into three distinct categories based on the strategies they use to manage the relationship with a significant adult.

The avoidant child

A therapist who notices that a child tends to keep his distance from her and attempts to be self-sufficient may understand this as a learnt way of managing proximity to an adult whom he expects to be rejecting. It will be helpful to communicate this observation to the child while at the same time encouraging him to connect with us. This child, verbally uncommunicative and quite hostile in an indirect way, may fit an 'avoidant' profile.

The resistant or ambivalent child

A child who had an unpredictable parent is more likely to present as 'resistant' or 'ambivalent'; his way of coping is both to cling to and angrily reject the adult in an effort to keep her connected to him. These children may be described by their teachers as 'mouthy' and rude towards them and tend to be more articulate than their 'avoidant' counterparts.

The disorganized child

A third and smaller category are called 'disorganized'. These children may not always benefit from therapy: they may be too chronically anxious to listen and it can be hard to keep them in the room. They have had carers who were frightened or frightening or suffering from mental health problems or drug abuse and the children have struggled to find a consistent way of managing the relationship. In class they are described by teachers as 'all over the place', 'highly volatile and unpredictable' or 'cut off and unreachable'. They tend to be very controlling. Such children present an enormous challenge to adults working with them, who must provide a highly consistent and safe environment. Therapists have to be wary of any comment they make that may arouse a feeling of 'shame' for these children who have felt so impotent and helpless. Such children may benefit from very simple, gentle and brief interpretations. The child's capacity to use these must be carefully noted as well as small, gradual changes in his responses.

When considering 'disorganized' children in particular, the neurological implications of lack of containment and chronic early trauma must be held in mind. Past experiences that cannot be remembered in words are held in a bodily memory and when children are in a context reminiscent of the traumatic one, they may respond with fear or panic. They may also be overly responsive to small hidden triggers in the environment. The therapist may help such children to develop an awareness of the triggers through close monitoring and observation.

Aggression

Picking up negative feelings and hostile impulses is an important part of the work with troubled children who, at an unconscious level, often feel that their aggressive feelings are destructive and inadmissible. Melanie Klein (1931) emphasized the importance of children reaching an understanding that both loving and hostile feelings are accepted and tolerated by the mother. Klein believed that in his phantasy the frustrated infant makes hostile attacks on the 'bad' mother and needs repeated experiences of a mother who remains benign in order to reach the stage of ambivalence.

> Lisa, who had suffered loss and illness in her family and had supported her fragile mother, was inhibited about trying out new tasks in school. She seemed to believe that she would deplete or destroy the therapist with her demands and neediness. In her sessions she watched her therapist's face anxiously to see if she was upset by her mistakes. She worried about breaking the pen and messing up her drawing book. She drew her family with the use of a ruler in an attempt at rigid control – as if free expression might be disastrous. She depicted herself with hands behind her back: a typical feature of children worried about hostile impulses. Her therapist demonstrated robustness and a capacity to bear her mistakes, hostility and messy feelings.

> Aaron, aged 15, was highly anxious about his aggressive impulses and had difficulty breaking things up or taking things apart. This passivity impacted on his capacity to decode words. He was helped to overcome this inhibition by being enabled, in the safety of the therapy room, to dismantle and rebuild construction toys, jigsaws and eventually words, which he cut up and stuck together again, while his therapist commented on how difficult he found it to believe he could put things right.

Observing defensive behaviour

The infant who is not emotionally 'held' may experience a feeling of 'going to pieces' (Winnicott 1990) or 'nameless dread' (Bion 1962a, 1962b) and fear disintegration. He seeks to find ways to manage these unbearable feelings and defend against psychic pain.

Troubled children use a variety of ways in the classroom or therapy room to manage difficult feelings or challenges related to learning and relating. Examples of this may be:

- using constant movement and activity to keep thinking at bay;
- escaping painful realities by going into a world of their own;
- regressing;
- adopting a helpless stance;
- projecting uncomfortable feelings into the therapist who is seen as getting things all wrong;
- adopting an omnipotent stance, knowing everything already and being in control;
- projecting destructive feelings into monsters and being preoccupied and persecuted by their imagined retaliation.

Winnicott (1990) pointed out an additional danger concerning defences. In order for a child to develop a real sense of self, his parents need to be able to recognize and respond to his unique personality. When a parent sees a child in a distorted way – not as the child really is but as the parent expects him to be – this may be the basis of a great confusion for the child who may then develop a 'false self'.

> Oliver's therapist noticed that he had developed such a 'false self'. He complied with her around activities but 'He was going through the motions of playing but was too frightened to have his own ideas.'

> Splitting off unwanted aspects of self and locating them elsewhere is a commonly used defence. Lisa drew a picture of an abusive adult male. She depicted him alongside a drawing of herself and a drawing of an imaginary friend. By giving this friend many features common to drawings of sexually abused children, her bad feelings were split off and located in the friend. By doing so, Lisa was also able to keep a picture of herself as healthy and free of abuse. Making connections in her mind was simply too dangerous.

> Another girl idealised her therapist and demonised her teacher. In order to challenge this 'splitting', her therapist had to be alert to subtle indicators of the girl's negative feelings towards herself and then to expose them. In this way good and bad attributes could be integrated into each individual.

Looking for clues

Children find an infinite variety of ways to convey information that may be held in implicit memory and are not necessarily available for expression in words. The unconscious communication in creative activities such as story-making, drawing and play provides rich information. Deprived children may be overwhelmed by too many materials or activities on offer – as may hyperactive children – and so it is often useful to have a limited selection. This facilitates close observation of a child's use of materials. Using familiar activities and materials with a range of children makes it easier to identify unusual responses.

An adolescent's preoccupation with external events can be telling. One boy who was not supposed to know that his father was in prison was obsessed with the film *Who Framed Roger Rabbit?* A teenage girl, full of repressed fury towards her stepfather, was fascinated by the potentially disastrous effects of a nuclear explosion. In a similar way, misreading words or slips of the tongue can be revealing. One boy always read 'monster' for 'mother'.

Stories

Children's own made-up stories inform us about their attachments and perceptions. In contrast to the stories of secure children, insecure children produce incoherent stories lacking resolution and with an absence of benign characters. In the case of 'disorganized' children, stories may be characterized by extreme violence, catastrophe and magical solutions – or no solutions at all. Alternatively a child may be extremely inhibited in using imagination. Any change in children's habitual stories during the course of the psychotherapy can provide a useful means of assessing emotional growth. For instance, characters may become more benign and there may be resolutions of conflicts. Choice of books too can be significant.

> Fearing that adults could see only the 'disgusting monster' side of her, Lisa was fascinated by the story of 'Mucky Mabel', whose parents eventually failed to distinguish her from a pig. Lisa found it very helpful when her therapist showed she could see the hidden 'real' Lisa and not just the bad behaviour.

Fearful responses to stories can give useful information about ideas that a child may not yet be able to manage. A story can be a metaphorical representation of aspects of a child's experience. In this way it can introduce thoughts that a child is not yet ready to deal with, or it can provide possible solutions to a child's problems.

> Oliver found that the repetition of a wolf story in the presence of a reliable adult enabled him to be less overwhelmed by his fears of being devoured. His therapist was mindful that Bettelheim (1976) saw the wolf in the story as a projection of the child's badness and his wish to devour.

Drawings

The content of children's drawings carries both conscious and unconscious material and because of this can be immensely revealing. But because there is always a subjective aspect in interpreting artwork, it is very important that drawings are never used as the sole evidence of any formulation. The process of making a drawing, too, will deserve attention. One adolescent continuously rubbed out the figure of her paraplegic brother, while saying desperately, 'I can't make him stand!' Her therapist talked to her about her guilt and sadness about his disability.

On an impressionistic level, aspects of drawings and paintings such as their colour, boldness, movement and emotional impact can convey a sense of a child's feeling state. Depressed children, for example, may use a great deal of black and over-scribbling and children with low self-esteem often depict themselves as very tiny and use faint colours. Koppitz (1968) maintained that any human-figure drawing by a child is a reflection of his inner representation of self. In addition we may look for indicators in human figure drawings common to groups of children with particular difficulties such as sexual abuse, learning difficulties and ADHD. For example, children with below-average IQs tend to draw figures that are poorly integrated, with 'petal-like' fingers on one hand, asymmetric limbs and transparencies. Standardized scales based on human-figure drawings can provide information on cognitive, emotional and developmental age.

Kinetic family drawings, where a child draws his family 'doing something', can be highly informative in terms of who is included or excluded, the interaction of family members, the position of the child in relation to others, and so on.

> Sam was developmentally ready to read but seemed to stop progressing suddenly. In his first therapy session he drew his entire family but depicted one of his brothers with wings rather than arms. Exploration with his family revealed a 'secret' supposedly unknown to Sam – that this brother was suffering from a terminal illness. Stumbling across information felt to be dangerous and taboo set up an internal conflict for this boy, for whom reading represented independent access to information. Opening up discussion about the illness in the family helped Sam to regain his confidence.

The changes in children's drawings can be a measure of progress: they often become more integrated and carry better narrative content as the therapy continues. Readers wishing to know more about children's drawings may find a book by Cathy Malchiodi (1998) useful.

Approach to activities and play

As therapists, we pay attention to general aspects of a child's approach to tasks and activities that indicate ego strengths. For instance, we will notice his capacity to persevere, ask for help, bear making mistakes, losing at games. We will also keep an eye out for unusual responses.

> Jake's therapist noticed that when attempting to complete a jigsaw, he focused on individual pieces, making no use of contextual information on other pieces or the completed picture on the lid of the box. When she suggested to him that he might look at the picture for help, he said that that would be 'cheating'. Material in his sessions suggested that at some level Jake was aware of a secret in the family about his paternity – and was afraid of looking at the 'whole picture'.

> Lisa's therapist understood that her struggle with regard to 'taking away' in arithmetic was connected to traumatic losses in her life. Some gentle linking helped to bring the resistance into her conscious thinking.

Some therapists use projective materials to gain information about the child's view of the world. These are tasks that stimulate a response and are designed to appraise aspects of a child's personality. The Children's Apperception Test (Bellack 1949) asks for responses to pictures and can show how overtly well-behaved children may be highly disturbed, deprived or harbour violent phantasies. In a similar way the Madeleine Thomas (1937) stories describe everyday scenarios that take place at home or school and ask the child to say what they think has happened or will happen. Adolescents often respond better to more 'structured' materials. For instance, they might give information about themselves through questions about what their friends would say about them or through sentence-completion exercises. They also appreciate having a task or activity that acts as a 'buffer', regulating distance from the therapist.

Making sense of the child's spontaneous play is an important part of the work. Sometimes experiences can be graphically conveyed:

> Lisa re-enacted her abuse by her father with figures in the doll's house. Her therapist was aware that while Lisa expressed no affect, she herself felt chilled and shocked.

> Jake's play was more symbolic. He repeatedly locked the child out of the house in his play – which seemed to be an expression of his feelings of exclusion from the emotional life of the family.

Aspects of children's play can inform us about hopes and fears:

> Oliver identified with a toy dog, separating it from other animals. His therapist understood this in terms of his separating off bits of himself in order to detach himself from chaotic feelings that might overwhelm him.

> Jasira's eagerness for hide-and-seek seemed linked to a desire to be found after being lost and, perhaps, to have her hidden self known.

Sand play can be particularly fruitful. Marion Milner (1950) has said that children seem especially aware of the symbolic nature of sand play within a frame.

Playfulness and play are an integral part of the closely attuned reciprocal mother–infant relationship vital to healthy attachment (Schore 1994). If, as a consequence of early adverse experience, playfulness is inhibited, the child's emotional development may be compromised. Winnicott said, 'where playing is not possible, then the work done by the psychotherapist is directed towards bringing the patient from a state of not being able to play into a state of being able to play' (1971a: 51). He reminds us of the different stages in children's play – from solitary play in the presence of an adult as described above – through to mutual play.

> Lisa initiated role play with her therapist. She was to be the baker and the therapist her assistant. In her role of baker's assistant the therapist was not permitted to influence the events played out in any way. Only later in the therapy was Lisa able to move to the stage of mutual play where she could allow her therapist to introduce some of her own ideas into her imaginative world.

Conclusion

This chapter has described some of the ways that children and young people reveal aspects of their internal worlds in the therapy room and has considered how we share our understanding of these with them. A main skill for all therapists to develop as trainees and then build over their years of post-qualifying practice is that of attentive observation. As this chapter has shown, the therapist notes all aspects of how the child is in her presence. She listens carefully, not only taking in the content of what the child tells her but also the tone and volume of his voice, the coherency of his narrative and the feelings evoked in her. At the same time, she will register how close he comes to her and when he keeps his distance, whether or not his play or use of art materials flows or is fragmented, when he allows himself to make a mess, and so on. What the therapist has seen, heard, felt and observed is thought about within the context of the child's particular history. The therapist's interpretation of this will reflect the sense she has made of the material and will be fed back to the child in such a way that his feelings and mental states are validated on conscious and unconscious levels, having been recognised and understood. The experience, taken as a whole, enables the child to respond to the world in a more authentic way and to trust that his feelings are acceptable and can be borne.

Study questions

- How does your client respond to the containment offered when you share your understanding with him?
- What are his expectations of you and what does that say about his early experience?
- What feelings does he elicit in you and what might they mean?
- What makes him anxious/upset and how does his attempt to deal with these feelings translate into his behaviour/responses?
- What is his 'story' about himself and his life?
- Does he respond to direct discussion as opposed to working through the metaphor?
- How does he use materials/opportunities to express and explore feelings and thoughts?
- Can he play and is he comfortable with imaginative activity?
- What are the main themes/issues arising in his material?
- Is he more comfortable with structured activities?
- How might he be described in terms of attachment patterns?
- What is his emotional developmental level?
- How do you understand the child's difficulties and relationships?

References

Ainsworth, M. D. S. and Wittig, B. A. (1969) Attachment and Exploratory Behaviour of One-Year-Olds in a Strange Situation. In B. M. Foss (ed.), *Determinants of Infant Behaviour*, vol. 4. Methuen, London.

Bellack, L. (1949) Children's Apperception Test (CAT). CPS, Larchmont, N. Y.

Bettelheim, B. (1976) *The Uses of Enchantment: The Meaning and Importance of Fairy Tales*. Thames and Hudson, London.

Bion, W. R. (1962a) A Theory of Thinking. *International Journal of Psychoanalysis*, 43, 306–310.

Bion, W. R. (1962b) *Learning from Experience*. Heinemann Medical, London.

Bowlby, J. (1969) *Attachment and Loss*. vol. 1: *Attachment*. Penguin, London.

Dale, F. (1992) The Art of Communication with Vulnerable Children. In P. Varna, *The Secret Life of Vulnerable Children*. Routledge, London.

Dockar-Drysdale, B. (1993) *Therapy and Consultation in Childcare*. Free Association, London.

Harris, M. and Bick, E. (1987) *Collected Papers*. Clunie, Perthshire.

Holmes, J. (2001) *The Search for the Secure Base*. Brunner-Routledge, Hove.

Klein, M. (1931) A Contribution to the Theory of Intellectual Inhibition. *International Jounal of Psychoanalysis*, 12, 206–218.

Koppitz, E. (1968) *Psychological Evaluation of Children's Figure Drawing*. Grune and Stratton, New York.

Malchiodi, C. A. (1998) *Understanding Children's Drawings*. Jessica Kingsley, London.

Milner, M. (1950) *On Not Being Able to Paint*. Heinemann, London.

Schore, A. (1994) *Affect Regulation and the Origin of Self*. Lawrence Erlbaum Associates, Hillsdale, N. J.

Thomas, M. (1937) Methode des histoire a completer pour le depistage des complex et des conflits affectif enfantine. *Archives of Psychology, Geneva*, 26, 209–284.

Winnicott, D. W. (1971a) *Playing and Reality*. Penguin, London.

Winnicott, D. W. (1971b) *Therapeutic Consultations in Child Psychiatry*. Hogarth, London.

Winnicott, D. W. (1990) *The Maturational Processes and the Facilitating Environment*. Karnac, London.

Part II

Working in schools

The context

Chapter 5

The symbolic function of a school-based therapy service

Lyn French

Understanding key psychoanalytic concepts such as those outlined in Chapters 1–4 provides therapists with a body of knowledge that can be drawn on in and out of the consulting room. Throughout our time as trainees and over the course of our working years, we continue to learn about how our unconscious thoughts and fantasies shape our conscious perceptions; how transferences manifest in all areas of our lives; the kinds of anxieties triggered by personal, social and professional relationships; and the defences we all employ in everyday life. This way of understanding the world can be transferred to how we think about organisational dynamics.

For therapists delivering services in either the primary or secondary school setting, the school itself moulds the context for the work. This chapter explores the many ways in which both positive and negative conscious or unconscious assumptions, associations, anxieties, defences, expectations and fantasies tint the lenses through which the therapy provision – and the therapist, by implication – is viewed. In preparation for reflecting on these themes, it is useful to begin by identifying the school's primary task and what it means to 'be a learner'.

The school's primary task

If asked, most of us would say that a school's main task is to educate children and young people. If pressed, we might give more definition to this broad-brush description by adding that what is to be learned is either fact-based or skill-based. But if we think back to our own school days, the enduring memories are often of our social and emotional experiences with peers, with admired or feared teachers or with the struggles and triumphs of the learning process itself.

Our relationship to learning

Learning engages us on all levels and invariably takes place in the context of relationships, including our internal relationships with parental figures we carry in mind. When we are children, we pick up our parents' assumptions and aspirations relating to learning, knowledge and achievement as well as cultural mores associated with them. For example, we may have deep-seated beliefs acquired in childhood about what we 'should' or 'should not be' reading or studying or about how intelligent or creative – or not – we perceive ourselves to be.

Learning involves putting ideas together, holding things in mind, challenging what has gone before and coming up with new ways of thinking. All these tasks can arouse powerful feelings. This may include anxieties linked to

- competition and rivalry between peers and with internal and external adult figures;
- succeeding and triumphing over a rival or leaving behind lower-ability siblings, peers or even parents or teachers;
- surpassing an older sibling;
- dealing with internal pressures and external expectations to keep on succeeding;
- discovering the perceived limits of our intelligence;
- an inability to meet our own expectations or those of others fully;
- potential humiliation and loss of face (even if our perceived 'lacks' are not public knowledge);
- failure and the attendant fear of deep or irreparable damage to our self-image;
- evoking the envy or scorn of others;
- displeasing those upon whom we are reliant for love and acceptance by rejecting their ways of thinking or the kinds of knowledge they value;
- fearing whether we will have the capacity and creativity to put our learning to good use.

The ways in which our earliest struggles to learn were responded to by those around us leave a lasting imprint. How we manage our relationship to learning and the various feelings it evokes will have an impact on how receptive we are to the learning process.

The quality of our relationships with peers and teachers, and their capacity to engage in the emotional and psychological tasks implicit in learning, will play a role as well.

These inter-generational networks are at the core of school life, forming the foundation and framework for academic learning. They also provide us with opportunities to build our understanding of how we see the world and adjust our perceptions and expectations so that they are not dominated by our conscious or unconscious fears and wishes.

Supporting emotional learning and well-being in schools

Therapy is a practice that is rooted in thinking about the nature, quality and function of relationships. Intrinsic to this is how we view those relationships and use them, both consciously and unconsciously. Psychodynamic therapies place emphasis on the connections between our internal and external worlds and how each shapes, and is shaped by, the other. The majority of schools have incorporated emotional and psychological learning into the curriculum as an acknowledgement of the importance of learning about our relationship with ourselves, each other and within our wider environment.

The extent to which a school is prepared to support this kind of learning, however, will vary. Each school has its own culture and related priorities, which means that the emphasis placed on learning about and working towards emotional well-being can vary considerably. There may be different ideas of how this can be achieved as well. For example, we might think that pastoral lessons in secondary schools could accommodate opportunities to learn about attachment patterns, family/group dynamics, social roles that can be taken up or avoided, the kinds of anxieties that are triggered when our capacities are being tested, and so forth. However, this can be at odds with our common wish to avoid the pain that is inevitably felt when we explore our own inner worlds and try to understand the parts we've played – for better or worse – in our relationships. Rather than facilitate discussions around such themes, there can be an unspoken or unconscious desire to avoid these topics altogether. At one end of the spectrum will be those schools where this kind of learning is not viewed as a priority within mainstream education, while at the other there will be schools led by head teachers and staff who create opportunities for it. Of course, there will be all those other schools in between these two poles. The place a school assigns emotional learning and well-being within its hierarchy of priorities will affect how a therapy service is viewed and the degree to which it is welcomed, accepted and supported.

Establishing a school-based therapy service

The very act of establishing a school-based therapy service conveys unspoken messages to the community. Even if the service is minimal, the school is communicating to its population that space is being made for thinking about distressing, unsettling or anxiety-provoking experiences, rather than denying, avoiding or in some way passing on disturbing material by referring the child or adolescent elsewhere.

School therapists take care to promote the idea that therapy is not just for the most troubled or troublesome children, emphasising that it can help all of us make sense of everyday experiences. But even when this message is clearly put across, there will be some in the school community who respond warily or suspiciously to what is being offered. There may be parents or teachers who feel that providing a service in a mainstream school is akin to saying that *they* are not able to meet all the needs of their children. While these initial impressions may be modified if therapists establish their service through collaboration with the whole school community, it is a process that can take time. Nurturing a culture that can support therapy in the school requires open and direct communication, a willingness to think about what are often complex organisational dynamics and our commitment to personal development through our own therapy, supervision and continuing professional development.

Room allocation

In all schools there will be demands on physical space that cannot be met. Allocating a dedicated room for therapy, whether the sessions are being provided by a trainee, a therapist on an honorary contract or a fully qualified professional can be read as a sign that value is given to psychological and emotional development. To some, this may be reassuring, conveying an unconscious communication that the school is robust enough to contain the more confusing, upsetting and even potentially overwhelming aspects of life. To others, conversely, it could be seen as a step in the *wrong* direction, symbolising a more lenient stance in response to the school's most challenging pupils: handing over much-needed space to students who are seen as unwilling to engage, hurtfully rejecting what teachers are trying to offer and making it difficult for others to learn.

Especially in inner-city schools where space is often at a premium, therapists may not be given a dedicated room but will instead be asked to book one that is free on the days when the service is being offered. For example, we may be requested to use a deputy head's office or, alternatively, we may be given a room used primarily by support staff. School therapists are generally willing to be flexible and adaptive in the first phase of setting up their service, accepting space that is less than ideal, such as a library or a community room, until a more suitable room can be negotiated. However, it is important to remember that room allocation will carry a symbolic message. Just as a business will work towards securing a prime location, so will the school therapist. It may be a gradual process that unfolds over a number of years; however, it is an important one. Pupils using our service will respond differently to us, depending on where we are seeing them. If we are based in a small, windowless room in a seldom-used part of the school, or in a deputy head's office where students are sent when in trouble or in a learning mentor's room, we may have to work harder to establish the therapeutic alliance with our pupils because of their associations with the space in which we see them.

Conscious and unconscious messages conveyed by a school-based service

As we will be seeing in the chapters to follow, everyone in the school – staff, parents, children and adolescents – will have differing conscious and unconscious reactions to a therapy service being provided during curriculum time. Understanding the meanings that are evoked by our presence in the school can be useful. For example, the role of the therapist could symbolise that of the idealised resilient and dependable mother to whom one can turn even in the most extreme moments, confident of a thoughtful and containing response. This may be reassuring or indeed envy-provoking. To others, the therapist – male or female – could represent an intrusive mother figure who wants to know everything, which itself can be a projection of the common wish to 'get inside'. Yet another image is that of a withholding or depriving mother who 'knows but won't tell'. And for those whose early experiences were marked by emotional absence, the image of a helpless mother with nothing to give, and nothing to envy, may be the dominant impression unconsciously associated with the school therapist.

Alternatively – or additionally – for some, the idea of a school therapist may evoke conscious and unconscious associations with either a wise father figure who has the capacity to step back, reflect and give a measured response or the kind of father who in fantasy is harsh, judgemental and to be feared. On a deeper, more archaic, level the therapist or the actual service provided could be seen as the wished-for receptacle into which primitive confusion, irrational wishes and unnameable fears can be deposited and left behind.

As well, cross-cultural associations will come into play. Some may perceive therapy as favouring an American or Eurocentric way of working with life's complexities; there may be mixed feelings about the value placed on a model linked with a particular culture's way of conceptualising child-rearing, family roles and what constitutes difficulties within the child or family and how to work with them.

All of us will view the concept of therapy and the role of the therapist through layers of associations, some that we are aware of and others that are buried in our unconscious. Everyone in the school community will experience a therapist working in an on-site service in myriad ways that reflect the dominant features of their internal world.

Whether or not individuals feel they can bear the kinds of anxieties sparked by bringing to the surface their hidden or denied parts will influence how the therapeutic aim of gaining self-knowledge is perceived. Learning more about ourselves will always be accompanied by varying degrees of anticipatory fear of what could be unearthed as well as curiosity about what makes us tick.

Self-knowledge may be sought or pushed away. We may retreat from the prospect of identifying personal shortcomings or coming to terms with life's limitations. The expectation of facing up to one's dependency needs can also reinforce defences. Moreover, all of us hold in mind an internal picture of an idealised self (the ego ideal). Discovering more about ourselves will inevitably tarnish this image. We all fear looking directly at what we might label our own form of madness and many of us might ask ourselves, 'Is it better, perhaps, *not* to know?'

What we imagine a therapy service can and cannot provide triggers fantasies originating in how we have experienced our own relationships, including what has been missing or has been missed out on, what has been lost and subsequently idealised in memory and what we long for or fear most about intimacy. For all these reasons, introducing a therapy service in school will probably be met with mixed feelings and not a little resistance.

Integrating knowledge-based learning and emotional learning

Establishing therapy services in schools has the potential to symbolise the bringing together of two different kinds of learning. One is more explicitly linked to the external or physical world. The other, which is about our inner life, encompasses naming emotions (in itself a form of containment); identifying what triggers them; mapping our relationship patterns; recognising anxieties and the defences we erect against them; and learning to change what impedes rather than supports our development. As therapists working in schools, we need to be prepared to challenge idealised notions of what therapy can achieve. We also role-model staying with uncomfortable feelings long enough to think about them. This is central to being able to learn, even if at times it is painful to do so. We convey this by tolerating, rather than reacting to, the negative perceptions and projections that we are the recipients of along with the positive ones. And we do it by thinking about and processing conscious and unconscious communications.

When setting up a service, we need to equip ourselves to talk about what we are offering in ways that can be understood and related to. This includes being open to a range of different responses as described above and not becoming too defensive or personalising the situation if critical or undermining views are expressed or conveyed. It can be difficult to be on the receiving end of negative projections; both supervision and our own personal therapy can help us to process our internal responses and think about how best to handle the situations that arise and deal with them professionally. It can be helpful, too, to bear in mind that teachers are also subjected to negative projections from some of their pupils, parents, peers and management. They may want to pass these feelings on and you, the school therapist, may be the next in line. For example, if a teacher is feeling particularly deskilled and disempowered by her challenging pupils, she may resent the implication that a therapist will possess the professional knowledge and personal skills to work more effectively and sympathetically with such students. The unconscious envy aroused may result in disparaging the service, homing in on those instances when pupils haven't attended regularly or seem to be making little or no progress.

Of course, such an explicit use of projection is easier to spot than that which is disguised. An example is the senior teacher who tells you how long it took to secure funding for a therapy service, expressing relief as well as pleasure at your appointment. However, this same teacher may double book the room allocated for your sessions or fail to remember to obtain parental consent for the children referred to you.

Conclusion

As will be apparent from the themes highlighted above, establishing and sustaining a school-based therapy service is a complex undertaking. The greater our awareness of the range of conscious and unconscious associations evoked, the more possible it will be to feel stimulated rather than daunted or overwhelmed by the challenges inherent in the task. Providing a school-based service will inevitably trigger all the feelings and mental states associated with both hope and despair. This in itself makes it a richly rewarding experience that benefits us as well as the school community – as long as we retain our reflective capacities, even in situations that seem designed to close down thinking.

Study questions

Think about your own transference to learning, to schools and to therapy services:

- How would you describe your relationship with learning?
- How do you perceive your own learning capacities?
- What do you remember most from your school days?
- What did the head teacher symbolise for you when you were a student?
- Have these perceptions changed over the years and, if so, what are your current associations to the role?
- What were your own initial assumptions and expectations of therapy and what informed your views?
- Have your views changed and, if so, what does the therapist symbolise for you now and what do you think therapy can and cannot offer?
- As a therapist working with children and/or adolescents, what are your anxieties and hopes?

Track your responses to the school(s) you're working in:

- What were your first impressions of the school?
- What have you noted so far about the teachers' relationships with the senior management team?
- Does the school come across to you as a supportive and facilitating learning environment?
- If so, what are the key features that convey this impression?
- What kind of room have you been allocated (where is it located in the school; do you read any meaning into the room you've been assigned)?
- Is the school pleased to have found you a space (even if you think it may not be ideal), or do you get the impression that they gave little thought to it?
- What have you been able to find out about the historical context; e.g. Where did the idea to establish a therapy service originate? How long did it take to establish the service? Were some staff perceived as 'for' the service and some as 'against' it? How has the service been presented to the whole school community?
- Is there a policy governing the service at the school?

Being able to describe what we can and cannot provide is part of our professional role:

- How would you describe your service to a head teacher?
- How would you describe to teachers what you are offering their pupils?
- How would you describe your key aims and objectives in general terms?
- How would you describe what you are *not* able to offer?

Chapter 6

Working in the primary school setting

Reva Klein

Primary schools are fascinating and enlivening places to work in as therapists. At their best, they incorporate good childcare practice together with pedagogy. At their most effective, they are caring institutions that give children a good enough sense of security and the affirmation they need to grow developmentally, intellectually, socially and emotionally.

They are also, increasingly more so than secondary schools, microcosms of the local communities they serve, reflecting the demographic of their neighbourhoods in all their diversity, challenges and inequalities. But ultimately, each school is unique with its own dynamics, ethos and procedures. Within a half-mile radius of each other you can find schools that will be distinctive in the way they communicate with children and parents, in their approach to education and in their interface with their communities.

Notwithstanding these differences, there are certain factors that primary schools have in common. Most head teachers, for instance, understand that educating children involves much more than delivering a curriculum and will have set themselves the task of addressing, as much as possible, the needs of the whole child. In the primary school setting, heads will be thinking about how children's developmental needs can best be met in the widest sense.

This will include deciding how to support the child in, among other things: learning to play creatively and with intent, communicating effectively, expressing their feelings healthily, relating to others openly, accepting differences, dealing with peer competition and rivalry, cooperating with adults and children, containing frustrations and being flexible.

In other words, schools have a key role to play in helping children to learn from a range of life experiences. In many schools, this extends to providing family learning opportunities so that parents can learn alongside, and in relation to, their child.

The profile of therapy in primary schools

Many primary schools are providing, or aim to provide, therapeutic services for their pupils during curriculum time. The school will assign significant status to such services by ensuring that the Head or a senior member of the leadership team has the strategic lead on the development of the service. It will include the therapy service in the school's strategic development plans, assigning a discrete budget for the service. While space can be an ongoing challenge, schools will do what they can to allocate a dedicated room or rooms for the therapy sessions. The service will be represented in relevant school policies and literature on the service will be available to the whole school community.

Advantages of providing therapy in primary schools

Due to their scale, their closeness to the communities they serve and the caring ethos of the vast majority of them, primary schools are particularly well placed to offer therapeutic services to their pupils. They provide a child-friendly context that is supportive and reassuring to children and their families. Because of being located in the familiar setting of the school, the stigma that some children, parents and school staff associate with therapeutic services will be reduced.

Therapists in primary schools are in a position enabling them not only to liaise with other professionals working in the school setting but to operate within a multi-agency framework with professionals in the wider education services as well as bodies such as NSPCC.

There is a symbiotic relationship between school therapy and the wider school that, when it works, is mutually beneficial. Therapy will be supported where the whole-school ethos promotes emotional literacy. This can work to embed therapy in the school's development plan, promoting the view that emotional support and emotional literacy are part of the wider curriculum. By doing so, the therapy service gains the confidence of parents and school staff, enabling a collaborative relationship to be developed with them.

The benefits to children of seeing a therapist at primary school are significant. Rather than being dependent on a family member to take them to appointments at their local Child and Adolescent Mental Health Services, they attend all sessions on site and don't miss sessions unless they are away from school. They are likely to have a less anxious transference to the room and what it represents, as it is located within a known and safe environment, and are likely to trust the therapist more readily, as she has the implicit backing of the school.

Limitations of working in primary schools

While some schools have senior managers and others championing psychological support for their pupils, there will be schools in which therapeutic services have not been embedded within the school ethos. In such schools and indeed in others where therapy is provided, challenges can arise from different bodies within the school system. These include the following:

School governors will hold views on whether or not support services additional to those provided under statutory services should be made available to pupils in curriculum time. Governors can influence whether or not services are commissioned each year and, if so, the level of funding allocated.

The school's leadership team and senior staff may not wish to prioritise therapeutic services, preferring an option in which emotional support services are delivered by existing school staff (e.g. learning mentors or support staff).

The whole school community may not view individual therapy sessions for referred children as the best way of meeting the needs of a multicultural/multi-faith community.

For reasons such as those given above, even if a therapy service is established in the school it may function as a 'bolt on' or satellite service. The school therapist working in this context may encounter difficulties in a number of different ways. There may be issues around room allocation. For instance, she may have to book a different room each half-term and/or may find the bookings changed or even be asked to use an alternative room at short notice. She may not be informed in advance about school trips, school closures or exam days that impact on her work with children. There may be a problem with being kept up to date on important developments within the child's family, such as parents separating, moving house or a death. She may find that she hasn't been invited to participate in or contribute to important meetings about the children she is seeing and may not receive any feedback from such meetings. As a result of these difficulties, she may feel that the therapy is undervalued by the child, the family and the school.

From the child's perspective

The child receiving therapy in a primary school will have his own views of what is being offered to him. He may perceive school as a safe place that provides a refuge from home life, especially if his family circumstances are distressing; consequently he may baulk at the idea of talking or thinking about home while at school, especially in the early weeks or months of the therapy. The child who is younger, traumatised or very anxious may feel frightened of being in a room he is unfamiliar with and alone with an adult he doesn't know. He may resist leaving the classroom or try to wander off en route to the therapy room

As opposed to receiving therapy outside school, the child will have to cope with repeated interruptions to the sessions because of the frequent school holidays. If he is suspended from school or sent to a pupil referral unit, this will often mean discontinuation of the therapy. And if he is re-referred each year, he may be given a new therapist each time because of change of personnel.

The child may feel self-conscious about being singled out and being seen leaving the classroom for sessions. Similarly, he may see the therapist collecting other children from his class or from different classrooms. As well as triggering a form of sibling rivalry, he may believe he is somehow being linked to the others receiving therapy and feel uncomfortable with the association with this peer group.

The role of the therapist may cause confusion to the child, too. He may think of her as similar to a teacher who will take the lead in sessions. There's also the possibility that, given the school context in which he is receiving therapy, he may think that there is a 'right' or 'wrong' way to use the sessions. This could lead to his experiencing ongoing anxiety about how he is doing.

Another confusion may be related to the therapy room, which could be used primarily by teaching assistants and because of that has the potential for unconsciously conveying a message to the child and the school in general that therapy is an equivalent support service. Alternatively, it may feel too much like a school room, which could leave the child confused about what to expect. If the room is also used as a 'time-out' or exclusion room, it could carry a negative association for pupils and staff. Finally, the location of the room may be in a busy or central part of the school, which, apart from being noisy, may impact on confidentiality.

The role of teachers

Teachers will have conscious and unconscious fantasies about what therapy is, what it can provide and what it signifies, based on their own experiences and cultural backgrounds. Those who have trained more recently will be especially aware of the importance of meeting children's emotional needs, as will many veteran teachers and senior managers. Where teachers express or carry ambivalence or uncertainty about the nature and value of therapy, vying priorities that pull them in different directions are often the cause.

Positive attitudes to therapy in schools

Many teachers will experience the service as a welcome intervention that complements their role. They will know their pupils well and can identify those whom they think would most benefit from therapy, providing the therapist with useful background information about the child's home and school contexts. They can ease the referral process by talking to the parents to assure them that therapy will support the child's educational, emotional and psychological development. Teachers' monitoring of the child's progress and giving feedback to the therapist can be helpful in tracking the impact of the work outside sessions. They can also helpfully de-stigmatise therapy by finding appropriate opportunities to talk to their pupils about what therapeutic support offers, how adults and children might benefit from it and how most people will have challenges in life with which they might want help.

Anxieties, projections and envy

Whatever their orientations, many teachers will have a complex response to the idea of a therapist offering services to their pupils during curriculum time. Conscious and unconscious associations will be triggered that we need to be aware of and for which we need to understand the reasons.

At the outset, teachers may interpret the presence of a therapist in the school as a negative reflection on their own professional ability to provide adequate or effective pastoral support. This can lead to different attitudes. One is that they might make unhelpful assumptions about whether or not a child will benefit from therapy. Another is harbouring unrealistic hopes, expecting a child to be quickly 'cured', with the expectation that therapy will impact positively on children's behaviour within a matter of weeks. This could mean that there is a focus on getting evidence-based results (e.g. improved concentration, increased toleration of frustration, enhanced capacity to learn, etc.). Others may be against therapy for underachieving pupils because they will see it as valuable lesson time being 'lost' in the therapy room. Because of misapprehensions about what therapy is and who might benefit, as well as the demands of classroom management, teachers may only refer children who present challenging behaviour in the classroom. This means that those who are under-functioning and/or have painful family circumstances (e.g. an ill family member or a recent bereavement) will be overlooked.

There will be those who feel that the therapist is taking on the kind of work that *they* would like to be more closely involved in, with all the attendant fantasies there are about the 'cosiness' of working one to one with a child. This can engender jealousy of the therapist's relationship with the child and envy, whether conscious or unconscious, of her role. Yet others will identify with the child referred for therapy, wishing they themselves had been offered support when younger.

Whatever the reason, unacknowledged envy can lead to unconscious attempts to sabotage the therapy, which can be enacted in several ways. For example, when the therapist arrives at the classroom door to collect the child, the teacher might begin a conversation about the child in his or her presence or instruct the child to tell the therapist about a particular incident. Or the teacher might try to give the therapist or the child schoolwork to be completed during the therapy session. Even an experienced teacher with a knowledge of therapy might ask that the therapist leave the child in the class 'just this once' so he can participate in a special lesson or project or test.

Supply teachers can present other challenges. For example, they might not have been told about the child's sessions and may question the therapist about the work in front of the child. Or they may consider the removal of the child from the classroom as a distraction they could well do without and express their disapproval.

Children's perceptions of therapy

Children too will have different views on therapeutic services offered in the school setting. These will be shaped by their parents' perceptions, cultural beliefs and, especially with older children, by the way therapy is presented in the media. They may experience therapeutic support offered within the school as a welcome extension of the school's parenting role. Or they may see it as an attempt by meddling professionals to make things difficult for themselves and/or their family. Whatever their perceptions, they will have conscious and unconscious fantasies about what therapy is, what it can provide and what it signifies for them.

Parents' and carers' views

Parents' views on what therapy is – and isn't – will reflect their conscious and unconscious assumptions, associations, fantasies and anxieties. They will have differing reactions to therapy services being provided in the school setting.

They may be relieved that the school is able to provide therapeutic input for their child. It can feel reassuring to them that it is being offered on the school site during curriculum hours rather than off-site at a CAMHS centre. They may be pleased to attend a pre-therapy appointment to talk about their experience of their child and any significant family issues or events and feel supported in the complex and challenging role of being a parent/carer.

In contrast to these positive responses, some parents may hold that the school's primary function is to deliver the curriculum. Bringing support services into this setting may, as can be the view of some teachers, take away from time better spent learning. Alternatively, they may feel that their child's referral means that they have failed as parents or are deficient in some way. This can set up defences with which the therapist will have to work.

In these cases and in other circumstances, parents whose child is referred to the service may believe their child is being singled out as a 'problem child' or conclude that he has a serious mental health issue. They may assume that the teacher, deputy or head will hear about the content of the sessions, which could intensify their fear that the child will present their family life in a negative light. Some parents will make the assumption that they are considered ineffective or bad in the school's view because of their child's referral. This could lead to anxieties that everyone within the school community, including other parents, will make assumptions about their child and about their private family life. These fears could result in their avoiding any contact with the therapist on the telephone or in person. They could also be worried about the impact on siblings at the school who may feel stigmatised by association.

Conclusion

Primary schools are vibrant communities with head teachers and leadership teams increasingly interested in supporting, enhancing and creatively contributing to the child's whole development. More emphasis is placed on building emotional competencies, expanding social and personal skills and providing targeted interventions for the most vulnerable. Initiating new ways of engaging whole families to participate in joint learning or recreational or cultural activities remains high on the agenda.

Therapists have much to offer in the primary school setting. As discussed in this chapter, working in such an environment involves entering a complex field. Everyone in the extended school community – teachers, pupils, governors, support staff, dinner ladies, visiting specialists, parents, and so on – will have their own conscious and unconscious understanding of and associations with what the practice of therapy entails and what even the word 'therapy' signifies. Being mindful of negative views as well as idealised notions of what can and cannot be achieved by therapy provided in schools is vital. This chapter has highlighted how crucial it is for the therapist to work in collaboration with school staff and parents so that a robust partnership can be forged that will be strong enough to withstand the challenges inherent in establishing and sustaining a therapy service. School therapists have the opportunity to make a significant difference while, at the same time, fulfilling a role that is stimulating, creative and ever evolving.

Study questions

The questions below will be answered in the chapters to follow. Try answering them now.

- Who will be the main source for referrals?
- Will you see the parents before beginning the therapy? What will you tell them about the service? What will you ask them? What may come up in this first meeting?
- Who will tell the child that he is being offered therapy? Will it be the teacher, the therapist or the SENCo? Will older primary school children be given a leaflet describing the service on offer?
- What explanation will be given to the child about why she has been selected for therapy?
- Will the child have a choice about attending?
- Will the child have a choice about stopping the sessions?
- How would you as the therapist react if the teacher tries to update you on the child's behaviour or well-being in front of the child when you go to collect him? How would you respond if the teacher expects regular updates or asks for specific information on the child?
- What kind of information would you be prepared to pass on to the child's teacher?

Chapter 7

Working in the secondary school setting

Stefania Putzu-Williams

Secondary school head teachers generally understand that many children are born into complex circumstances and that schools are well placed to address some of the resulting deficits. It is therefore likely to find them as committed as primary school heads to supporting their students' social, emotional and psychological growth as well as progressing their academic learning. Most have given careful thought to how best to achieve this. For instance, lessons during curriculum time cover some of the basic themes related to navigating adolescence. In addition, the majority of schools have introduced support services which ensure that all pupils have the opportunity to participate fully in school life regardless of their cognitive abilities, life skills, social or emotional needs.

Providing therapy sessions during curriculum time on the school site is one way of ensuring that those students most in need can access services. Many of the advantages and limitations outlined in the preceding chapter on working in primary schools also apply to working in secondary schools. However, there are differences, not least because the young people receiving the service are facing different developmental tasks.

Whole school development

Another aim of school-based therapy can be to support the promotion and development of a more therapeutic school environment. Depending on the amount of time allocated to the school therapist, there may be opportunities to contribute to wider school aims linked to the social and emotional aspects of learning. There are many ways the therapist can collaborate with school staff to meet this aim. For example, the therapist's role in school may include group work and other interventions delivered with teachers and support staff. There may also be opportunities for direct work with parents and families as well as providing one-off discussion groups covering themes relating to adolescence and parenting in general. Some school therapists may also provide work discussion groups, consultation and/or support sessions for school staff, or they may contribute to relevant aspects of curriculum delivery, workshops on mental health or similar initiatives. However, this chapter will not be covering this aspect of the school therapist's role. Instead, the focus of the sections to follow will be on individual therapy with adolescents and the benefits and challenges of providing a school-based service.

Meeting the needs of adolescents

The role of the therapist working in the secondary school setting is to support students as they attempt to weather the changes associated with adolescence. This means, among other things, enabling them to bear their difficulties or emotional pain in ways that are not self-defeating, maladaptive or destructive. The contemporary world is a complex one and adolescents face a wide range of challenges. They will be negotiating their path towards independent living, which involves beginning the separation process from parents or carers and home life. This in itself triggers anxieties. Everyone suffers from teenage stresses but in many cases traumatic experiences, self-doubt, deep vulnerabilities stemming from low self-worth and a lack of internal resources in general will impact in painful ways. In addition, peer pressures often seem more acute in the secondary school setting than those encountered in primary school.

Accepting and better understanding what is happening in their lives can be a positive outcome of therapy with adolescents, an age group often more prone to action than reflection. Some refrain from introspection out of fear of discovering that there may be something very wrong with them. At the other end of the spectrum are those who ruminate too much and become paralysed by their doubts and fears. Avoiding the necessary pain involved in reality testing may be an aspect of their difficulty and they will need to be supported so they can take more risks.

Therapy can help them to step back and think about their day-to-day experiences, identifying the feelings evoked and giving words to their internal fantasies about themselves and their relationships. The therapist can help adolescents to modify and contain some of their most disturbing thoughts, feelings and memories by understanding and considering them together with another thinking mind.

Impact of the unconscious

The school therapist needs to be aware of the unconscious life and dynamics, not just of the individual client, but of the organisation as a whole and to have an understanding of the rules, tasks and culture of the school. Like individuals, institutions develop particular defences against emotional and mental pain. These can be reinforced in response to external pressures, internal conflicts between staff or departments, competition over scarce resources, or as a result of the nature of the work.

It is helpful for the school therapist to be perceived by students and staff as occupying an 'in-between' space, neither fully part of the school milieu nor completely separate either. The therapist takes up a stance that prioritises observation, reflection and the capacity to think. This space can be unconsciously internalised and experienced by students as a neutral space in their minds, a place where they can reflect. This can also be true for school staff.

This 'neutral' space can be better achieved if there is enough trust in the management of boundaries and confidentiality, a trust that can only be built over time. Adolescents need us to maintain and communicate clear and appropriate boundaries, which allow them to feel safe and know what to expect.

Managing self-destructive fantasies or behaviour

Risk management in secondary schools is discussed in more detail in Chapter 10 (The Assessment Process). However, it is worth noting that morbid thinking, a desire to act out revenge fantasies (along the lines of 'when I'm dead, they'll be sorry') and talk of self-harming behaviours, both emotional and physical, are quite common in adolescence. When it seems a young person is at serious risk, the conscious and unconscious impact on the therapist can be powerful.

In such instances, the therapist is left feeling very unsettled or even deeply concerned about whether or not there is an underlying intention to act on the fantasies. The young person may be unconsciously attempting to elicit alarm or to induce guilt and confusion in the therapist without having any intention of taking real action. The therapist, for her part, may find herself compelled to act, stepping out of role and 'doing' things for the young person, rather than trusting that thinking is usually more effective than giving in to the impulse to take action.

Working directly with the young person to identify the motives and consequences of his suicidal intentions or self-destructive behaviour can be a way forward. Trying to understand the symbolic meanings underpinning his thinking can be more effective than external containment.

Chapter 10 highlights how important it is to view the first few sessions as an assessment phase in which a clearer picture can be formed of the young person's presenting issues. As emphasised in that chapter, school therapists are working within a wider network. There are designated staff in every school who have the responsibility for safeguarding children and are available to work in collaboration with the school therapist. They will be able to access support and will hold final responsibility for referring the young person on. This, combined with the school therapist's own supervision, will provide a containing framework for thinking about how best to support the young person in the longer term.

When different professionals are involved, it is important to understand which part of the client is being 'carried' by each member of the wider team. Inadequate communication within the system can lead to conflicts of interest and polarisation that can easily be experienced by the adolescent as confirmation of his own destructiveness. However, most school therapists find that professionals from networks both in and outside the school are also aware of these risks and are able to work through difficult patches when communication is confused, contradictory or breaking down. They are, to some extent, inevitable processes in all communication systems.

The service context

The therapist who is entering a school where a counselling or therapeutic service has been established for some time can find it helpful to learn about its background and history. By doing so, you will begin to form a picture of the service's 'birth and infanthood', including who in the school took responsibility for the initial conception, who championed it, and whether achieving it involved a struggle. As well, you will want to know the extent to which the service has been embedded and how securely anchored it is. Understanding the context will enable you to identify what the strengths and shortcomings of the service are so that you are better positioned to anticipate difficulties and build on what works well.

Those therapists who are setting up a service for the first time are advised to bear in mind that this process involves a number of key tasks including those outlined below.

There needs to be agreement on

- a working contract between the therapist or therapist's organisation and the school – establishing a clear understanding of the service aims; clarifying the distinct roles and responsibilities of both the therapist and the school;
- booking a suitable room – identifying a room in the school, preferably a soundproof one that offers some privacy; confirming whether or not there will be access to a telephone and a computer;
- how the therapy service will be accessed – setting up a referral system and agreeing on how the service will be promoted in school;
- how the young person will be told about his referral to the school therapist – who will inform the young person; what will be said;
- confidentiality – clarifying the procedures around pupils at risk; discussing and agreeing what kind of feedback the therapist will provide on her clients and any work undertaken with parents or school staff, along with what form this feedback will take (e.g. termly or annual written reports and/or verbal feedback);
- liaising with school staff including Special Educational Needs Coordinator (SENCo), senior staff (heads of year, child protection [CP] or safeguarding officer) and with relevant external professionals from statutory and voluntary organisations;
- service evaluation – how it will be conducted and in what form it will be fed back to the school.

Service structure and management

School therapists who are working either independently or linked to an external organisation usually ask the school to name a member of staff as a link worker. It is this person's role to coordinate jointly the service with the school therapist, which generally involves managing the room bookings, the referral system and the waiting list. Some schools will allocate two link workers: a senior staff member in the management team to provide higher-level input and a teacher or a school support worker to liaise with about day-to-day matters. This might include organising appointments, checking to see if a student is in school, collecting a student from class, and so on. A good alliance with the link worker is essential to avoid double bookings and to stay informed about school trips, exam days, suspensions, exclusions and absences.

School therapists employed directly by the school and viewed as a member of their staff team often find it easier to maintain communication channels across the whole school network. It is useful to note that schools may commission therapeutic services from more than one therapist or organisation. The school therapist will need to be aware of other related professionals and be prepared to work collaboratively with them, jointly coordinating services.

Key aspects of working in secondary schools

Referrals

- School therapists liaise with their links in school either to find out how the existing system works or to set up their own system in collaboration with the school. (See Chapter 9.)
- The systems for self-referral vary. For example, a school therapist's practice might include a drop-in session during part of lunch break or after school. A postbox with referral forms placed in the library or close to the canteen can be used for self-referrals. Alternatively, students may be invited to talk to a designated support staff member in the school who will then arrange for an appointment with the school therapist.
- In contrast to the primary school setting, school therapists may receive very little information before seeing their pupil for the first time, which is why including an assessment phase is important. (See Chapter 10.)

Parental consent

- In the UK, young people under the age of 16 require parental consent unless they are considered competent under the terms of the Fraser Principle (formerly known as the Gillick Principle). The Fraser Principle states, 'As a general principle it is legal and acceptable for a young person to ask for confidential counselling without parental consent or against their parents' wishes, providing they are of sufficient understanding and intelligence.'
- Parental consent may prove difficult to obtain from parents who are hard to engage. Another complication may be that the young person does not want the therapist to have any contact with his parents. In such instances, and in collaboration with an experienced supervisor and the school, the therapist

will take a view on whether or not to see the young person at least for an assessment. Competence in young people can be impaired by circumstances such as special needs, extreme stress and drug misuse.
- Some schools deal with the issue of parental consent by telling parents and pupils about the therapy service in the school prospectus, presenting it as part of the wider curriculum and school ethos. Nevertheless, it may be legally advisable for the head teacher to ensure that all parents are notified that their child may receive support while in school. A statement of this kind is often included in the Year 7 starter pack given to all parents.

Contact with teachers and parents

- Primary schools are structured to provide children with a main attachment figure in the person of their class teacher. This matches the developmental needs of the age group. In secondary schools adolescents are encouraged to be more independent. Teachers are less directly involved with their pupils and will, therefore, know less about them.
- Secondary schools are complex organisations and teachers have other responsibilities in addition to teaching. Teachers are less directly involved with their pupils and will, therefore, know less about them. Even those teachers who know many of their students very well will rarely have the time to liaise with the school therapist. Teachers may also have mixed feelings about sharing their students with the therapist, which need to be respected and understood.
- Adolescents generally prefer to keep therapy confidential and usually do not want to involve others. Therefore contact with parents is mostly in the lower school (i.e. pupils aged 11–14). For this age group parental permission is sought and the school therapist tries to develop a working alliance between school and home.

Appointment systems

- The school therapist needs to follow the school's lead on structuring appointments. Some schools allow pupils to miss the same lesson each week in order to attend their therapy session. Others will ask the school therapist to rotate appointment times. The school therapist will need to develop a system for this, such as printing appointment slips that can be given out in registration or putting a sticker with the next appointment written on it in the pupil's school diary. For instance: _____ (student's name) has an appointment with _____ (therapist's name) on _____ (date) in (period) _____.
- While in primary schools children are usually escorted to sessions, students in secondary school generally, though not always, make their own way to sessions.
- If students don't arrive in time for their session, there will be a system for checking if they are in school and, if so, what lesson they are in. The school therapist will need to decide what her practice will be. For example, will she

consider collecting students from their class who do not turn up? Will she send the link worker or a duty student to do so? Or will she decide on a case-by-case basis? There are advantages and limitations to each of these approaches, so it is useful to discuss with your supervisor and with the school how to respond to those who are in school but do not show up.
- In primary schools, it is usually easier to let a child know in advance that he will be seen by the school therapist. His teacher or parent will be encouraged to tell him, or else the school therapist herself will let the child know. In the secondary school setting, it is not unusual for a first appointment to be offered on the same day the referral is received. It may be an urgent referral, or there may simply be a cancellation that allows a student on the waiting list to be offered an assessment session. In clinical terms, this means, for example, that the time and space of an ongoing client's appointment will be taken by another.
- The student and the therapist need to discuss attendance and punctuality. Usually this conversation takes place in the first session or initial stages of the work. For example, some schools or agencies specify that the case is closed if the student misses two or three times without giving notice. In such instances, the student can self-refer or be referred again at any time. When students are consistently late or miss sessions – every time seemingly with a plausible reason – it is important to remember that this is also a communication about their ambivalence towards therapy and the thought of making changes. It can usefully be addressed with the student in the session.
- At the end of each session, the student has to re-enter the school environment, returning to class, to teachers, to peers. The therapist may need to bear this in mind so that some time is left before the end to prepare for the transition back into the school day. A session length of 50 minutes often suits a school timetable, leaving students 10 minutes before the bell for their next class. It also helps to preserve confidentiality, so students do not meet each other at the therapist's door.
- The length of contract with secondary school students can vary considerably. While trainee therapists may see students for the whole academic year in order to meet their course requirements, school therapists often offer a 6–12 session contract to each young person, usually including two initial assessment sessions. Depending on factors such as the therapist's caseload and, where relevant, the external agency's requirements, a quarter of cases can be longer term so that the needs of more vulnerable or complex clients can be met. Balancing short- and long-term contracts is an important aspect of managing a caseload.

Urgent referrals
- In schools where there is a steady flow of referrals with a number highlighted as 'urgent', it is advisable to keep a time slot free for short-notice consultations. This slot can be used to assess the most pressing referrals, ensuring that priority can be given to more serious cases.

- If it is possible to arrange a meeting with the referrers, especially if they have categorised the case as 'urgent', then the free slot can be used for this. It is useful to find out what other interventions have already been tried or can be considered. Sometimes a consultation with the referrer(s) is enough to contain a situation without the therapist even meeting the adolescent. Or, if the young person refuses to see the therapist, the parent(s) or a teacher may be offered a consultation. Trainees are usually not obliged to see parents or offer staff consultations, but qualified school therapists may make this option available.
- This free time slot can also be used for liaison work with school or external staff. For example, when other professionals or services are already involved with the young person referred, it is important to discuss with them whether or not offering therapy sessions is appropriate and relevant.

Waiting lists

- Most schools will introduce a waiting list even by default, as there are usually more referrals than time slots available. The list is best managed by the school therapist and the link worker in consultation with the staff/referrer. Decisions will have to be made about prioritising the pupils referred.
- When the waiting list builds up, the therapist can feel under pressure from the school to stop working with existing clients so as to make space for new ones. There are ethical considerations involved in such situations. Once the school knows about a young person's needs, then appropriate support should be offered. Some therapists use slots created by cancellations or absences to see students for an assessment. While this conflicts with the more traditional therapeutic stance, which emphasises holding the space for an absent client, school therapists need to be flexible and responsive to need.

Managing expectations

- School therapists need to balance their profession's standards and ethics, those of their own organisation when relevant (e.g. if working in a voluntary agency or as a member of a statutory service), the expectations of the school and those of the client. In some cases, the parents or carers are involved and their needs and expectations need to be considered as well. As a general guideline, school therapists will try to role-model reflective thinking about any request made by the school, a young person or a parent rather than succumbing to pressure to give an immediate reply or come up with an instant solution. Sometimes this is best achieved by saying, for example, 'Let's think about what the impact would be if I did change the appointment time and what would happen if I didn't.'
- The kinds of pressures inherent in the job include those generated by the school's own sense of being overwhelmed or panicked and the wish to hand this on to the therapist. For example, the school might refer a young person to therapy as a 'last resort' before an exclusion is applied. Containing the projected anxiety,

staying calm and agreeing to have an initial conversation with the young person is often the most useful course of action. Such a response will implicitly convey that you may not be able to offer more than a first discussion. To be able to carry this off successfully depends on being able to resist taking up the role of 'rescuer' and also being able to make good use of your own inner authority.

- As will be apparent, school therapists need to feel comfortable with what they can and cannot offer. Not all young people will be receptive to the process. During the assessment phase, the therapist is especially aware of differences and how this might impact on the work. For example, some young people and their parents may perceive therapy as being the exclusive province of the middle classes or specifically the *white* middle classes, and may initially feel patronised or undermined by being referred. An important core task is to convey to the client that whatever the differences in age, gender, class, culture and race, relationships can be built and understanding achieved.
- Managing our own expectations of what 'doing a good job' entails is another consideration. School therapists need to maintain their professional role, even under pressure, yet remain open to adapting and modifying their provision when this is required. We all have an 'internal supervisor' who needs to be managed so we don't feel caught between what we think we 'should' be doing and what we cannot do because of the school context.
- Finally, we all have our own transferences to school as an institution and need to be aware of what positions we might unconsciously identify with. For example, the therapist who internalised teachers as 'good objects' may unconsciously align herself with school staff and identify less easily with the young person who feels persecuted by them. A different transference will be experienced by the therapist who experienced teachers as demanding or punitive – in other words, primarily as 'bad objects'. This kind of therapist might catch herself over-identifying with the pupils referred to her at the expense of seeing the school's point of view.

Review sessions

- A review session with students can be offered about six to eight weeks after the end of therapy to provide an opportunity to hear about new developments and changes as well as raise any concerns that may have come up. It also gives the student the chance to ask for a 'top-up' and to have another block of sessions if needed, though he may have to be placed on the waiting list if there is one. The time-limited nature of the therapy inevitably stirs up issues around individuation and separation, which are experienced in the transference and so need to be considered and addressed with the client.

Conclusion

This chapter has provided an overview of some of the main features of working in the secondary school context. As has been observed, every school is different and each will have a unique ethos carefully shaped by the head teacher in consultation with the leadership team. Consequently, the boundary and scope of the school therapist's role will be different in every secondary school. In some, the therapist will contribute to child protection or safeguarding children procedures, the development of whole-school policies especially around emotional learning and well-being, the delivery of in-school training for teachers (INSET), the provision of work discussion or support sessions for school staff and/or the delivery of peer support or peer counselling for pupils or group work with them. In others, the therapist's role will be very much that of a specialist practitioner coming in to provide individual sessions for referred students and liaising with school staff to support the work. As the provision of one-to-one sessions is central to any therapeutic service, this was the focus of the chapter. However, the points raised in discussion of the role that in-school therapy can play in the lives of adolescents has a wider application.

Study questions

- What kinds of defences might schools develop against emotional and mental pain?
- What defences have you observed at play in your school?
- How does the therapist work effectively when these defences are strongly enforced?
- What is the history and stage of development of the therapy service you are providing?
- What does this history tell you about the conscious and unconscious views of the school on offering therapy to its pupils?

As a school therapist, how would you respond if

- a teacher knocks on your door at lunch and asks you for feedback on one of your clients;
- the head teacher stops you in the corridor and asks if you can let a senior staff member use your room for a consultation with a parent at a time when you see a client;
- a young person tells you about a suicidal fantasy?

Part III

Practical approaches to the work

Chapter 8

Preparing the room

Camilla Waldburg

Introduction

Before looking at the practical aspects of the room – what's involved in booking and preparing it for sessions – it's useful to think about the symbolic significance of the space, both on a conscious and unconscious level.

Using the same room each week communicates to the child that the physical boundaries framing the work are reliable and dependable, echoing the consistency and availability of the therapist for the child. Ensuring that the same room is available each week contributes to creating a therapeutic culture both within the room and outside, in the school at large. Staff and pupils come to know what the room is used for and when sessions take place. This should result in fewer disruptions, especially once the school therapist has established the service.

As the therapeutic relationship unfolds, the room in which the ongoing narrative takes shape acts as a symbolic container. The room itself holds the client's story as well as the emotional history of past and present relationships, including both the real and the transference relationship between client and therapist. On a deeply unconscious level, the room comes to stand for the outer receptacle holding the contents of the client's mind, a concrete manifestation of the therapist's mind, which contains and processes what is revealed, both verbally and non-verbally, as well as all that is fantasised about in that particular space. Because of the symbolic power of the room, most practitioners choose to arrange it in the same way each week and have a fixed set of art and play resources available. This conveys the message that in the face of powerful primitive feelings, fantasies and mental states, the room – and, by association, the therapist's mind – can function as a robust enough container. It goes without saying, however, that the most important component of this process is the therapist's mind: her capacity to go on thinking and not be overwhelmed by the material presented. So, while a dedicated and secure room is the ideal, many therapists do their work day in and day out in less than perfect circumstances ranging from different rooms every week in the school setting to providing out-of-door sessions in refugee camps.

Negotiating space within the school

Negotiating with a school for an appropriate room and for a booking that is respected throughout the academic year is often best viewed as a long-term process. School therapists usually have to be very flexible to begin with and make do with whatever physical space the school is prepared to offer, which initially may be far from our idea of an appropriate room. Over time, the school's management team will hopefully build their confidence and trust in the service and come to value the contribution it is making, paving the way towards a more suitable room allocation. A successful outcome often relies on the school therapist being able to explain clearly what is required and why.

In both primary and secondary schools, different types of rooms will be made available. In some schools, the therapist may be given a dedicated therapy room that is used only by the school therapist, external agencies and professionals for individual sessions, small therapy groups and meetings with parents. However, in the first instance it is probably more common to be allocated one of the following:

- a parent room
- a community room
- a general meeting room
- a multipurpose room used for a range of school-based activities (e.g. learning-support interventions, booster classes, one-to-one lessons, etc.)
- a deputy head or SENCo's office
- an adapted space such as a converted walk-in cupboard fashioned into a small consulting room
- a small, partitioned-off area in a larger room, such as an under-utilised classroom, art room or library

The school therapist may need to be prepared to embark on an ongoing dialogue around the room booking, explaining what kind of space is most suitable and what the reasons for this are. It is best to keep the description simple. Such conversations can help to frame requests within the wider context of school therapy services in general. Some suggestions on how this can be approached are provided below.

> 'School therapists are usually given the same room to use each week. There is a purpose for this kind of consistency. Pupils need to get used to what is a very new experience. This process is made easier if they become familiar with the one room. It also makes it more likely that they will see me as trustworthy and reliable if we don't move from one place to the other. Pupils need to feel able to talk about private feelings and personal experiences and having the same room to come to each week helps them feel safe and contained.
>
> 'I know there are many demands on space in this school and that most staff have to take whatever room is available. I'm happy to work with this

arrangement but it would be useful to think about longer-term possibilities. Maybe we can review the room booking at the end of the term and see what else might be available.' At the end-of-term review meeting, the school therapist might say, 'Professional guidelines recommend that school therapists aim to have a room that is relatively soundproof and is on a quiet corridor. This protects confidentiality and can help the pupil open up more freely.'

Every therapist will have her own unique relationship with school staff and the management team. The way you choose to describe your practice and room preferences will depend very much on the kinds of relationships you've developed within the school and with whom you are negotiating.

It may take a year or two to secure a room in a school that is best suited for therapeutic work. If there is a change in head teacher or even in government policy or educational priorities, a secure booking can be changed. The therapist needs to be aware that provision in schools is almost always a 'work in progress'.

It is professional, and sometimes a challenge, to contain our feelings about the room allocated for therapy services. There are times when others are allocated a 'better' room in the school. This can provoke difficult feelings such as jealousy or hurt at not being appreciated. If we can see these incidents not as a personal affront but as part and parcel of establishing and maintaining a service in a school that has its own preoccupations and changing priorities, they will be easier to manage.

Even once a regular room booking has been established for therapeutic work, there may be instances when it is needed for a special occasion. The school therapist who finds herself in this situation will need to gauge how best to respond. It is usually most helpful if the therapist is prepared to move rooms as a one-off arrangement. Perhaps afterwards she can find the right moment to repeat to the staff member she usually liaises with how important it is to be able to offer the pupil consistency and reliability. It can be emphasised that those referred for therapy are usually children who find it hard to trust and to believe that their needs can be both respected and met. Sudden changes can shake their trust even further.

If the school has to alter the room booking on a more permanent basis, it's best for the therapeutic process if the change coincides with a natural break in the school timetable, such as after a school holiday or at the start of a new half-term. Room changes should always be communicated to the client, giving as much notice as possible to allow time to acknowledge the feelings stirred up as well as to prepare for the change. At times this may not be possible and in these instances it is advised to communicate something along the lines of the following to the child:

> 'You probably remember that I told you in your first session that we'd meet in this room every week. The school has now asked me to change rooms. From next week we will be meeting on the other side of this building in Room A10. So while I like to keep to what I told you will happen, sometimes unexpected changes have to be made, just as in life outside this room. How do you feel about what I've just said? What does it bring up for you?'

The therapist may need to do more of the processing work if she is seeing a younger child. It can be useful to make links to other changes the child has gone through as well as ensuring that the pupil can freely express his views on what the change of room means to him, including how it affects his perception of the therapist.

Some questions that can be reflected on include:

- If the child or young person doesn't seem to be impacted by the change, how does the therapist work with this?
- How does the therapist acknowledge the difficult feelings without dramatising the significance of the change or seeming to be making too much of it?
- How can the child or young person's adaptability be reinforced without side-stepping feelings that might be minimised or denied about the impact?
- How does the therapist work with the child or young person who might still be suffering from the impact of traumatic changes and the losses incurred? How might a sudden and unexpected room change be experienced by such a client?

The multiple-use room

The school therapist might have been allocated a room that has multiple uses. Sharing space with another professional such as a specialist teacher, social worker or parent worker can be complex. Successful collaboration depends on the different professionals liaising with each other about scheduling their appointments and being prepared to negotiate around timetabling. On the other hand, it creates possibilities for relationship building and even future partnerships.

Shared spaces can be more prone to interruptions as different professionals may have their own guiding principles around how they use the room and whether or not interruptions are permitted. For example, a specialist teacher may work with children for shorter time slots, which could set the scene for other school staff to pop in and out at frequent intervals between appointments. Or if the person using the room prior to the therapist gets off to a late start and the session over-runs, it could make a significant impact. Again, flexibility and holding one's professional role is key.

It is useful for the school therapist to find out whether the children she sees are taken to the same room for purposes other than therapy. For example, if the therapist is using the deputy head's office, the child may be requested to go there when he has not been able to work within the school's rules. The child's unconscious transference to the room may be to perceive anything that takes place in it as associated with being in trouble. This may not be referred to directly by the child or the therapist but will need to be thought about by the therapist.

Practicalities

Once an appropriate room has been allocated, some basic strategies will help create a culture that respects the fact that sessions are not to be interrupted and that protecting clients' confidentiality is crucial. Printing a simple sign saying, 'Session in Progress – Please Do Not Disturb', laminating and placing it on the door can work. It won't necessarily prevent unconscious acting out, though, especially in the early weeks and months of establishing the service. Often there is an unconscious desire to 'get inside': a shut door behind which an intimate encounter is taking place triggers deeper fantasies relating to the child-like wish to gain access to the parents' private relationship. As well, staff may take it for granted that they can walk straight in, as most rooms, especially in primary schools, are accessible. An example follows.

A teaching assistant knocks on the door, and immediately walks into the room, saying, 'Sorry but I just need to get that box of toys in the top cupboard. It will only take a minute.' Often it is helpful to address the child first, saying something along the lines of 'Let's pause for a moment until Sandra's finished collecting the toys', and then sit quietly with the child. Often silence communicates more effectively than words that the session shouldn't be interrupted. After the teaching assistant leaves, you will probably want to re-establish the boundary, saying 'I'm sorry we had to stop just then. I'll speak to Sandra afterwards and remind her that we shouldn't be interrupted. You were just telling me about what happened at break time yesterday. You were saying . . .'

Whether you choose to explore what the interruption meant to the child will depend on the age of the child, how long you've been seeing him and what it felt like during the interruption. When the external boundary is briefly ruptured like this, it is useful to try to continue to hold the internal boundary by staying with the child in your thoughts and keeping the focus. It is not so helpful to speak to the staff member then and there but instead to wait until afterwards and perhaps go and have a short conversation to suggest that the toys are stored elsewhere or collected just before a session. To help with this process, you may want to post a timetable on the therapy door that clearly states what times sessions take place. Usually school therapists will see their clients for 45 or 50 minutes, leaving at least 10 minutes between sessions, during which time the room can be accessed by other staff.

Senior staff in particular may understandably feel they have a right to enter any room on the school site when necessary. For example, a head teacher could tap on the door, opening it as he does so, and say he wants to talk with you about plans for using the room in the afternoon. In such situations, the school therapist needs to feel comfortable about holding her professional role and saying something along the lines of 'This isn't a good time. Can I come to see you at 10.20 when I'm finished with John?' If the Head replies that he won't be free then, you may need to be prepared to be flexible, saying to the child, 'I'll just have a short conversation with Mr Smith and then we'll continue our session.'

How you proceed to manage this interruption will have an impact on both the person who's interrupted and the child you've had to move away from momentarily. By leaving your seat and going over to the door, standing within the door frame or just outside it and holding the door open so you are not leaving the child on his own, you will be communicating to the Head that the room boundary needs to be respected. You'll need to keep the conversation very short and be prepared to pick it up later if necessary. Again, our actions often convey more effectively than words that the room boundary needs to be respected. A quiet, calm manner and a general ease with the situation can help, even if you are talking to an executive principal in a secondary school. Keeping our cool in such situations can be particularly difficult to achieve in the early stages of working as a therapist: we are all bound to have internal reactions to such interruptions which can be quite powerful, depending on the strength of the unconscious material that may be in play both in the school staff member and in ourselves. We all carry our own historical relationship to authority figures, and complex internal responses can be triggered in such situations. One can use personal therapy and even supervision to express freely what cannot be communicated in the moment along with processing the experience.

You can help ensure that room bookings are respected by posting the timetable in the school staff room. It can also be emailed to relevant staff such as the front office, administration and management team. A sample timetable is provided below:

School Therapy Sessions in _____ (insert room number/name)
TUESDAYS

9.00–9.50am	Session 1
9.50–10.00am	**Free access**
10.00–10.50am	Session 2
10.50–11.00am	Morning break: **Free Access**
(etc.)	

Setting up the room

Arranging the therapy room will vary from school to school, depending on whether or not the room is used for other purposes and what those purposes are. If you are given a dedicated room, it can be set up at the start of the academic year. A lockable cupboard in which materials and children's folders can be stored should be made available in the room. However, if you're working in a multifunctional room, this may not be possible. Your materials might be stored in a different location in the school so you will need to collect them before your first session of the day and then set up the room.

There are many ways of setting up a therapy room. For example, a room in a primary school might be equipped with a sink, a sand-tray area, a small table and chairs and a comfortable corner, with different types of material openly visible in boxes on the floor (see 'Materials' below). On the other hand, a therapy space in a secondary school, where the therapeutic process is often more conversation based, might consist of two adult chairs and a basic set of resources, such as pen, pencil, eraser, felt tips, paper and perhaps some plastic figures.

Some school therapists may choose to keep a separate material box for each child or young person, ensuring consistency of equipment. This often depends on whether or not there is adequate storage space and enough materials to create individual boxes.

If several professionals are sharing the room, each may have their own way of organising the space. It is advisable for you to think carefully about this in the first instance, as the arrangement will need to be recreated each week. It may entail moving several pieces of furniture and rearranging them into a workable environment.

An attractive piece of cloth or a colourful spread can be used to cover items in the room such as computers, bookshelves, someone else's work desk and other work resources belonging to school staff such as toys and books, as they may be distracting. When setting up the room for therapeutic work, all materials should be kept in the same space each week in order to convey consistency. It is worth keeping in mind how accessible the resources are. For example, a five-year-old will need the materials to be placed lower down or even on the floor, whereas an older pupil would be able to reach them if placed on a shelf or in a cupboard fixed higher up on the wall.

Materials

Therapeutic toys and materials will vary according to each therapist's working paradigm and training. The basic list of resources provided below includes toys and materials that can usefully facilitate free expression and encourage child-led play.

A basic therapeutic kit can include the following:

- Toys that easily relate to real life such as a dolls' house and furniture, doll family, puppets and clothes, farm animals, cars, trucks, boats, food, shop toys, money, etc.
- Toys that permit the expression of more aggressive feelings such as toy soldiers, wild animals, monsters, spiders, plastic swords, etc. Some school therapists choose to include play guns and knives. They can allow for explorations of real-life events as covered in the press as well as mobilise discussion around what triggers the need to carry them.
- Toys for creative expression and emotional release such as sand, water, building blocks, Lego, paints, chalk, play dough and sensory material such as plastic 'goo' and 'slime'. Many school therapists choose to avoid bottled paint as it can be tempting to overuse it. For example, a child or young person with a history of deprivation might want to use it all up by pouring it out in pools onto paper. (For a further discussion, see below under 'How to deal with different materials'.)
- Toys for projective play, such as animals, fantasy figures, superheroes, and other items, such as a medical kit, small-world houses, etc.
- Art materials including a range of paper in different sizes and colours, cardboard, soft tissue paper, shiny paper, foil, patterned paper for collages, drawing materials, scissors, glue, paints and tape.

- Miscellaneous materials which might include soft toys, cushions, blankets, postcards, random household items, such as pegs, corks and string, small empty boxes, books, etc.

School therapists who prefer using sand and water in their sessions are reminded to keep two containers, one for dry sand and the other for wet sand. If the room is carpeted, the area where the sand is used or where art is made will need a plastic sheet or waterproofed cotton spread for the floor. If, as is likely, the therapy space does not include a sink, low plastic water containers can be used with one designated for dirty water and one for clean.

It is not necessary to provide all the toys and materials listed above. School therapists will be limited by budget, space and storage restrictions and will need to select their materials carefully based on these considerations. However, toys should be varied and include a range of different types so children or young people are able to play out different roles and emotions using a particular toy as a catalyst. Older children may need to be 'given permission' to play with toys. The school therapist may want to say that toys and resources in therapy can be used by children and adults alike to express aspects of their life experiences, especially those that relate more specifically to their earlier years. This can free up older clients to use play materials that they otherwise would feel inhibited from touching.

Roles that might be played out via dolls or using props could include those that are power-holding, abusive, aggressive, frightening, friendly, caring, nurturing, calming or soothing. The chosen toys should represent different ethnicities, cultures, classes, religions and lifestyles, enabling the diversity of children and young people you will be working with to feel represented in the therapy room. For example, it is helpful to buy more than one set of family figures so that same-sex parents, step-parents and stepsiblings can be represented. As all children are part of a family constellation, sets of animal families will also be conducive to exploring relationships and acting out scenarios via play.

How to deal with different materials

Some school therapists may feel that materials are so important that they are tempted to provide too much. When the therapist feels a pull in this direction, it may be helpful to explore where this impulse is coming from. Is it to distract from the school therapist's own anxiety of how she will cope with the therapeutic space and relationship? Could the therapist be feeling under-resourced internally in anticipation of starting the work and is she compensating for this by over-providing? Might it be easier for her to hide behind a large selection of materials so she does not have to deal with the client's feelings, especially the most painful, aggressive or conflicted ones?

Providing a full array of resources may be counterproductive. For example, it can be experienced as overwhelming. Alternatively, the sessions may represent an idealised space where all needs are met (akin to a sweet shop where one can choose whatever one wants). Providing too much can overlook the reality principle: people (even important family members, favourite teachers or best friends) can be disappointing, life doesn't always give us what we want, some people *do* get more than others, and so on. Similarly, there are certain materials that can prove difficult to contain within the therapeutic space. As noted above, it is suggested that materials such as squirt-paints in bottles or tubes, pots of glitter and wet clay are not included.

Paints in plastic bottles or tubes are attractive as they can literally be squirted onto paper, which can feel cathartic. However, it is important for the therapist to be able to contain the situation. Some children with a history of unmet needs and complex circumstances cannot stop themselves from giving in to regressed impulses such as squirting the paints on the floor, walls or therapist, or using so much that the paper is soaked through and cannot hold the paint. If the child's play becomes uncontainable like this, it is not helpful for either the child or the therapist. And if the next client is coming straight after such a session, there is simply no time to clean up the mess it will leave.

The use of glitter presents another potential dilemma. It is a material that can evoke feelings of jealousy and greed, symbolising what the child imagines those who are more privileged have in their lives. This can lead to acting out in the session by, for example, using all the glitter up in one go, leaving the child to take away unconscious guilt. In addition, no matter how careful the child is, glitter has a propensity to get everywhere and is very hard to clear up. This means that the next child or young person using the room may be stepping into a space that still holds traces of the preceding client.

Clay is an eminently versatile material but most therapy rooms are not equipped for wet-clay work and few have adequate storage. Play dough or modelling plasticine may be used as a substitute. Both can be returned to the container at the end of the session, side-stepping any storage issues. This has the added advantage of providing a material where the expectation is that whatever is made will be dismantled at the end of the session. This means that, for example, difficult feelings can be fleetingly expressed without having to be fully owned and held in the conscious mind. They can be symbolically returned to the unconscious by putting whatever has been made back into the play dough container. Sometimes clients make something quite sophisticated, expressive or touching and the therapist may be tempted to keep the piece of work as a one-off. This isn't helpful, as it gives the client a mixed message.

If a child is presenting as very chaotic and uncontained within the school, it is recommended that the therapist initially reduce the materials available in the room. Working with fewer materials will alleviate the pressure on the child of having to decide what to play with next, which might be experienced as distracting and overwhelming. A contained environment can be created with carefully selected toys or art materials. Over time, these can be added to as the child begins to feel held and has a more satisfying experience of the sessions.

Over the academic year, consumable materials such as paper and play dough can be used up. It is recommended to stock up the room just before a school holiday following the last session of the term or just before work commences after the break. This is the least disruptive to the process.

There might be occurrences where children will take/steal toys out of the playroom without the therapist's realising it at that time. The loss of the toy might be noticed by another client and a replacement may need to be provided. This is something that can usefully be discussed in supervision.

Storage

In the primary school setting and often in the secondary school setting as well, the school therapist will create a folder for each child. Regardless of whether or not they use it for paper-based work (drawings, writing, mixed media pieces), it will need to be stored and brought to each session. Even an unused folder symbolises containment.

Depending on the set-up of the therapeutic room, the school therapist will have different options around storing materials and the clients' work. Resources can be kept in boxes or cupboards in the room which are labelled clearly as belonging to the therapist or the therapist's organisation, so that school staff do not use them. If there is no room or adequate storage, another space has to be found within the school. The therapist needs to ensure that the resources and the folders containing clients' artwork can be stored safely and so that confidentiality can be maintained. The folder is taken home after the last session. School therapists will need to make arrangements for storing folders belonging to children or young people who are continuing after the summer break.

Conclusion

This chapter has provided a basic introduction to themes relating to setting up a therapy room within the school setting. Each school therapist's preferred working style and professional discipline will influence how they arrange their room and what is provided. Budget restrictions will play their part as will room and storage availability. As has already been emphasised, school therapists need to be flexible and creative. In the best possible circumstances, therapists may be given a dedicated room, which they can decorate and organise as they see fit. However this is increasingly rare, especially in inner-city schools where space is at a premium. All therapists appreciate the fact that the most important aspect of the work is their relationship with their client. One does not need a fully equipped and dedicated therapy room to provide a meaningful experience and the opportunity for authentic expression. Just as children can play creatively inside with kitchen pots, pans and a wooden spoon, or outside with natural materials, so too can the therapy client use basic resources for deeply felt self-expression.

Most expectant parents will create a physical space in their home before the birth of their baby, equipping it with a small cot, baby clothes and perhaps soft toys or play things. So too does the school therapist give careful thought to preparing a room for her client before commencing work in the school setting. In both instances, this parallels creating a space in mind for the new infant/client. We all know that the most luxurious room for a new baby counts for very little. The relationship that forms between baby and mother or carer and, in time, the rest of the family, is the most important element, just as the therapist's relationship with the client is the agent of change.

Study questions

The therapy room

- What suggestions would you give the school regarding what kind of room they might consider booking for therapy sessions?
- Track your own responses to the room you are allocated. How did you feel the first time you stepped into it? What were your first associations? What might the room tell you about how the school perceives your services?
- If the room is less than ideal, what plans can you draw up for working towards negotiating either changes to it or a new allocation?

Providing resources

When selecting resources, you can ask yourself the following questions.
   Do they

- facilitate a wide range of creative and emotional expression;
- engage children's interest;
- allow exploration and expression without verbalisation;
- allow for open-ended play?

   What would you say if a child or young person

- requests materials that are not provided;
- wants to bring their own materials or toys;
- discreetly puts a small toy or felt-tip pen into their pocket just before the end of the session;
- goes through all the coloured paper and selects out the best pieces to put in their folder 'in case they want to use them next time'?

   What feelings might come up for you in the above examples?

Chapter 9

The referral process

Camilla Waldburg

Introduction

The referral process consists of a number of phases. The quantity and content of those phases is determined by several factors, not least of which is whether the child is in primary or secondary school. We refer throughout the book to the distinctions between the two sectors in terms of how school therapists are viewed, the functions we serve and how those functions are carried out. The referral process, which signals the beginning of our work with individual children, is no exception and in fact crystallises those very distinctions. Perhaps first and foremost is the reality that in primary schools we are often able to confer with a number of teachers and other school staff about prospective clients, but this is not generally the case in the secondary sector – staff are often less accessible and time more at a premium. Pressures of time may also be a factor when attempting to see parents who, by the time their children are at secondary school, are often working outside the home. There will be a further discussion of this in Chapter 11.

This chapter breaks the referral process down into its component parts. The school therapist's professional skills and approach are as important to the process as the therapeutic skills we draw on when working with a client. As we have emphasised throughout this book, the boundary and scope of the school therapist's role is much wider than delivering sessions. Engaging with school staff and, where possible and appropriate, with parents or carers, is an essential aspect of the work and one that requires diplomacy, solution-focused thinking and flexibility.

The referral process can take some time and may be spread over several weeks. Some therapists may start with one or two clients at the beginning of the academic year and build up their caseload over several months as more appropriate referrals come through the system. Others may face the opposite situation and will be given a daunting number of referrals at the start of the new term, which will need to be gone through carefully and prioritised.

General principles

It is good practice to develop collaborative working relationships with key school staff, especially when setting up a therapy service for the first time. In order to clarify the school's expectations from the beginning, some time should be devoted to discussing what changes or outcomes would be most desirable. There can be marked differences between primary school teachers' and managers' ideas of what therapy can achieve for individual children and how secondary schools view therapeutic intervention. The former may be more focused on children's social and emotional development issues, while for the latter seeing the school therapist may be laden with the expectation that the student will be kept in line. Through the initial assessment and ongoing conversations with the school, these expectations can be seen to be either realistic or else in need of modification. Projected outcomes can be gradually re-formed as the therapy takes shape and the therapist is in a better position to assess what can and cannot be achieved.

As you might expect, this involves thinking about referrals in the context of the school in which you find yourself. A common issue to be prepared for is that the school's view of who would most benefit from seeing someone may differ from the therapist's. Clarity about the criteria for referrals from the start is essential in order to avoid misunderstandings as well as to manage expectations. This can be achieved by talking to the lead professionals within the school. The challenge is finding a balance between a 'light touch' approach and professional thoroughness. Conversations with school staff around appropriate referrals, expectations and outcomes are part of an ongoing process that includes gradually educating school staff on the opportunities that a therapy service provides and also on its limitations. This chapter will outline suggested approaches to setting up the referral process.

Referral structures

Each school will establish its preferred referral system, which may change over time as the therapy service develops and becomes embedded in the school culture. Ideally, one lead professional, such as the Special Educational Needs Coordinator (SENCo) who is often – but not always – the inclusion manager or deputy head, coordinates the service and liaises with the school therapist. Some schools will encourage teachers to refer children and young people in the first instance to the SENCo or inclusion manager. These referrals may take place during termly inclusion surgeries, pastoral care meetings or student review meetings. In attendance at such meetings are likely to be the inclusion manager or lead professional, class teachers and other school support staff, and sometimes external professionals such as the social worker or family therapist. It's recommended to hold regular meetings between the school therapist and the lead professional(s) throughout the academic year; they can be useful for updating the therapist about the more vulnerable children in the school and for reviewing the existing provision.

Another potential referral route is parents contacting the Head, SENCo or class teacher directly to ask for support for their child. It is advisable for the therapist and the lead professional together to decide how these referrals will be managed. It is most likely that the therapist will build up a waiting list of prospective referrals over time, which can be ranked according to the level of concern and identified need.

Primary school referrals

Speaking to each teacher personally in order to gather referrals is generally the prerogative of therapists working in primary schools, where contact with staff is more likely to be possible than in secondary schools. By talking directly to teachers, the therapist can describe her service and gather appropriate referrals at the same time. This can be done in a directive way. For example, each teacher could be asked to refer two pupils: one child whose behaviour clearly shows underlying emotional difficulties as well as one child who may be very quiet, withdrawn, low in mood and at risk of being overlooked. This allows for a range of referrals to be secured, rather than the focus being too firmly placed on overt signs of distress such as behavioural difficulties or on the pupil who is always drawing attention to himself. Because it is time-consuming, this 'hands on' approach to gathering referrals is likely to be limited to work in primary schools, although it is also possible in small secondary schools or secondary schools where the therapist is working only with the upper or lower school pupils. The strength of working in this way is that it provides opportunities for the therapist to start building relationships with all teachers. It also ensures equal access to the service.

Secondary school referrals

Because of the difficulties of finding a mutually convenient time to speak to teachers in busy secondary schools, arranging a presentation at a staff meeting can be an alternative way of making contact with teachers, giving them information about the service and inviting them to refer students. Referral forms can be brought along to the meeting and staff can be invited to complete them there and then. (Sample forms are provided at the end of this chapter.)

Liaison and collaboration

Some schools will have termly multi-agency professional meetings already in place. These meetings generally bring together professionals from the wider support network representing services such as social care, mental health, welfare and family provision. The needs of individual children and families are discussed and the most appropriate service provision agreed upon. It is useful if the school therapist is able to attend these meetings, as children who are under discussion can be directly referred to the service. However, when she is not available it is helpful if she can provide written input for the meetings as well as questions or requests for referrals. She could ask her school link worker to take notes for her so that she has a record of the discussions that have taken place. It is useful, too, if she can ensure that all professionals attending the meeting have information on the referral criteria. That way, the most effective use can be made of what is invariably a limited resource.

Referral guidelines

It is a good idea for the therapist to raise the school's awareness of why children might be referred to therapy. For example, therapists may prepare a handout for staff along the following lines:

> Pupils can be referred to the school therapist for short-, medium- or long-term work. Reasons for a referral may include one or more of the following:
>
> - a perceived high level of need (e.g. pupils who are clearly depressed or excessively anxious or who are frequently coming to the teacher's attention);
> - a perceived low level of need (e.g. pupils who are extremely shy, self-conscious, withdrawn, have few friends and who are often 'invisible' or 'without a voice' in the class; those who are consistently under-achieving and/or disengaged);
> - gaps in development or lagging behind;
> - significant family or personal life experiences (e.g. bereavement, family break-up, a significant move, new step-family, conflict at home or any form of neglect);
> - unusual or antisocial behavior which suggests there are underlying emotional issues (e.g. children who are confrontational, bullying, compulsively lying, etc.);
> - difficulties accessing the school curriculum because of distractions due to internal difficulties (e.g. preoccupation with unsettling or anxiety-provoking feelings, fantasies or mental states);
> - signs of very low self-esteem and poor self-image.

The handout might include instructions on making a formal referral by filling out a referral form and/or booking an appointment with the school therapist to talk over the potential referral.

Building a picture of the child

In order to make an informed decision about whether a referral is appropriate, the school therapist is encouraged to gather as much information as possible about the child.

As noted, in the primary school setting this will involve liaising closely with school staff and particularly with the present class teacher and the teacher the child had in the previous year, who will hold a good deal of valuable information about the child's development, social interaction, academic progress and family background. A referral form with detailed questions can be used to support this process. As already noted, examples of forms applying to both primary and secondary school therapy services are given at the end of this chapter.

Meeting complex needs

There will be some children whose needs are sufficiently complex to merit referral to specialist teams such as the local child and adolescent mental health service or social services. They include those who have undergone traumatic experiences or who are seriously acting out their distress through risk-taking behaviour, such as severe eating disorders, substance misuse or sexualised acting out. In such cases, the therapist will explain to the school that these children require referral to specialist services. The school will then take over and refer such children on to the appropriate agency. It is a good idea to have a grasp of local provision including statutory and community resources.

The needs of children in the throes of family crisis or disruption must also be thought about carefully. Those who are living in an unstable situation, such as being moved between care placements or being housed in a refuge, may not be able to work therapeutically for a time. Therapy would need to be delayed until they are settled.

If several children from the same class have been referred to the school therapist, it is recommended that consideration be given to the impact this might have on the therapeutic process.

Thinking about the school context

Because teachers are often pressed for time during the school day, whether in primary or secondary school settings, meetings you set up with them can be rushed. Similarly, you may receive back referral forms that are only sketchily filled in. While this can be frustrating, it's helpful to think about the teacher's needs and pressures. Try to accept that it may be more realistic to organise a number of very short meetings in close succession each of which can focus on particular questions or themes during that time.

Children's well-being in general is supported when teachers can be encouraged to think in a more focused way about the children in their class. This enhances their understanding of students' problem behaviours and helps to identify when the difficulties were first noticed as well as what might be at their root. It is through conversations with the therapist that the teacher's compassion for the child can be fostered. Often the language used by the teacher to describe the child will change in the course of these conversations, becoming less value-laden. For example, a child who might initially be labelled as badly behaved in class may eventually be more accurately described as a child who can't manage himself when he doesn't understand instructions.

The therapist might be given sensitive information about a child's family background, such as alcohol addiction or domestic violence. It is possible this information won't appear on the referral form for reasons of confidentiality and may instead be passed on verbally. It is the therapist's responsibility to reflect on what will be shared with other professionals and/or with the family itself. As this can be complex, it is recommended that time be given over to discussing it in supervision.

Ensuring that the therapy service is valued

Part of the ongoing job of the therapist is to raise the profile of the service and de-stigmatise the notion of seeing a therapist. A display board giving general information about the therapy service that is visible to staff, children and parents will aid in creating an environment where therapy is perceived as a welcome contribution to school life. General information about the service and the referral process, including the name and contact details of the lead professional, can be given. The information displayed on the board can be summarised in a leaflet or handout to be made available to school staff and parents. Some schools invite pupils to self-refer. This aspect of the service is covered in more detail in the next chapter on the assessment phase.

Sample referral forms

As discussed earlier in this chapter, a referral form can be a useful tool. It can be completed either by the referrer or by the therapist, who will record the relevant information over the initial referral and assessment phase. Sample forms are given below.

IN-SCHOOL THERAPY SERVICE
REFERRAL FORM for use in PRIMARY SCHOOLS

This form is to be completed by a school staff member

Name of the school staff member completing this form:
Date:

Pupil Details
Child's name:
Child's age and gender:
Ethnic background:
Child's class/year group:
Name of parent(s)/carer(s):
Child's home telephone number:
Parent(s)/carer(s) mobile number(s):

This Child

is known to social services	Yes	No
is looked after	Yes	No
is eligible for free school lunches	Yes	No
has a Safeguarding Plan	Yes	No

Additional Support
Is there anyone else in the school or from an external service providing support for this pupil? If so, what support is currently being offered and by whom?

Level of Concern
(please indicate)
Low 1 2 3 4 5 6 7 8 9 10 High

Please provide details of this child's background and family history

Family Context
Are both birth parents living with the child? ____ Yes ____ No
If not, do you know when the separation occurred?
Is the reason for the separation known?
Is there still contact with the absent parent?
Does a parent or relative come to the parent–teacher meetings? If so, how well do they engage?
How do they interact with the child?
Are there siblings? Older? Younger? At home? Living elsewhere? Stepsiblings? Recent birth?

Significant Events
Has the family moved (country, city, house, school)?
Any deaths? Illnesses?

Parents/Carers: School Context
Is the child's parent/carer working in the school in any capacity (e.g. voluntary or paid or on the Governing Body)?

Detailed Reasons for the Referral
In as much detail as you can, please describe why you have referred this child for therapy:

IN-SCHOOL THERAPY SERVICE
REFERRAL FORM for use in SECONDARY SCHOOLS

This form is to be completed by a school staff member
School:
Name of school staff member completing this form:
Date:

Pupil Details
Young person's name:
Gender: Ethnic background:
Year group + form:
Name of parent(s)/carer(s):
Young person's home telephone number:
Parent(s)/carer(s) mobile number:

This Young Person
is known to social services	Yes	No
is looked after	Yes	No
is eligible for free school lunches	Yes	No
has a Safeguarding Plan	Yes	No

Additional Support
Is there anyone else in the school or from an external service providing support for this pupil? If so, who is it and what support is currently being offered?

Level of Concern
(please indicate)
Low 1 2 3 4 5 6 7 8 9 10 High

Please provide details of the young person's background and family history

Family Context
Are both birth parents living with the young person? ____ Yes ____ No
If not, do you know when the separation occurred?
Is the reason for the separation known?
Is there still contact with the absent parent?
Does a parent or relative come to the parent–teacher meetings? If so, how well do they engage?

> How do they interact with the young person?
> Are there siblings? Older? Younger? At home? Living elsewhere? Stepsiblings? Recent birth?
>
> **Significant Events**
> Has the family moved (country, city, house, school)?
> Any deaths? Illnesses?
>
> **Parents/Carers: School Context**
> Is the young person's parent/carer working in the school in any capacity (e.g. voluntary or paid or on the Governing Body)?
>
> **Detailed Reasons for the Referral**
> In as much detail as you can, please describe why you have referred this young person for therapy:

Conclusion

To recap, the referral process is the beginning of the therapeutic experience. Preparing to see a child means, first and foremost, thinking in a focused way about the most appropriate intervention for him, based on the information you glean from teachers and support staff. The school's expectations of what you can achieve may be rather removed from reality and it's important that those expectations and the parameters of therapy are made clear from the outset. Hopes for obvious or quick, measurable outcomes, for instance, need to be moderated and more manageable outcomes put in their place.

Communication with the school and the forging of positive professional relationships are all-important as we embark on the referral process. It makes for a solid foundation, one from which we can build an understanding that therapist and school are involved in a working partnership to enable children to feel better about themselves and thereby achieve their potential.

Study questions

- How will you ensure that the school provides a range of referrals and not only from the pupils most obviously in difficulty?
- If you make a presentation to school staff, what will you say about your service, your role in the school and how to refer pupils?
- What kinds of referrals do you feel most anxious about? What might this link to in your personal background?
- What will you feed back to the school if a child or young person simply does not want to engage and you cannot move the work forward?

Chapter 10

The assessment process

Stefania Putzu-Williams

Introduction

The term 'assessment' can have different meanings in different contexts. It might refer to a particular style of interviewing, structured or directive, or more analytical and free associating that the school therapist uses to gauge her clients' level of disturbance, ability to relate and capacity for psychological insight. The term could also refer to specific assessment tools used by school therapists working for an external agency, which may include set guidelines and forms. However, when we talk about assessing a child within the context of working in schools, we often use it as shorthand for describing the process the school therapist undertakes to form a full picture of her client. The focus in this chapter will be on the latter, from the position of the school therapist who is working within a psychodynamically informed model.

A key assessment task is gathering information from the Special Educational Needs Coordinator (SENCo), other school staff, parents and the child himself. At least as important is getting a feel for what it is like to be alone in the room with the child. As school therapists, we will be monitoring ourselves and noting whether or not – or when – we feel comfortable in their presence, unduly anxious, lost for words, self-conscious, overwhelmed, blocked in our thinking or, conversely, free to think creatively, able to make links and associations and so on. Our experience of time will also be of interest: does it creep along slowly or speed by? We will be observing, too, how receptive the child is and whether he can usefully engage in therapeutic work or whether he seems disengaged. The answer to this comes from a number of sources but, most usefully, from the child himself. Talking openly and directly about the relationship that is forming over the assessment period is a key part of the work.

With older children, we look for signs of their capacity to *mentalise*; that is, to form mental constructs of what they feel, what they imagine their impact on others might be and what others could be feeling or thinking. Can they take a step back and see that there are always a number of different ways of interpreting situations, feelings, mental states and relationships? The younger the child, the less developed this capacity may be. But keeping in mind his capacity to analyse himself and others within an age-appropriate framework is a useful yardstick in assessment.

Piecing together a picture of the client

Generally the information-gathering that is a basic component of the assessment process is more easily managed in a primary school setting, due to the simple fact that teachers are often more accessible and usually able to provide useful information. Some however may resist any kind of dialogue, often for practical reasons such as lack of time or thinking space. By the same token, while many parents are used to coming into primary school and will make themselves available for initial meetings with the school therapist, there will be those who will be too intimidated or anxious to meet with the school therapist. It can take careful work to build a bridge in these instances.

It usually takes time to piece together a full picture of the child's circumstances and what has brought him to the school's attention. This is especially so in the secondary school setting where students have many teachers, each of them with a large number of individuals to hold in mind. Engaging in conversations with parents of secondary school pupils, whether on the telephone or in person, is generally undertaken in consultation with the young person, as adolescents will have their own views on whether or not they want their family involved.

Adolescence, as we know, is a time of significant change, often accompanied by internal upheaval. At a time when adolescents are experiencing increasing pressures at school, they want to test out new kinds of relationships, experimenting with different identities and striving for greater independence. In a complex world, stress and anxiety can seem to be consistent features of young people's lives in this phase of their development, whether the feelings come from sources within or without. Increased impulsivity, experimentation and risk-taking are part of adolescence and because of these complexities, assessing risk in the secondary school setting may seem a daunting task. It's worth noting that often the majority of students at significant risk will already be known to the school and will have been passed on to specialist teams.

Given that the school therapist works in collaboration with others in the school, viewing the first phase of the work as an assessment block will allow her time to consult regularly with the school SENCo and with her supervisor about any new information that comes to light. Generally, it is not the school therapist's role to work with children or adolescents who present with more complex needs. Those whose presenting issues mask deeper pathologies and high risk need to be referred on. This will be the result of careful thought and consultation with an experienced supervisor, not a sign of professional weakness or lack.

A crucial component of a school therapist's role is containing anxiety-provoking material that students bring with them and being able to think about it. It may be quite uncomfortable at times; personal therapy, supervision and experience are vital resources in helping the school therapist work through these difficulties. Ultimately, the school therapist needs to feel that her professional assessment is valid.

The first encounter

Some therapists may choose to conduct their first session as a form of one-off assessment. If so, they will usually ask specific questions about the presenting issue (which may turn out to be something other than the issue of utmost concern for the school), the family's circumstances and the child's personal history. As well, the therapist may choose to describe what therapy can and cannot offer, including the limits of confidentiality, and how the sessions will unfold in future. At this point, she might want to explain that subsequent sessions will progress along less directive lines and why this is so.

Whether or not the therapist uses the first appointment as a form of stand-alone assessment, each first encounter is unique. In a less structured introductory session she may invite the client to start where he wants to, thereby introducing the idea that the sessions are theirs to use as they wish. Some young people have 'nothing to say' and may remain silent, while others engage well and may talk freely about their issues and problems. Those who are more anxious may try to fill the time with non-stop talk that seems to have little relevance to why they were referred. Alternatively, a torrent may flow from them about their key issues, as if they cannot contain them a moment longer.

Therapists regulate their interventions according to what the client communicates. The first meeting is usually marked by degrees of anxiety for both therapist and child. The tone and quality of the emotional contact to come will be coloured, to some degree, by this first encounter. The anxiety of facing the unknown has to be balanced with the hope of a new beginning and belief in the possibility of some change for the better, even if the changes that can be achieved are in ways of thinking rather than in external terms. The initial meeting provides the starting point for forming a working relationship and therapeutic alliance. Inviting the child to use toys, art materials or conversation to express himself freely will lay the foundations for this. Inevitably, vulnerabilities will be touched on or even exposed if it is the kind of vulnerability that comes from feeling oneself at a loss or feigning indifference. The therapist's attentive, non-judgemental listening and, when appropriate, reflecting back on the material, will give the child the experience of being in the presence of a thinking mind, an essential dimension of any therapeutic encounter.

Being dynamic, the therapeutic relationship is made up of interactions that hold conscious and unconscious meanings, reality-based considerations or concerns and complexities in the areas of social and cultural identities and language. The therapist and client communicate through words – which may reveal social class – as well as through vocal tone, volume, facial expression, eye contact, body posture and general manner. Communication is also made through the feelings that are evoked in the other. The therapist mentally notes all her responses, especially the feelings she detects in the child and in herself.

It is also important to consider what the school as an institution may represent for both the therapist and the young person. As discussed earlier, we all have conscious and unconscious reactions to school, learning and our own intellectual capacities. The stage of development of the therapy service and its place in the school is another factor to bear in mind. How well it is established in the school culture and how valued and supported the school therapist feels within the organisation will add another dimension to the overall experience.

The assessment takes account of all that is observed, felt and spoken about both in the first session and in the initial phase of the work. Every aspect of the child's presentation will be thought about. This includes his attitude to therapy and to the therapist in general, how he manages the beginning and end of each session, what he makes of the room and of the wider school setting, the uses he makes of the school therapist and, of course, both what is talked about and what is avoided.

In summary, a key aim of the assessment process for school therapists is to clarify the presenting problem, gather information about the child's current life situation and history and observe how both present and past situations shape the 'here and now' of each session. Careful thought about what we hear, feel, think and imagine is going on in each session helps to build a clearer picture of the young person and to learn about the kinds of relationships they form.

Assessments in the primary school setting

If a school therapist has the privilege of working on a long-term basis with children, the assessment process may stretch over a number of weeks. This initial stage of work involves gathering information from the school, the child and, whenever possible, the parents.

From the school

The class teacher can be asked to provide his or her views on the child's relationship to learning. This may include answering some or all of the questions posed below:

- Is the child a high/low achiever or an inconsistent achiever?
- Does the child prefer to work in small groups or on his own?
- Is the child overly dependent on the teacher for support?
- Can the child tolerate making mistakes?
- Is the child anxious or curious when faced with a new task?
- Can the child sustain his engagement with a task?
- Can the child hold onto and make use of learning?
- Is the child able to be reflective and thoughtful?
- How does the child function under pressure?

In addition to the class teacher, learning mentors or classroom assistants are well placed to answer questions such as those below about the child's social development:

- How do other children respond to the child?
- Does the child make friends easily?

- Can the child keep friends?
- Do they generally play well with others or do they keep to themselves?
- What kinds of difficulties does the child get into at playtime or lunchtime?
- How often do these difficulties occur?
- In general, how would you describe the child?

From parents

The school therapist will also want to form a picture of home life. Information can be sought from the class teacher, the parents and the child on the family circumstances. It's not always possible to obtain answers to the following questions but they provide a useful guide:

- What causes them the most concern?
- What is the family composition? Are there siblings? Where is the client in the birth order?
- How do the siblings get along?
- Who lives at home?
- If either parent lives elsewhere, when did this separation occur?
- What was the child's response to it?
- Is there contact with the parent living outside the family home?
- If so, how frequently and where does the contact take place?
- How does the child respond to these occasions?
- Has the family moved country/city/home and if so what was/is the impact?
- What are the family's most significant experiences (e.g. deaths, significant losses, family break-up, illnesses [physical or mental])?
- What are the child's most positive features?
- What do the parents value most about their relationship with the child?
- What do they do together (what gives them shared pleasure)?
- What would they like the child to get out of the therapy sessions?
- How do they think school and home can best work together to bring about change?

In the initial meeting with parents it is important to emphasise confidentiality while clarifying its limits. With some parents, it may be possible to move into personal exploration even in the first meeting. Some are comfortable talking about all aspects of their experience with their child. Others will need the framework of a more evolved relationship with the school therapist before they are ready to bring up more intimate material. Therapists learn to gauge the comfort levels of parents and attune themselves accordingly. The following questions are ones that you may be able to ask with tact and sensitivity:

- Was the child planned?
- What was the birth like?

- What kind of baby was he?
- What was the child's response to weaning?
- How did you find the weaning process?
- Who took primary responsibility for caring for the child as an infant?
- What kind of toddler or young child was he?
- How did you find the separation when the child started school?
- How did the child respond?
- What methods of discipline do you use with your child?

The information gathered through these meetings will be compared and contrasted with the therapist's own experience of the child built up over time. As well, she will think about the child's presenting issues, key anxieties and defences within the context of the information provided by the school and the family about the home circumstances and the child's early life.

It may be that the therapist is given only sketchy or patchy information on the child's current circumstances and history. There are some children about whom very little is known and where no further information can be obtained. This in itself is valuable information, for it tells us that there is no adult in the child's life who is holding him in mind and that he may feel unknown and not thought about. In such instances, having a therapist who can find a place in her mind for him and who is able to feel, think, reflect and mirror back can make a significant contribution to that child's development.

Assessments in the secondary school setting

The assessment process in the secondary school context usually progresses along a different pathway to that in the primary sector. Because they are such large and complex organisations, it is not unusual for referral forms not to be completed in detail and for meetings between the therapist and teachers not to take place. If a meeting can be scheduled, the teacher may not have much information to pass on, as it's not possible to hold in mind personal details of individuals. Contact with parents may also not occur; the appropriateness of this will be given careful thought in supervision. If a meeting or phone conversation does take place, it will usually be scheduled in when the work is already underway so that the young person can be consulted about it first.

Assessment of risk

The initial assessment phase gives the therapist the opportunity to find out from the young person how he manages his more difficult feelings, experiences and mental states. Within this context, the therapist might need to encourage her client to talk about his drug or alcohol use, sexual behaviour or tendency to self-harm in other emotional or physical ways. This kind of conversation can be most containing when the therapist speaks from a position of compassion. For example, she may try to find something in the young person's story that is too painful for him to hold in mind. Working with an adolescent who has lost a parent and presents with 'anger management' problems, she might say something like 'It sounds like you've never had a chance to talk about how angry you are at your mother for dying when you still need her. I think drinking too much may be a way of numbing your pain.' Contextualising risky behaviour by giving it meaning can open up the possibility for further exploration.

Every school will have guidance on the procedures that need to be followed if a child reveals suicidal feelings, self-harm, eating disorders, severe depression, abuse or any form of mental health issue that might require higher-level interventions. Developing a trusting, collaborative working relationship with the school staff member who holds responsibility for safeguarding children is essential for any school therapist. In addition, an experienced supervisor will also be able to support the therapist in holding difficult material and knowing whether or not to break the young person's confidentiality.

Boundaries of confidentiality

The meaning and limits of confidentiality in the school context need to be given careful thought. Confidentiality is an essential element of the therapeutic process and a core feature of any trusting relationship. However, it cannot be absolute.

There may be times when it is necessary for the school and the school therapist or other professionals involved with the child to open up a dialogue with the family even without consultation with the school therapist or prior consent of the young person. This is most likely to occur if the adolescent is known to be engaging in self-harm, he has suicidal thoughts that are intensifying, he has an eating disorder that is starting to cause serious concern, he requires a psychiatric assessment or he is experiencing some form of abuse outside school. In such instances, the therapist needs to collaborate with the school. This may involve working hard to contain the anxieties of other school staff involved with the young person while still providing a therapeutic space for him. The school therapist needs to have the ability to preserve the therapeutic alliance with her client while also considering the requirements of both the inner and outer worlds.

Sometimes a teacher may be very concerned about a young person and will ask for feedback. Or the school therapist may be stopped in a corridor and asked to comment informally about a student she is seeing or one who has recently been referred. It is good practice to have some idea of what you might say in such instances. For example, you could reply, 'I'd be interested in hearing about your experience of this student as well. However, this isn't the best time for a conversation. Can I come and see you today or tomorrow at lunch or after school?' When you do get a chance to talk in a less 'off the cuff' context, you can explain to the teacher that it is not helpful to give specific feedback because students need to know their confidences are respected. However you can say that your client is using the sessions well and seems committed to coming (if this is an accurate description). If it isn't, you can say that you're still building the relationship and it can take young people some time before they feel they can trust adults.

Issues of confidentiality can arise at the referral stages as well. Although most school therapists would prefer to avoid seeing two or three students from the same class or friendship group, this isn't always possible. You may not know of the connection beforehand and it may take some time for it to come to light. Receiving referrals to see siblings and even twins can also arise. Well worth discussing with your supervisor is the context of the referral, the implications for the work and what the options might be before committing to take on such cases.

Taking histories and the use of the genogram or family tree

Drawing a family tree as part of the assessment process is usually responded to with curiosity and interest by children and adolescents. The process of history-taking involves striking a balance between collecting factual information through asking key questions and letting the child lead the session. This process allows the therapist to observe and attune herself to the way the child tells his story and speaks about his family and relationships. She will be listening to the emotional content and meaning that can offer important insights into his internal world and patterns of attachment. If the narrative is coherent, if appropriate emotion is shown or talked about at salient points and if the child or young person is able to hold this 'map' of his family in his mind, then is it more likely that he has experienced a secure attachment. If he cannot remember much, doesn't seem to know a great deal about his family and the story or information given is muddled and lacks any sequential pattern, it is more likely to reveal an insecure attachment (Coren 2001).

Interesting work in the field of attachment theory has been carried out. The Adult Attachment Interview grew out of the work of Mary Main and her colleagues (Main 1985) who identified links between the quality of the narrative and the quality of the attachments. The categories of attachment that have been developed by attachment theorists are described below and can easily be used to help us think about any age group:

- *Autonomous* (i.e. the young person speaks of the past, including painful past experiences, in a coherent manner that reveals an appreciation of his own and other people's mental states).
- *Dismissing* (i.e. the young person dismisses or devalues the significance of relationships or minimises the impact of traumatic experiences).
- *Preoccupied* (i.e. the young person reveals confused feelings about childhood experiences and relationships and their impact on current functioning, displaying anger, fear and confusion).
- *Unresolved* (i.e. the young person has experienced trauma and still feels emotionally entangled with it as it has not been processed).

The assessment process   107

While drawing the family tree, the child is invited to think consciously about his family relationships and to make links between the present and the past. This can create a platform from which the therapist can draw attention to the way the past influences the present. It also gives a view of the client's sense of self, of his significant attachments and of relationship patterns. The genogram usually includes three generations: grandparents, parents and the current family, whether this is the nuclear family, stepfamily or foster family. Traumas and misfortunes that have impacted on previous generations and the continuing effects of unprocessed or undigested material often comes to light through this mapping exercise.

When working with young people, the school therapist can gain insights into the kinds of relationships they most typically form. The above categories provide a useful starting point for thinking about this.

Practical suggestions for assessment work

So far, this chapter has explored what is involved in the initial assessment stage of therapy. The section to follow summarises the key elements of assessment work and provide some practical suggestions.

Introducing the therapy

In the first session or the initial phase of work, the school therapist will usually undertake the tasks listed below. More information is given in Chapter 14 on suggestions of what to say and how much to cover in the first session.

The therapist explains to the child or young person what therapy entails and what may go on in sessions. (Again, please refer to Chapter 14 for detailed examples.) If relevant, the difference between the first, introductory, session and subsequent sessions will be explained, such as, 'Today I'll be asking you questions and I'll probably be talking more than I will in our sessions to follow. This is because I'd like to learn more about your life and what's most important to you.' The age of the child or young person you are working with will determine how you word what follows from here.

With an older child, you might explore why the referral was made. This could include reasons why the school thought therapy might be useful. If the student referred himself, the reasons for his decision and his expectations of therapy can be discussed. The history and severity of the presenting issues can be explored; a mixture of direct and open-ended questions may be useful. Examples include the following:

- 'When did this difficulty begin? Did you seek help? How old were you at the time? What happened? What happened next? How did you cope in the past? What helped/relieved the difficulties/symptoms? How concerned are you about the problem now?'

From here, you may move on to say something along the lines of:

- 'It would be helpful to know a little more about your family situation. Who lives at home? Who are you closest to? What do you like to do together? We all have difficult feelings or experiences from time to time. Can you talk to anyone in your family when you're going through a bad time? Can you tell me about one of your most difficult experiences? Who helped you?

Or you could suggest that a map of the family is made. You may invite the child or young person to use the drawing materials to make a family tree. You might say, 'Why don't you sketch out who is in your family? If you want, you can use boxes for the males and circles for the females.' And so on.

This can open up possibilities for further elaboration. For example, you might say:

- 'I see you've got a father and a stepfather – when did your dad move away? Do you still see him? How about your stepfather? When did he come into your life? How's that been?' And so on.

When starting work with a younger child, you may invite him to use resources:

- 'You can see that there are toys and art materials here for you to use. Do you want to have a look? I suggest you draw a picture that shows me who is in your family. If you don't want to draw people, you can use shapes to show everyone in your family. I see you've made your older sister bigger than your mother. I wonder if she is quite important to you.' And so on.

Acknowledging the emotional content of the client's story and any negative feelings evident in the first meeting or initial sessions will help to build rapport between the two of you:

- 'It sounds like you went through a difficult and painful time when . . .'
- 'I can see you're close to tears. I imagine it wasn't easy for you to hear about . . .'
- 'I think you're telling me you're still angry about . . .'
- 'I notice you're finding it difficult to talk here. It's common for young people to have mixed feelings if their teacher suggests they come and see someone like me.'
- 'Maybe it's beginning to feel as if I'm asking too many questions.'

In addition to sensitively eliciting information, the therapist will be using observational skills to note the following aspects of her client:

- Physical appearance (e.g. level of self-care, dress style, general presentation or state of school uniform).

- Verbal skills (e.g. how language is used, ability to communicate thoughts and feelings, capacity to reflect upon the impact of his behaviour on others and on other people's feelings).
- Non-verbal communication (e.g. whether or not there is much eye contact, tone of voice, composure, gestures) and general presentation (restless, uncomfortable, excitable, relaxed, tense, anxious, etc.).

Managing expectations and exploring his motivation for change will be important and can be facilitated by asking a few carefully timed questions:

- 'How do you think coming to see me might help you?'
- 'What do you want to get out of the sessions?'

To clarify the child or young person's preconceptions of therapy (in other words, the pre-transference), the therapist may want to explore the following:

- Expectations and fears about the therapist and the therapy (e.g. how realistic are his expectations of therapy? Is he supposed to take a passive or more active stance? Does he appreciate his role and know that he will need to participate in the change process – that it is not just down to the therapist?).
- Current or past involvement of other services (e.g. social services, health services, educational welfare services, youth courts). What was the experience like?
- 'Here and now' anxieties (e.g. you may want to explore what they feel when with you in the room and whether or not it is as they expected).

Patterns of behaviours, noticeable themes, defences, anxieties and emotions displayed will be observed by the therapist. The following list captures some of the general themes that you might explore over the initial phase of the work:

- *Naming and understanding emotions*: Ask the client, 'What makes you happy, angry, sad, jealous, relaxed or stressed? How do you let off steam? How do you express your sad or hurt feelings?'
- *Identifying strengths and aspirations*: Ask the client, 'How would you describe your personal qualities? What are your strengths (socially, academically, as a family member, as a student)? What are your hopes for the future? What might get in the way of achieving your goals? What do you perceive as the areas you most need to work on?
- *Understanding core anxieties and defences employed*: How flexible/rigid does your client seem? Can he think differently about his way of seeing things? What are his preferred defences? (E.g. does he change the subject, use denial, blame others, clam up, want to leave the session early and so on when painful feelings or vulnerabilities are triggered?)

- *Emotional receptivity*: How close to the surface are your client's feelings? What is the degree of anxiety or pain with which he is invested? How much mental pain can be borne? Can he allow himself to have feelings about you and/or the therapy?
- *Capacity for self-reflection*: Is your client willing to think about himself? Does he have the capacity to mentalise (i.e. to think about his mental processes)? To what extent is he psychologically minded? What is his potential for building psychological insights through the therapy?
- *Capacity for reflecting on others*: Can your client see others' points of view? Or does he refuse to acknowledge the validity of perspectives that are not his own? Does he show a lack of empathy? To what extent does he protect himself by using self-deception?
- *Level of self-esteem*: Does your client come across as confident or insecure? Does he seem to be lacking in self-worth, ashamed or in some way self-deprecating or self-denigrating?
- *Capacity to form a therapeutic alliance*: Do you think your client keeps you at a distance? Or tries to get too close? How often do you get a sense of connectedness in the session? Can your client take in what you are offering?
- *Ego strength*: Can your client tolerate anxiety and frustration? What feelings seem to come up in response to experiencing his dependency on you or on the therapy? (E.g. do you sense that he feels humiliated by 'having to come' to see you or does he feel relieved and supported? Does he feel resentful or misunderstood because the school asked him to see you? Does he come across as 'never getting enough'? Is he eager to go at the end or does he stall and try to stay longer?)
- *Developmental perspective*: What development stage does your client seem to be at? Does he convey the need to control you and the session? Or does he seem to be taking everything in indiscriminately? Is he holding on to information and his feelings, refusing to let go? Is he wanting to be held and contained and pushing you to do all the work? How do you think he is negotiating the developmental task of separation and individuation that features throughout childhood and adolescence? What developmental stage was the client at when his difficulties were first experienced?

Conclusion

Assessment is a complex, multifaceted and vital preliminary stage in the process of working therapeutically with clients. It requires being able to liaise effectively and gather information with relevant school staff and parents as much as being able to think about the child sitting in front of us and to relate to him in ways that are open and direct. As a diagnostic tool as well as a structured way of gaining an understanding of whom we are working with, assessment is of inestimable value.

Study questions

Throughout therapy, especially in the first phase, it's important to track the dynamics of each session by thinking about the following questions:

- How does your client relate to you? (E.g. who are you to him? Are you perceived as a figure who is likely to be judging him and will find him lacking? Does he feel that you are intimidated by him? Are you experienced as someone who is withholding all the 'good' and tantalising him? Or as someone likely to get angry and reject him? Or someone who has to be pleased and even looked after? Or too vulnerable to hear painful material?)
- Do your client's expectations or projections prompt you to think or even react in a judgemental or persecuting manner? (E.g. do you catch yourself thinking something like 'Well, maybe you could have tried harder'? Who are you representing for your client in such instances? Are you someone from his external world such as a teacher who is experienced as demanding and critical? Or are you an internal father figure whose standards and expectations can never be met?)
- Are you colluding with your client's wishes for comfortable and easy-going sessions? (E.g. do you find yourself 'forgetting' the more painful aspects of your client's story? Do you feel you don't want to upset your vulnerable client and that you rationalise staying away from more challenging or emotionally charged material?)
- What kinds of feelings are aroused in you? (E.g. are there times when you feel flattered, worried, frustrated, bored, envious of his youth or privileges, anxious, warm, connected, confused, etc.? Do one or two feelings seem to dominate or do you find yourself pulled in different directions?)
- What might you be carrying for the client? (E.g. did you find yourself close to tears when your client seemed to be telling you something painful in a matter-of-fact tone of voice? Did you feel deskilled and inarticulate? Are these feelings ones the client wants you to experience on his behalf so he can distance himself from them?)
- Was any of your own material triggered? Who might your client represent for you? (E.g. did your client's story remind you of aspects of your own history? Does your client remind you of one of your siblings or one of your own children – or of your younger self? Is your client coming across in a way that reminds you of the way in which your father, mother or a teacher seemed to treat you?)
- How does your client respond to your therapeutic interventions? (E.g. are your observations, comments or suggestions ignored, accepted uncritically or taken further? After an intervention or interpretation is there a shift or a deepening level of rapport? Or a silence or change of subject that might signal a defensive withdrawal?)
- Does your client expect to be understood or misunderstood? Liked or disliked? Believed or distrusted?

- Does your client feel helped by an observation or comment you've made, or by discovering a link between one thing and another? Or does he seem to feel threatened or criticised?
- Does your client seem interested in knowing more about how his mind works? About his feelings and thoughts? Does he seem responsive to your being interested in him? Is there a desire for deeper understanding (which may initially be limited to the desire to be understood)?

References

Coren, Alex (2001) *Short-Term Psychotherapy: A Psychodynamic Approach.* London: Palgrave.

Main, M., Kaplan, N. and Cassidy, J. (1985) Security in infancy, childhood and adulthood: a move to the level of representation. *Monographs of the Society for Research in Child Development*, 50, 66–104.

Chapter 11

Meeting with parents or carers

Reva Klein

Why do we meet them?

While some children will be open to the idea of your meeting with their parents soon after therapy has begun, others won't, and there will be cases where it's simply not appropriate for a variety of reasons. Some of those reasons have to do with the age and developmental stage of the children you are working with, while others won't necessarily be apparent. Some Year 7 or 8 students may find it containing for parents to come in to see their therapist, while others will make it clear that it's not desirable or appropriate. As they get older, this is more often than not the case and for sound reasons: in their striving for greater independence and separation from home, the notion of parents being involved in their therapy is just not acceptable. There are also those younger children who have difficult relationships at home who may insist that their parents aren't seen and this must be respected too and handled sensitively. In short, we may meet with primary school parents for an initial conversation before seeing the child. However, we must always confer with children and young people before subsequent meetings with their parents, making clear that confidentiality guidelines are in place and considering their responses as useful information for the therapy itself.

Needless to say, despite resistance we may encounter, there are good reasons for wishing to meet with parents and carers. Getting parents' perspective on their child is enormously helpful in constructing a picture of who the child is at home, with siblings, with parents. It tells us about the parent–child relationship and also about where some of the child's emotional or behavioural problems may be coming from.

But while the process of speaking to parents may be enormously helpful to us as school therapists, we need to keep ourselves open to how parents experience these meetings and, even before that, to the news that their child is being referred. The situation is bound to trigger conscious and unconscious reactions in parents or carers of children who have been referred for therapy sessions by their school. They may feel that their child has been unfairly identified as having 'problems'. They may feel guilty, believing that the referral indicates inadequate parenting – or worse. Feelings like these can stir up defensiveness, in which they believe that the school sees them as lacking. On the other hand, they could be relieved that another adult will be supporting them and sharing some of the responsibility for the well-being of their child. The very act of sitting in a room and having a conversation can do much to alleviate parents' anticipatory anxieties about both the therapist and the therapeutic process. However they approach the meeting, we must remember to treat them with sensitivity and reassurance.

In the primary school setting an ideal situation is for meetings with parents to occur at the start of the work, midway through and at its completion when the therapist is working with the child over the school year. In these sessions she will have the opportunity to gather both basic and also more detailed information about the child. It also gives her an opportunity to explain and answer questions about the service the child will be getting. The therapist has to tolerate the fact that it's never possible to know everything about the child's situation. She will also be aware that parents will have reactions to her along with their own ideas of what therapy represents, as noted previously.

Parents' transference

On an unconscious level, parents, like all of us, will have some forgotten or repressed feelings about school and what it symbolises for them. For example, some of us may look back on our school days as a time when we felt understood, thought about and stimulated both educationally and socially. Perhaps school offered *a safe base* from which to explore the world, which has led to *a positive transference* to all that school represents. For others, school could be remembered as a place where, on the whole, expectations could never be met and teachers were perceived as demanding, critical and unsympathetic. It may also have been a place where it was difficult to make or keep friends.

Parents carrying an unconscious positive transference to schools may well have unrealistic or idealised expectations of what therapy in the school setting can offer. Or, conversely, they may experience a *negative transference*, which may affect their ability to see their child's experience as different from theirs. In both instances, their reaction may not reflect their own childhood experiences in their entirety. As discussed in the introductory chapter to this book, we all have *an internal world* in which our responses to everyday life are influenced by our own fantasies. For example, we might idealise our school years because we don't want to remember instances when we felt inadequate, humiliated or unjustly treated by school staff or peers.

All the residual negative feelings that are transferred onto the school could also screen more painful memories. For many, people in positions of authority such as teachers or head teachers will represent parental figures. Perhaps we recall only the demanding or critical teachers because we don't want to remember our favourite one who unexpectedly moved on and whose loss was too painful to mourn because it echoed the death or departure of a parent or grandparent.

Alternatively, in our internal world our negative responses to school could be coloured by fraught or conflicted feelings about authority figures in general. Our ability to take in and make use of what is being offered in the learning relationship can be affected by leftover infantile feelings that haven't been fully digested or processed. For example, unacknowledged *envy* can make it difficult to accept that teachers have good, mentally nourishing 'food' to offer. Excessive envy can mean it's difficult to feel *gratitude* for what is being freely given. Parents with unresolved feelings of this kind may feel envious towards what the therapist is offering or what their child is receiving.

As will be clear from these few examples, parents will have their own unique reaction to schools and their own thoughts as to what schools can provide. These reactions will be shaped by conscious and unconscious memories, feelings and desires as well as by what is *projected* onto the therapist. Parents meeting us for the first time may project onto us their wish for the perfect mother who can make everything better. Conversely, they may project their fear of the all-seeing parent who will expose their shameful inadequacies or weaknesses. In most cases, a combination of conscious and unconscious wishes and fears will be triggered even before they meet us. It's useful to note their reaction to us as it could provide valuable information on the child's environment. If, for example, a parent is suspicious and wary of whatever a school has to offer, this will be conveyed in a multitude of ways to the child. The therapist's non-judgemental, sensitively attuned and mindful reaction to parents can go a long way in modifying their harsh internal picture of schools and those who work in them. This, in turn, will eventually filter down to the child and can also modify his response.

Anticipating anxieties

Every parent meeting is different: some, more than others, are willing to discuss their child's difficulties openly and to share their views on schools with us. But whatever the parents' level of openness, all meetings will trigger both the everyday anxieties stirred up by a first meeting and the inflated anxieties driven by unconscious material. Psychoanalysts have noted that people alone in a room together for the first time with no social task are bound to feel varying degrees of terror and anxiety. This is entirely normal as a first meeting represents the unfamiliar and we all project onto the unknown our greatest fears and wishes. The difference between the therapist and the parents in this instance is that the therapist will anticipate such anxieties and will be better equipped to contain them.

Being told by the school that their child would benefit from therapy is a sensitive issue for most, if not all, parents. It's important that they are made to feel validated and understood. Therapists can convey this by listening attentively and communicating interest and care. This is achieved by using reflective listening skills, by being non-judgemental and by giving positive and supportive feedback.

Therapists should also be alert to their own assumptions, theories and generalisations about the family. Research indicates that many therapists have a tendency to formulate their impressions within the first 30 to 60 seconds of meeting their clients (Gauron and Dickinson 1969). We all need to be aware that the contemporary family takes different forms and that roles within families are shaped by many factors including cultural, economic and social. For instance, a mother may be the sole breadwinner of the family while the father stays at home as the primary carer. Keeping an open mind and focusing on the quality of relationships within families rather than the composition or role divisions is a useful approach.

In the secondary school context, contact with parents is far more variable. They may not be seen at all, they may have one introductory meeting only or they may have ongoing contact with the therapist. Each situation has to be assessed on an individual basis, taking into account the age of the young person, why he was referred and whether or not he would welcome the therapist having some contact with his parents. Often it's more appropriate for the work to remain focused on the young person and for the contact with parents or carers to be kept to a minimum.

What do we talk about at the first session?

It's useful to prepare for your first introductory meeting with a parent. This will help you to contain your anxiety and also help you to begin the process of developing a therapeutic language. You can use the suggested format below as a starting point. As your experience builds, you will find your own words to describe your role and the work you do and you'll develop your own ways of framing questions.

Start by introducing yourself

'My name is . . . and I'm working at this school supporting children.' If you are a trainee, you might want to add 'for this academic year'. It's not necessary to mention that you are a trainee but if you would like to define your role, you can identify yourself as a school therapist, art therapist, play or drama therapist.

Clarify what the structure and aims of this session are

'We have up to an hour today to think together about your child's needs and also for me to learn a little more about him.'

There will be important information you will want to record

Bear in mind that it can be threatening for parents to meet with a professional, and note taking can make it even more so. It's preferable to try to hold things in mind and then have up to an hour set aside after the meeting to write up what the parent(s) have told you as well as noting down your own observations of their reactions to you, the situation and anything else that might strike you as interesting, including what you felt during your time with them. If you feel you need to take notes, you can say, 'Do you mind if I take a few notes for myself? I may not be able to remember everything we discuss.'

Provide some insight into what you are offering to their child

'Your child has been referred to me because the school felt he could benefit from working with an understanding adult who is not a teacher or family member. I can give the children I work with the opportunity to talk about what's important to them and make sense of some of their experiences. If they want to, they can use art or play materials to show me what's on their mind.'

You may wish to add the following: 'Research shows that art and play are important for all children. Making objects and using toys helps them to work out how they relate to others in their world. Drawing pictures about what is bothering them or acting out scenarios through play can enable them to make better sense of their experiences. As a therapist, I can look at your child's picture or observe his play and say, for example, "It seems you're showing me what might hurt your feelings" or "I wonder if this means that you're feeling angry about something."'

Clarify practical issues, such as day and time

'I'll work with your child every ___ day from ___ till ___. I'll pick him up from his classroom and return him after 50 minutes. We'll be working in _____ (the designated room).'

Explain confidentiality

'I'm providing a confidential service, which means that what your child and I talk about won't be passed on to any of the school staff or to other parents or carers. There are reasons for this. Children benefit from being able to talk about whatever preoccupies them without having to worry about it being discussed with a teacher or a parent. For example, children can be quite sensitive and embarrassed or concerned about things that adults aren't very worried about. Also, giving children a private space makes it safe for them to try things out without the fear of others hearing their thoughts or learning about their vulnerable feelings. The only time that the content of our work would not remain confidential is if I had serious concerns either about your child's well-being or that of someone else he tells me about. Then I would have to share this with a senior staff member in my team [or in the school if you are in an independent role] and possibly with the person who deals with child protection at the school.'

Managing expectations

It's important to touch on the parents' expectations, since they may have unrealistic hopes about what can be achieved. It's not unusual for therapy to be idealised and viewed as the longed-for solution to all their problems.

You may wish to explain that the child's difficult behaviour is his way of communicating that there's something bothering him and that it may take time for changes in him to become visible.

What information do we need to gather?

Family situation: It's useful to ask the following questions to clarify the family and housing situation:

- Who is the child living with?
- Are there any brothers and sisters?
- Who holds parental responsibility?
- Who else is part of the family?
- Have there been any significant changes in the family (i.e. moving house, separations, deaths)?
- Has the child always attended this school? If not, how long has he been here? Why did he change schools? How did the child respond to the change?
- Are there any future plans (i.e. moves, marriages, new baby)?
- Is the family working with any other professionals (i.e. social services, CAMHS)?

Support system:

- Who do they go to for support?
- In a difficult situation, who would help them?
- If they've had a bad day, who do they speak to?

Perceptions of their problems: It's useful to ascertain how the parents perceive their child. Sometimes you will find that they will start off the meeting claiming that there are no problems. But once they feel comfortable and supported, they are likely to open up to discuss their worries. The following are useful questions to ask:

- What are the most worrying difficulties?
- Why do they think the school suggested their child see someone?
- What is their child's main problem?
- Did the child always have this problem or these problems? What might have started it/them?
- What impact or consequence has the problem had on the child or the rest of the family?
- What would the parents like to ask the child?

Scaling questions can be useful for working with children and adults when trying to establish the severity or impact of the difficulty. You can ask the parent or the child to place the problem on a scale from 1 to 10, with 1 having very little impact and 10 a great deal. This can be adapted to other situations.

Presentation of problem: You may wish to explore the following issues in this session:

- Is there an established sleeping pattern and bedtime routine?
- Is the behaviour different at home to what it is at school?
- Does the child have key friendships?
- Are there any concerns around eating?
- What activities (e.g. sports, games, video games, cycling) does your child engage in?
- What is your response if your child doesn't behave?
- What consequences or punishments do you impose?

Focusing on the positives (these can be interwoven into the conversation):

- What are three things that your child really likes?
- What are three things that your child is really good at doing?
- What do you really like about your child?

Goal setting: It's important that the therapist assesses the parents' wishes for the future of their family. If you are using a pre- and post-therapy evaluation form, the answers to these questions can be noted on it:

- What would they like to be different in a few months' time for their child?
- How would this make things better?
- What changes would they like to see? (It's important to remind the parents again that change is a process and can take time. Also, you can ask the parents what they can do to bring about their hoped-for changes.)

Coping mechanisms or degrees of resilience: It's useful to try to assess how capable the parents are of managing life's challenges. This can be done by asking the following questions:

- Can you think of any events that you as a family found difficult but have coped with?
- What were the circumstances and what enabled you to manage?

How should the session be ended?

At the end of the session you can summarise what you are offering to the child and ask the parents if they agree to the service suggested. If they do, ask them to sign the consent form. By signing, they are giving permission for the child to be taken out of class to see you for support work.

Assure them that they can contact you through the school's staff member who is responsible for pastoral care (you can name the person) if they have any questions or difficulties or if they wish to arrange another meeting. You can conclude by saying, 'I'll get in touch again in about two months to arrange for a review meeting if that sounds all right with you.'

Further support for you in working with parents

It's common to use supervision time to discuss any themes relating to meetings with parents.

Conclusion

Generally we'll see parents of younger children. Working with adolescents is a different process that demands other ways of eliciting information and supporting them. The teenager struggling with his own identity may find the notion of his parents meeting his therapist infantilising, threatening or a breach of confidence.

For us, meeting with parents for the first time can seem a daunting prospect too, especially if the school has experienced them as unsupportive or antagonistic. We will have our own transference to the situation of sitting in a room with angry or concerned parents that we'll need to be aware of. But explaining to them why we are seeing their children and what benefits may be achieved is as important to the therapeutic process as getting any information we're able to glean from them about their child and the family dynamics.

Study questions

Explore your own response to meeting with parents by writing down your thoughts and feelings and/or discuss them with a peer:

- What anxieties or expectations do you have about talking to parents?
- Do you think it's useful to get background on the families from school staff?
- How might you deal with possible defensiveness?
- What do you think are the main aims of these meetings?

You may want to discuss some or all of the vignettes listed below or try to come up with your own responses.

Vignette 1

Ramina is a Year 6 girl who has been referred because she sometimes cries without provocation or warning in class and in the playground. Her mother, whose English is basic, comes into the meeting clearly nervous and ill at ease. 'What's wrong with Ramina?' she asks, her face etched with worry. 'Is she a bad girl at school? Why does she have to miss lessons?' *What would you say?*

Vignette 2

Titus is in Year 5 and gets into frequent trouble because of his attention-seeking behaviour, which can sometimes be aggressive towards other children. His mother was reluctant to come for a meeting and, once present, comes across as antagonistic. 'There's nothing the matter with my boy. He's just lazy and all he cares about is football. But he's not a bad boy. It's the school that brings out the worst in him and now they're punishing him by showing his whole class that he needs special attention.' *What would you say?*

Vignette 3

Miriam, in Year 8, has been acting out in ways that have spurred her form tutor on to ask for a referral. She has been uncharacteristically rude to teachers, her grades have been slipping and so has her hygiene. Her father appears to be depressed. Miriam's mother left the country four months ago and now it's just him and her in the house. He gets tearful when he talks about being out of his depth with her and with life in general. *What would you say?*

Vignette 4

Jason is in Year 10. The school has been concerned about the rumours that he is involved in a gang. His mother remarried after a long period of being alone following the death of Jason's father. She has had three children in quick succession and Jason feels resentful, angry and alienated. She comes into the meeting heavily pregnant with a fourth baby and expresses her fury at Jason for making problems for her. 'I don't have time for his stupidity. He does everything he can to irritate me or else he says nothing at all for days on end. He's not going to say anything to you, either.' *What would you say?*

Sample responses

Vignette 1

'It's understandable that you're concerned but there's nothing wrong with Ramina. The school doesn't think she's bad. It's just that teachers have noticed that she cries easily. Children are very sensitive and crying easily isn't a problem but it's a sign that something may be worrying Ramina. Having her own time with me will give her a chance to explore what may be troubling her.'

Or 'There are many children in school who find things a little difficult from time to time. Right now it seems that Ramina is a bit unhappy and it would be good to try to improve things for her before she goes off to secondary school.'

Vignette 2

'You're right – he's not a bad child and the school doesn't see him that way. However, teachers have noticed that he's behaving in ways that could suggest he has hurt feelings or that perhaps there is something troubling him. The school wants to help him, not punish him. Often children, especially boys, feel quite sensitive about talking about how they feel in front of others. Seeing me on his own will give him the chance to open up about his feelings.'

Or 'Children often find it hard to talk about their problems, so they behave in ways that say there's something they're unhappy about. Titus is doing that at the moment, so the school is keen to give him a chance to talk about what's bothering him and how he might express himself in different ways.'

Vignette 3

'It sounds like you're going through a painful and difficult time. You and Miriam have a lot to cope with. Miriam's mother moving away is a loss for both of you and you'll be feeling it in different ways. But the fact that you've come today to see me suggests that you're managing and that you're thinking of Miriam. I'd like to know a bit more about her. Can you tell me how she got on with her mother and whether there is any contact with her now?'

At the end of the meeting, you might want to say something along the lines of 'As we've discussed, it's clear that you and Miriam are both going through a painful time. I can provide some support for Miriam but I'm thinking about what kind of support you may be getting. If you don't have friends or family members who you can talk openly to, it may be a good idea to ask your GP for a referral to a counsellor.' (If the school has further information on adult services, you can pass this on. You might also ask if he wants you to speak to the school about accessing more support from Child, Adolescent and Family Services.)

Vignette 4

'I hear what you're telling me about how you see Jason. It's not easy being a mother of a teenager, especially as you have younger children to look after. However, I think it's important for both of us to try to see things from Jason's side. His behaviour is telling us something. It sounds like your family has gone through a lot of changes over quite a short period of time and more to come with another new baby on the way. The changes may, on the whole, be positive for you, but change always brings up mixed feelings. I think it would help if Jason has his own time with me to reflect on how it feels to have lost his father and now to have a new stepfather and half-siblings. We often find that young people can talk to someone who is outside their everyday life if they know that the sessions are confidential. I think it's worth a try. We don't know yet how Jason will react to me or to having his own time. I suggest we give him the chance to see me and let him decide what he makes of it.'

Or 'When we're under a lot of stress and feel tired and overstretched, it's natural for our fuses to be very short. It sounds like you're having a difficult time at home with Jason and that must be exhausting for you. But it sounds like Jason's having a hard time too, dealing with the changes in the family and with another new baby who will take up a lot of your time and attention. Giving him some space here with me to express his feelings might help him and it might help the situation at home too.'

Reference

Gauron, E. F. and Dickinson, J. K. (1969) The influence of seeing the patient first on diagnostic decision-making in psychiatry. *American Journal of Psychiatry*, 126, 199–205.

Chapter 12

Meeting with teachers and other school staff

Angie Doran

Introduction

Children or young people who the school thinks would benefit from working with a therapist are usually known to the school's Special Educational Needs Coordinator (SENCo). However, as has been noted, there are variations from one school to another, so it's important to be clear from the start which member of staff you are expected to liaise with. Depending on the arrangements and job titles within the particular school, it may be the SENCo, Learning or Behaviour Mentor, Pastoral Care Coordinator or Inclusion Manager, for example, who acts as your key staff contact. Whatever their job title, it will be this person with whom you will liaise for new referrals, assessments, client attendance, report writing, evaluation, and liaison with external agencies. For the sake of simplicity, let's call this person the SENCo.

While you'll be thinking about the overall management of your caseload as well as the clinical content of your work in regular meetings with your clinical supervisor, maintaining regular contact with the SENCo throughout the school year is vital. As well as liaising with her about new referrals, school-specific matters and submitting reports, it is a good idea to arrange a short formal meeting with her at the end of each term if possible. You can use these meetings to review how the therapy service is going in general, to discuss any concerns you have about the therapy setting, to consider changes to the service within the school's service contract and other related issues that come up.

Building on the referral information

As previously noted, different schools will arrange their referral procedure in different ways. At some, the referral form will be completed by a class teacher or other member of the staff team and will be given or sent to you via the SENCo. At others, the SENCo will fill in the initial referral form herself.

Referral forms should be focused enough to provide useful information about the child you'll be working with and at the same time avoid being an added pressure on staff who are asked to complete them. At some schools, staff will fill out a form; at others, you may need to take notes from a conversation and condense that into your own referral information.

Schools hold a file on each pupil which you can ask to access if you're not invited to see them. There are different views about accessing student files or not before you begin work with a young person: while some prefer to have background information to contextualise the client from the outset, others prefer to look at the student's file only after several sessions, when clarification about essential details would be helpful. The latter approach means that the client becomes established in your mind on his own terms and through his existing relationships, before a written, formal school-based history is incorporated into the picture you have of him.

Although the SENCo may have filled in the referral form and know the student well, she may not be the person at school who knows your client best. Although school staff often feel pressed for time, it's always useful to be able to have at least one conversation early on in the work with a staff member who works closely with the child. This helps create a fuller picture of the presenting issues of the child and can give you a sense of the feeling-responses he evokes for the adults around him – all useful material for you.

It's generally easier, as mentioned before, to make contact with class teachers or teaching assistants in primary than in secondary schools, which are larger institutions where teachers come into contact with many more students and tend to have less personal knowledge about each individual young person. Referrals are often given at the beginning of the academic year, so, in a primary school, the person who best knows the child being referred may be his class teacher or teaching assistant from the previous school year. In a secondary school you may need to talk to the form tutor, head of house, student support officer, learning or behaviour mentor, or the client's learning support assistant, for example.

What to cover at the first meeting

At the initial meeting with a member of staff who knows your client, you will want to cover a number of areas and gather detailed information. You will find it useful during this initial discussion to take notes or fill in a Strengths and Difficulties Questionnaire (a behavioural screening tool, see Goodman 1997), or your therapy service's equivalent. Often, however, because of the pressure of time, the pre-therapy profiling form will be completed over a few weeks rather than at one sitting. Becoming familiarised with the main themes contained in the profiling form will enable you to cover these areas in conversations with the teacher.

Usually these forms include sections focusing on the pupil's school-based experiences (e.g. approaches to learning, relationships with peers, attitudes towards adults, etc.) as well as information the staff member has on the young person's family background, which will be useful. Asking the member of staff about what she would like to see change for this child or young person over the course of your work with him can be illuminating too. After the meeting it can be helpful to identify for yourself three key concerns that the school has in regard to this child, and draw from those what the main aims of the therapy will be. Information from your meeting will also help when you come to evaluate the therapy and write up a review of what has changed at the end of your work with the young person.

The climate of secondary schools can be very different from that of the primary sector. Some teachers will be receptive and open to dialogue, and in such cases the therapist can gather as much information as the teacher has access to, using this information to set goals for the work and to evaluate the outcomes. More usually, though, profiling forms are used as a tool to help you think about themes to bear in mind during your work with young people. An example of a profiling form can be found in the final chapter of the book.

Close liaison

Maintaining regular contact with the staff member who works most closely with the child and checking in informally with her every few weeks to get a sense of how things are going for the client can be helpful in noting whether there are any changes or whether things appear to be the same. It will be useful to talk to this staff member at the end of your work with the young person in order to review your profiling information and to acknowledge the end of the work with that member of staff.

Meeting with other staff

At the time of referral you will want to find out which other professionals support this young person and if possible develop working relationships with them too. The school-based or peripatetic general nurse employed by the NHS and/or a mental health nurse (part of the local CAMHS team) may be supporting your client or may have done so in the past. You may find that you are working alongside parental involvement or family liaison workers, educational psychologists, social workers, speech and language therapists and/or drugs and alcohol awareness counsellors, any of whom may have an interest in your client's welfare and experience of working with him. It requires sensitivity to work in parallel with other professionals who have an interest in the health and/or mental health of your client. Conscious and unconscious feelings about the boundaries and responsibilities of your work alongside one another will be at play. However, such professionals should have a good understanding of the confidentiality aspect of your work.

The SENCo will be able to tell you if multi-agency meetings or core staff meetings concerning your client are taking place and you may find that you can contribute to these meetings in person or by submitting a written report on the work you are doing. The report can cover the general progress of the work and the themes that have been explored, the client's level of engagement and your observations about the process of therapy for the client. Remember that you are the young person's advocate and should always safeguard the confidentiality of your sessions in such reports. If you believe you have information that is essential for another professional to know about your client, you must be sure to inform your client that this information needs to be shared before you do so. When in doubt about the appropriateness of sharing information with others, seek the advice of your supervisor.

Keeping in the loop

Changes to school timetabling can affect your session times. School visits and trips, special projects, PSHE days and student review days can crop up suddenly and you may find that you are not informed about these events. The SENCo should be able to tell you if timetabling changes are school-wide but talking to individual class teachers may be the only way of finding out if a class is off-timetable. You will want to ensure that you have a high enough profile in the organisation and that you are visible enough to school staff to be kept informed. It's a good idea to spend some time in the staffroom each week, as this is where you get a sense of the school as a system, as well as where you'll hear about forthcoming school events. It also gives you the opportunity to have informal conversations with staff – not forgetting to maintain a boundaried and professional manner at all times.

Conclusion

Previous chapters have noted that teachers and other professionals will bring to their working relationship with you both conscious and unconscious fantasies about what therapy is and what it can provide. Some may feel that the therapist is privileged in working closely with children in a way the teacher wishes she could do. Others may see the presence of a therapist in school as a negative reflection on their own professional ability to provide adequate pastoral care. However they view us, it is a fact that the member of staff you talk to about a child will have an existing relationship with him. It's possible that this person has been a confidante to the young person in the past and may have unconscious envious feelings about 'handing' him over to you. On the other hand, this teacher may be relieved at the opportunity to share responsibility for this child. This may come with unrealistic hopes about the changes you will be able to bring about. Some may also identify with the young person referred for therapy, feeling they would have benefited from therapeutic input when they were younger. In addition to managing the staff member's transference to you, an awareness of the dynamics that exist around the young person being referred can offer insights into the quality of interpersonal relationships that exist for him.

Study questions

Explore your own response to meeting with teachers by writing down your thoughts and feelings:

- What anxieties or expectations do you have about talking to school staff?

- How might you deal with what you see as efforts to undermine your work?
- What do you think are the main aims of meetings with teachers?

Discuss some or all of the vignettes listed below.

Vignette 1

Occasionally you'll need to answer enquiries from school staff that would lead to a breach of client confidentiality. Without disclosing private information from your sessions be as specific as you can about any non-confidential material from your work, especially if it's relevant to the outcome the school hopes to see (in Billy's case, below, improved attendance), acknowledge shared information and ask for the members of staff's thoughts about the student.

Billy was referred because he is frequently absent from school and is disruptive when he does attend. His form tutor knows from the SENCo that his father is in prison. You meet his form tutor in the staffroom just after a session with Billy. She says to you, 'So, how's Billy doing? What exactly did happen last year with his dad?' *What would you say?*

Vignette 2

It's worth bearing in mind in your exchanges with teachers that the language you use will differ in some ways from that of educationalists and, as a result, the expectations of what therapy can address may be misunderstood. You will want to try to develop some common language with teachers, so that although they may be talking about targets and achievements you will want to think about these things within the terms of the therapy and the child's relationships.

Louise has returned home to her mother after a period of respite foster care. You've arranged a parent meeting and, by way of preparation, say to the teacher, 'I'm meeting with Louise's mum next week. I wonder if there's anything you think it would be helpful for me to say to her about Louise and how things are for her now?' The teacher replies, 'Yes, she's doing OK, but can you say something about homework to Mum? Louise often doesn't do it – the Head's asking us to monitor it at the moment.' *What would you say?*

Vignette 3

A member of staff's unconscious feelings about a child you're seeing may emerge outside the professional meetings you have with each other. For example, the teacher may feel envious of the exclusive, confidential one-to-one time the therapist and child have together and may act this out around the child's sessions.

When you go to pick up Corey for his session, the teacher says to him, 'Tell the therapist about what happened in the playground at lunchtime – come on, Corey. I know what happened!' *What would you say?*

Vignette 4

The frustration a teacher feels about the behaviour and attitude of a pupil in her class can be transferred on to you and your work with that young person. It's helpful if you can respond by managing and containing the teacher's projections, while giving clear and realistic information about the work you're doing.

Harry's father died two years ago and his mum has three teenage boys to look after on her own. You've been working with Harry for a term. At a short review meeting with his class teacher, she says, 'Harry's still as badly behaved in class as he ever was, and I just can't get him to focus on his schoolwork. Your meetings with him just don't seem to be helping.' *What would you say?*

Vignette 5

Some members of staff may feel uncertain about the usefulness of therapy. If you can describe the main benefits of therapy and, moreover, how these can help the young person you're discussing, you'll help the teacher to see the value of the work you're doing.

You have an initial meeting with a teacher and she says, 'How is this going to help Georgia anyway? What she needs is some discipline. I don't see how talking about herself is going to get her to learn anything – personally I'd like her to talk a lot less!' *What would you say?*

Sample responses

Vignette 1

'Billy's been to four of the six sessions we've had so far and is really making good use of his time with me. We're beginning to develop a good working relationship. What happened with his father last year has clearly had a big impact on the whole family and Billy's just beginning to make sense of it. He's slowly starting to settle into the work we're doing. How do *you* think things are for him at the moment?'

Vignette 2

'It sounds like you think Mum's still finding it difficult supporting Louise at home and that it would help if she could spend more time with Louise, including helping her prepare for school at the start of the week. Perhaps I'll have an opportunity to mention this to mum.'

Vignette 3

To the teacher: 'It sounds like something happened at lunchtime. I'll take Corey for our meeting now – the lunchtime incident may be something he wants to talk about in his session today.'

Vignette 4

'Harry is attending his sessions with me and we aim to continue next term, which is a good sign. His restlessness in class shows just how unsettled he feels. He's starting to calm down in his sessions and is beginning to talk about his family experiences. This work can take some time to have an impact and if we can continue to support him together, we may be able to help him get more out of school than he does at the moment.'

Vignette 5

'When young people continually get into trouble, it's not because they're bad but because they're trying to communicate something – like anger, frustration or sadness – to the people around them. Talking about what's troubling her might help Georgia to understand why she's feeling the way she is and behaving as she does. If she can take the opportunity with me to talk about these things on a regular basis, we may find she won't feel the need to be so talkative in class.'

Reference

Goodman, R. (1997) The Strengths and Difficulties Questionnaire: A Research Note. *Journal of Child Psychology and Psychiatry*, 38, 581–586.

Chapter 13

Informing the child or young person about the first session

Lyn French

The previous chapters have covered pre-therapy tasks including talking to teachers, other school staff and parents about why the child or young person came to the school's attention. Whenever possible, information will have been sought on the family circumstances and the therapist will have discussed with key teachers as well as with parents what the sessions can and cannot offer.

This chapter focuses on what stage in the referral process – and how – the child or young person is informed about the school's decision to offer therapy to him. As every school is different, the therapist will need to think through how this task is best approached.

The therapist new to a school may 'research' its ethos, getting a feel for it by attending meetings as an observer, reading policies, spending time in the staff room, looking on the school website and talking to a range of personnel including teachers, support staff, dinner ladies, caretakers and administrative staff. The therapist may want to ask them what makes their school unique, what they enjoy most about working there, what they find most challenging, what they think the school does best, what the school is most concerned about, and so on. Using the same skills as she does to create a picture of her clients – that is, observing, listening, asking questions, reading reports, talking with staff and parents or carers, monitoring her own feelings in response to being in the school, noting what feelings come up in conversations with staff, and so on – the therapist will begin to build a picture in mind of the organisation. This picture will be added to, reconfigured and reshaped again and again over time. In the first instance, the school's 'personality' or ethos will inform how the therapist develops her own protocols.

If, for example, the school prioritises a more organic approach, with ways of working continuously evolving as a result of formal and informal dialogue and paperwork kept to a minimum, the school therapist may follow suit. In such a school, the therapist might gather referrals through talking directly to key staff, schedule a brief introductory meeting with the child referred a few days before the first session and then keep the school informed of the work through conversations that take place as and when the moment is right, whether it be in the context of a meeting or in an ad hoc encounter during a break or after school.

In contrast, if the therapist is based in a school where most aspects of teaching and learning follow standard guidelines and the work of the organisation is highly structured with defined communication channels, lines of accountability and term-by-term target setting, then the therapist may devise her own written policy framework for her service delivery. This could cover the themes already discussed in the preceding chapters, including how referrals are made, who makes them, whether or not parents are met with, what the assessment process compromises, how risk assessments are carried out, whether or not reports are written and if so at what stage in the therapy, and so on. Regarding the theme of this chapter – informing the pupil – a policy of this kind might also make clear the following:

- at what stage in the process the pupil is informed about the proposal to see the school therapist;
- who explains to the pupil why the referral to the school therapist was made;
- whether the therapist has an initial, pre-therapy discussion with the pupil so that his views can be taken into consideration;
- whether or not pupils are given a choice about attending their first session or initial block of sessions;
- whether a standard procedure will be agreed upon regarding the above points with exceptions made as and when cases warrant it or whether each referral is treated on an individual basis.

There is no right or wrong way to structure a therapy service in school. What is most important is that the therapist puts in the initial work required to get a sense of the school ethos, including both a 'feel' for how things are done as well as a more concrete understanding based on reading the school development plan and becoming familiar with key policies. She then attunes her service to fit well enough with the school's working model without distorting basic therapy principles. Some therapists consider it good practice to ensure that a way of monitoring the service is introduced even if the school does not request it and is relatively easy-going about data collection of this kind.

Regardless of whether the therapist writes up a guiding policy for her service, she will need to consult with the school on whether to establish a procedure that is always adhered to regarding informing the pupil. For instance, it may be agreed that the SENCo will always tell the child or adolescent of the referral and about the first session. Or the therapist may recommend a 'case by case' approach with a teacher, support worker or the parents, or the school therapist herself carrying out this task, depending on the circumstances.

When and where the conversation with the child or young person takes place, how much he is told, how much advance notice is given before the initial session and whether or not he is given the option to attend will also need to be thought about. Various approaches to informing children in both primary and secondary school settings are outlined below.

The primary school context

In primary schools, there are a number of ways in which a child will hear about his referral to a school therapist.

The child may be informed by the

- class teacher
- classroom support worker or SENCo
- parents
- therapist
- therapist and teacher together
- therapist and parents together

The staff member who is chosen to tell the child will convey a message. For example, if a pupil can perceive of his class teacher only as someone who is 'always picking on him', then the teacher might not be the best person to inform him. In such an example, the child might assume the therapy is a form of punishment or a sign that the teacher cannot cope with him any longer and wishes to pass him on to someone else.

Informing the child will take place either in the

- classroom, when whoever is telling the child can be alone with him, or
- therapy room, when the therapist is informing the child either on her own or with the parents or the teacher also present.

This conversation should take place

- whenever there is no one else around (e.g. the teacher can ask the child to stay behind for a few minutes at break time, at lunch or after school, or the therapist can come along at one of these times);
- in advance of the first session, preferably no more than a week before.

The class teacher

Depending on the child's age, the class teacher may have a conversation with him even before making the referral. For example, a child may confide in his teacher or the teacher may know that the child's parent is ill or has moved away. The teacher might say, 'I imagine what you're telling me is upsetting for you. I think it would be useful if you met with Jane [school therapist]. She understands children very well and can help you think about this. What do you think – shall I arrange a time for you to meet with her?' Or the teacher might tell this same child, after the referral has been passed on, 'I've arranged a time for you to see Jane next Tuesday morning after our reading lesson.'

A class teacher may refer a child whose behaviour is causing difficulties. In this instance, once the referral is made, the parents and therapist may meet and the therapist may have more than one discussion with the teacher before the child is told. The teacher could say to the child just before the first session, for example, 'Your parents and I think it would be useful if you could meet with Jane. She understands children very well and can help you to think about why it's so hard to sit still in lessons and to stay out of fights at playtime. I want you to enjoy class time and have fun during the breaks. Jane will be coming for you after lunch today. I'd like you to meet her and spend some time with her.' Note that the teacher in this example is coming from a position of wanting to make life better for the child rather than conveying a sense that the therapy is linked to punishment or some form of behaviour management.

The classroom support worker or SENCo

When a child's disruptive behaviour has led to the referral, the therapist may feel that the class teacher is too impacted by the child to be the person to tell him about the sessions. Perhaps the child knows how to 'get under the teacher's skin', which makes it almost impossible for the teacher to have a straightforward, non-emotional conversation with him. Or the teacher may be disparaging and feel discouraged, believing that nothing can help this particular child. There are many other versions of this kind of dynamic between the teacher and the child. In these instances, the therapist may conclude that it is counterproductive to ask the class teacher to inform the child. If the therapist knows that one of the classroom assistants or the SENCo is perceived to be supportive by the child, then the therapist may ask one of them to inform him.

The parents or carers

There may be times when parents or carers have been in to have an initial conversation with the therapist and will talk about this meeting at home with the child. This can mean that it will be from them that the child first hears about the proposed sessions. Usually when this happens it is because the parents are interested and engaged. Less frequent are those instances when they want to warn the child not to reveal too much to the school therapist. In such cases, the family might have had a bad experience of external help or be particularly distrustful. The therapist needs to work hard to reach these parents so that they can have a good enough experience and can take a more relaxed view of their child's therapy.

The therapist

Many therapists take care to inform the child themselves in order to ensure that he knows the sessions have been arranged and that she will be coming for him at a specific time and day. At one end of the spectrum will be those times when both the teacher and parents have already told the child, making the therapist the third person to tell him. This can work to the advantage of the therapy, as it shows the child that the adults in his life are thinking about him together. The child also gets a chance to meet the therapist before the first session, which is helpful. At the other end of the spectrum will be those times when no one has spoken to the child, even though there may have been conversations between the school and the parents about the proposed therapy. The therapist, too, may have met with the parents. In these situations, it is important for the therapist to introduce herself and let the child know she'll be coming the following week to collect him.

Seeing the therapist and teacher together

Some therapists might choose to see the child together with his class teacher in the classroom for a brief introductory conversation. Again, this performs the role of linking the school with the therapist in the child's mind, which can be positive. However, it may make it harder for the child to trust that what he says or shows the therapist in the sessions will be kept confidential. While this can be worked with, it needs to be handled with a degree of caution: some teachers will be uninformed about therapy and with the best intentions may say something to the child in this initial meeting that misrepresents the process or leaves the child with the impression that there is 'something wrong' with him.

Seeing the therapist and parents together

One of the most useful approaches is for the therapist to invite the parents to come in for a three-way meeting together with her and the child. It gives her the opportunity to observe the parents interacting with the child and vice versa while also providing a picture for the child of the adults coming together to support him. In reality, this is not always possible to set up. If it can be achieved, some therapists have found it useful to see the parents on their own first for 10 or 15 minutes, then to collect the child and, with his being present, to have a short conversation about why the school and his parents think therapy might be useful. The child is then taken back to class and another 10 or 15 minutes is spent alone with the parents. Chapter 11, 'Meeting with Parents', provides useful examples of how to conduct these sessions so that there is less possibility of stigma or shame attached to seeing a therapist.

Sample vignettes

The following vignettes highlight ways in which the therapist might talk to the child about the referral and proposed sessions. You might want to work out what you would say in each instance before reading the suggestions made.

Vignette 1

Ella is eight years old and an only child. She has been referred because her mother died a year ago, at which time she moved in with her father. Prior to this, she had been seeing her father one Sunday afternoon a month. She is listless in class and her friends have drifted away due to her withdrawn behaviour. *What would you say to this child when telling her about your first meeting?*

> *Sample response*
>
> Therapist: Hi Ella. I'm Jane. You may have seen me around the school. Did your teacher mention that I'd be coming by to say hello? (Ella shakes her head.) No? Well, I wanted to tell you that the school thinks it would be helpful for you and me to meet on our own. I'll be coming for you next Tuesday at 1.30 p.m., right after lunch break.
>
> Ella: Why?
>
> Therapist: The school wants to be sure that children feel supported, especially when they go through big changes in their life. Your teacher thought you might find it helpful to see me on your own.
>
> Ella (*rather depressed sounding and in a hopeless tone of voice*): I don't want to.
>
> Therapist: We can talk more about this next week. I'll be coming for you after lunch on Tuesday and then we can spend some time together. Let's meet next week and just see how it feels. I look forward to seeing you then, Ella.

Observations

Note how the therapist does not get drawn into a longer conversation at this stage. She doesn't explain her role or use the word 'therapy' to describe what she is offering. She keeps what she has to say simple and straightforward. When Ella asks why, the therapist shifts to speaking more generally about 'the school' (not about Ella's teacher, the SENCo or the Head) and about 'children' (rather than about Ella directly). Beneath an unresponsive or withdrawn presentation, a child may be desperate for support yet afraid to trust that the therapist really wants to help. A low key, detached response such as Ella's may be a test to see if the therapist will be able to tolerate depression or hopelessness and if she will persevere in the face of it.

In exchanges such as this one with Ella, it is helpful if the therapist uses facial expressions, tone of voice and body language to communicate a soft, gentle approach. What is to be avoided is a more teacherly or parent-like stance that conveys to the child that he *has* to listen to adults and do what they say.

Keeping track of how we feel when engaging with a child in the first instance is a good idea. For example, the therapist talking to Ella may have had to resist strongly trying to win her over. Perhaps she could sense Ella's deep loneliness and vulnerability and wanted to reach her, even if it meant slipping into a more seductive or 'charming' manner. Or the therapist could have felt a little irritated or frustrated by what might have felt like Ella's passive-aggressive response and was possibly tempted into taking up a more authoritative position, stating quite emphatically that she would be starting her sessions the following week.

The therapist's feelings provide important information about the child and, over time, she will have opportunities to see how every child who asks the question 'Why?' in this first encounter will trigger a different response.

Vignette 2

Aki is ten years old. He has been at the school for a year. He lives with both parents and a younger sister. His behaviour has deteriorated and the school described him on the referral form as 'violent towards his peers and dismissive of adults'. The teacher has told you that he has a younger brother who was ill for a year with cancer and died six months ago. *What would you say to this child when telling him about your first meeting?*

Sample response

Therapist: Hi Aki. I'm Jane. I imagine you've seen me around the school.

Aki: I know who you are. You're a kind of 'psychologist' (this is said in a mocking voice as if to convey scorn).

Therapist: I've come by to introduce myself. You may know that the school wants to support its pupils, especially when they go through things in life that might be quite difficult or challenging in some way. It's been suggested that we meet together—

Aki (cuts in, trying to wrong-foot the therapist): Who suggested it?

Therapist: This is something we can go over when we meet next week. I've come by to let you know I'll be collecting you from class next Wednesday at 9.30. We'll have a chance to talk more then.

Aki: What if I don't want to come?

Therapist: It's common for children to have mixed feelings about coming to sessions. I always suggest that they give it a

> chance and come for a couple of sessions to see what it's like. I'll be here, as I said, next Wednesday at 9.30 and we can pick up from there. I'll see you then, Aki.
>
> *Aki (imitating the therapist in a mocking tone):* 'I'll see you then!'

Observations

It is evident from this short encounter that Aki is highly *defended* and trying to make the therapist the one to feel uncomfortable, deskilled and on the edge of losing control of the situation. Naturally, the therapist may have all these feelings but her aim is to contain them and, later, on her own or in supervision, will decode them as information about how Aki experiences his position in the world. Clearly, he is trying to make the therapist feel under the spotlight and inadequate, feelings he himself is probably determined to avoid.

As in Vignette 1, you can get a sense of how the therapist gently but firmly resists having to explain herself or what she is offering. She tries to convey a thoughtful but friendly, warm and practical attitude. She doesn't try to convince Aki that she's offering him something good, but instead acknowledges his feelings in a neutral way. In fact, the therapist refers to the 'mixed' feelings children commonly have, alluding to the fact that underneath the bravado and superiority Aki probably has other reactions, including, perhaps, a great deal of fear about what the focus of the work might be.

The two vignettes above provide examples of possible responses from children on first meeting a therapist and being told about their sessions. A useful learning exercise can be to write up other scenarios and, either on your own or with peers, think about the feelings that could come up and what the therapist might say. Role play can help therapists prepare for the challenges that are bound to surface, and even more experienced therapists find it useful in enhancing their 'therapy vocabulary' and refining their child-friendly language.

The secondary school context

In the secondary school setting, as already noted, referrals can come from a range of sources. Informing the young person of the therapy is a task that could fall to the original referrer, the SENCo, a school support worker or the therapist. Or it may be that the school informs the pupil via an appointment slip, which could take the form of a written note or email.

The referrer

The referrer may be a teacher, form tutor, school support worker or the SENCo. If the referrer is the one to inform the pupil about the sessions, then it is useful if the therapist can provide basic guidance on what might be said to the young person. For example, the therapist might have produced her own leaflet on what she is offering and this can be given to the young person. Or the therapist may suggest to the referrer that she keep it simple and tell the pupil that he has an appointment to meet the school therapist on the date and time agreed and at that time the student will be able to ask the therapist anything he wants to.

Sometimes the referrer will have been working with the student, providing low-key support. In this instance, she may talk through the differences between her provision and the therapist's. Alternatively – or additionally – she might take the pupil to the first introductory meeting and introduce him to the therapist.

Whoever informs the young person will carry a symbolic meaning. For example, if a support worker is going to carry out the task, it is advisable if she is someone like a learning mentor rather than a behaviour mentor. However, if the behaviour mentor has an existing relationship with the pupil and it is a positive one, then she may be the best choice.

The school therapist

It is less common in the secondary school setting for the therapist to be given the task of informing a student of his initial appointment. When this is the system the school chooses to implement, the therapist will need to decide what the best way of handling this might be. For example, she may need to have a look at his timetable and select a class from which she can take him out. In such instances, the therapist may want to take an appointment slip and also perhaps a leaflet on her service with her. She can then introduce herself to the student and give him the slip and the leaflet if she is using one. As in the primary school context, it is not so helpful to engage in a conversation about the referral or whether or not he has a choice in the matter. At this stage, the main point you will want to get across is that you will be meeting later that week (or the following one) for an initial conversation. It is useful to emphasise that at that meeting the student can ask you whatever he'd like and you will tell him more about what you are offering.

Appointment slips

In some schools, the student will be informed of his introductory meeting via an appointment slip, which could be a standard form with the student's name and appointment time filled in. This might be sent via email. In the majority of cases, the student will have had at least one conversation with either his form tutor, a teacher, the SENCo or a support worker so that that there is a context for the appointment.

Preparing for the first session

The chapter to follow discusses ways to approach the first session. However, it is important to note that the way in which the pupil is informed of the first meeting with the therapist will shape the *transference relationship* that begins to form even before the student sees or speaks to the therapist.

As discussed in previous chapters, *transference* is the term used to describe what we transfer onto the present from the past. In other words, all of our current or new experiences take place within our own historical context. We read meaning consciously and unconsciously into the present based on what has happened in the past and also make assumptions about the future, which are tinted by the past. We *project* what's gone before onto what is to come.

For example, the pupil who had a difficult time in primary school and felt his teachers consistently focused on him out of the whole class to be told off may assume that being singled out always has a negative context. This pupil's conscious response to being informed of an appointment with the school therapist may be 'Here we go again – it's always me. What did I do *this* time?' He may dislike the therapist before even setting eyes on her because, like the teachers in his primary school, she has 'picked *him* out' to speak to.

Unconsciously, something altogether different may be going on. This pupil may deny the extent to which he would like adults' attention. The only way he can get it without feeling infantilised by his neediness is to act out. This succeeds in making him visible – but with negative consequences.

Useful information can be gathered, if possible, from the school staff member who informed the pupil of the appointment:

- What was his response?
- Was it predictable?
- Did he express curiosity?

Conclusion

It is usually the case that the majority of pupils who see a school therapist are referred for sessions rather than self-nominating, which brings up the question of who tells the student about the referral and how it is done. As this chapter has shown, this seemingly straightforward task has multiple layers of meaning once it's broken down. Whether or not the therapist takes responsibility for informing the child or adolescent will need to be thought about in the context of the school ethos. Every school – like every client – has its own history, a way of seeing the world coloured by past and present experiences, aspirations, anxieties and defences both conscious and unconscious and ways of doing things that reflect these influences. The school therapist carefully negotiates how she will approach telling students about the initial referral and the first meeting, balancing her own professional orientation, ethics and standards with the way the school prefers to handle the process. Whatever method is decided upon, it is most helpful if the person informing the pupil about the referral thinks through what will be said, how much will be discussed there and then and whether or not the student has any choice in the matter. At the core of developing and refining therapy skills is the need to evolve a sensitive language suitable to the task at hand. Any communication with a pupil about therapy will trigger the transference process. As discussed in this chapter, taking care over what is said to the pupil in the first instance and how the message is conveyed can either help or hinder the unfolding of the therapeutic alliance.

Study questions

- If you can choose who informs the child or young person about his initial appointment with you, who would you select? Why?
- In the primary school setting, if you decide to see the parents and child together first, how might you conduct the session? What will be your main objectives?
- In the secondary school setting, if you decide to use a leaflet to describe what you offer, what will you say on it? What kind of language will you use to ensure that it is accessible and child-friendly?

Thinking about your own experiences of the earliest stages of your personal therapy can help you to gain insight into how transferences evolve:

- How did you find your therapist? What did you assume about her based on this?
- What impressions did you take away from the experience of setting up the first appointment? (E.g. if you had a telephone conversation, what did you imagine your therapist's tone of voice conveyed?)
- What did you think she would look like?
- Did you make any assumptions about her dress sense?
- What does this tell you about how you thought she would be?
- Were your fantasies borne out?

Chapter 14

The first session

Reva Klein

The primary school setting

How does the child arrive at the therapy room?

Whether or not we choose to collect the child from his classroom for a therapy session is an important decision. The choice we make will be understood by the child consciously as well as unconsciously as a symbolic communication. The meaning the child gives to our action may change throughout the course of the therapy depending on how the child is experiencing us – and the therapy room – at any given time.

The therapist may be tempted to invite the child to come to the session on his own. This can be an attempt to convey to the child that he has a choice of whether or not to attend and that he is trusted both to exercise his preference and to make his own way if this is his chosen option. However, it may be difficult to know whether the child experiences this as an opportunity to make a personal decision or whether he feels he is being left in a confusing situation where ambivalent feelings are at play. On a conscious level, some children may want to come yet at the same time resent leaving their class if, for example, they are missing a favourite lesson. Children can also feel anxious about what to expect each week: therapy is not like a lesson where clear instructions are given. For this reason, they may wish to avoid anticipatory anxiety and take the decision not to come.

The child whose parent gives him too much responsibility for looking after himself may feel that being asked to go to the therapy room on his own is simply another instance of being left to self-manage. Or the child who is very insecure may be fearful about arriving at the room to find that the therapist is not there.

What are the unconscious factors to be thinking about when children come on their own?

If left to make their own way to the session, children may 'forget' to come. 'Forgetting' may well be disguising other less-conscious motivations for missing the session. For example, on an unconscious level, for some children, the therapist might represent a demanding, hard-to-please parent figure whom the child may wish to avoid contact with. For the child who experiences his parent figure as tantalising but withholding, leaving the therapist wondering whether or not he will show up might represent an opportunity for the child to act out a form of retaliatory revenge on the parent. Motivations for missing the session will, in all likelihood, be disguised by the child under a more acceptable and everyday explanation such as 'forgetting the time of the session' or 'forgetting to come' altogether.

Leaving the child to make his way to the session raises issues for the therapist. If the child does not appear, does the therapist stay in the room or go to check to see if the child is in school that day? How will her time be used? What unconscious meaning does the therapist give the missed session? Does the therapist feel rejected, relieved or not good enough?

Why collecting the child is advisable

We may want to think that letting the child come to the session on his own is the ethical choice to make because it appears to honour the rights of the child. However, this view underplays the role of the unconscious. Some children may feel positively empowered by having the freedom of making a choice each week but, at the same time, will feel consciously and unconsciously pushed and pulled in different directions by competing desires and conflicting wishes. Even adults who have chosen to commit to weekly therapy sessions which they pay for will find that they have a 'good reason' not to attend when, for example, there is something they may wish to avoid thinking about or if they have feelings towards the therapist that they are uncomfortable with, such as envy or anger.

Although it is important to consider the situation from the child's point of view, when the advantages and disadvantages have been weighed up, it is generally thought most advisable to collect the primary school-aged child from the classroom.

How do we collect the child and escort them to the therapy room?

Collecting the child from the classroom will feel – and probably will be – different with each child and with each teacher. This reflects the simple fact that every teacher will have her own conscious assumptions and unconscious feelings about therapy, which will colour how the therapist is perceived. Chapter 6, 'Working in the Primary School Setting', elaborates on this.

As has been emphasised, setting aside time to talk with the teacher before the first session, even if it is in the form of a few short conversations, is always useful. It both helps the therapist gain more information about the child and has the potential to dispel preconceptions in the teacher's mind about who therapists are and what therapists do. This is discussed in more detail in Chapter 12, 'Meeting with Teachers and Other School Staff'.

It also provides time to think about the best approach to collecting the child for his session. How the collection is managed will reflect a number of factors, including the layout of the school, whether or not the session takes place just before or right after a break and what lesson the child will be missing.

You might arrange with the teacher to knock at the classroom door or open the door quietly and catch the teacher's attention. But be aware that even the most carefully laid plans are subject to unexpected glitches in schools. The teacher may have confirmed that you will be expected at a particular time and day, but then will forget about the session because of preoccupations with the complex business of being a teacher.

However, while it is common for teachers to forget the therapist is coming, they will usually recall the arrangement when you arrive at the door and will signal to the child to leave the class. If there is a supply teacher present, you may choose to say something very simple such as 'I've come to collect George.' If the supply teacher asks 'What for?' you can respond with a clear statement, such as 'He has an appointment with me.' Children are often taken out of class for various reasons and supply teachers should be familiar with this practice. It is unlikely that further questions would be asked.

Leaving the classroom to go with you to the therapy room is bound to stir up conscious and unconscious reactions in the child. Does the child experience the therapy as a 'looked forward to' event, as special time? Are you and the therapy valued or idealised, dreaded or denigrated? Is the child pleased to see you? Suspicious of you? Wary? Distrustful? Ashamed or embarrassed about having to leave the class? Angry about being singled out? Your thoughtful observations when collecting the child will be useful in the consulting room, helping to offer insight into how the child is relating to the therapy.

Practical approaches to the first session

The following steps function as a general guideline for conducting your first therapy session with the child. As you build your experience working with children, your own approach and therapeutic language will evolve.

Introduce yourself and ask the child to do the same

Therapist: 'I'm Jane/Joe. As your teacher may have told you, we will be meeting every _____ day from ____ o'clock to _____ o'clock in this room until the end of _____ (month/term). Can you introduce yourself to me, please?

Child: 'I'm Sade. I'm in Year 4.'

Explore with the child why he was referred

You can ask the child directly why he thinks he was referred and then move on to discuss why you are meeting weekly. Examples are listed below.

The first session   145

'Do you know why the school suggested you and I meet together?' Here the child may say 'because I get into fights/misbehave in class', and so on. Often the child assumes he or she has been referred to see you because of bad behaviour. If this is so, you might say, 'Sometimes we have strong feelings that cause us to behave in certain ways. We can talk about this here and try to understand what might be upsetting or troubling you. When a child breaks the school rules, it's not because they're bad but because they're trying to communicate something. Perhaps it's anger or frustration that causes them to break the rules. In here we will be talking about what feelings might be leading to you getting into trouble with your teacher.'

It may be that the child has suffered a bereavement, in which case you can refer to this openly. For instance: 'All children can benefit from having the time and space to express their feelings when something life-changing such as a family death occurs. This is something we may wish to talk about here along with more general subjects such as how you are getting on at school and at home.'

The child might have been referred because he is not able to make friends. You can mention this using sensitive language such as 'Your teacher said that it would be helpful for us to talk about how to make friends in school – this is something we might want to explore together. Often, it's not that easy to make friends.'

Sometimes the child doesn't know why he was referred and also doesn't recall anyone telling him that he would be meeting with you. In these instances you can tell him why the school suggested you meet weekly. Whatever the reason for the referral, you will want to explain the confidentiality contract from the outset.

How to explain the confidentiality contract using child-friendly language

Let the child know that you will be respecting confidentiality. For instance:

> 'I won't be talking to your parents or your teacher about what you tell me. You can feel free to talk about whatever you wish to here. However, if you tell me something that I need extra help to understand, I'll talk to your teacher or another school staff member and maybe even to your parents. But I'll tell you if I'm going to do this so don't worry. I won't talk about what goes on here to other adults unless I tell you first.'

How to introduce the way sessions work

You will want to find your own way of saying something along the following lines:

> 'When you meet with me every week, you can use the art materials and toys here if you wish to. Sometimes it's easier to show what's on your mind through making pictures or playing rather than talking. However, you don't *have* to use the materials here – we can just talk. Or you can choose to talk and play and make art. We're meeting to explore different feelings and

emotions that can come up for everyone at different times in our lives. It can help to talk about how we feel, especially at those times when we might feel sad, frustrated, hurt or angry.

'Our time together is not a lesson, so I won't be telling you what to do. I may make suggestions from time to time but you have the chance to tell me what it's like to be you and what you feel.'

Invite some feedback

You may wish to ask 'Does what I've told you so far make sense?' and have a short discussion about his thoughts on what you've spoken about.

Complete the introduction to the sessions

You may want to complete the introduction by saying, in your own way,

'I have just a few other points to make. As we only have an hour together once a week, it's important that you use the toilet or get a drink if you need to on the way here so you don't have to leave the room halfway through the session. If you do feel you want to go out of the room for whatever reason, let's agree to talk about it first.

'I mentioned there are toys and art materials here. It's important that you express yourself freely but try not to hurt yourself or me or break the toys or art equipment or damage the room in any way.

'I've made a list of the dates we are meeting. I've also made a folder for your work. The list of the dates will stay in the folder so we can look at it. If you make any artwork here, it will stay in the folder as well, in a safe place, and you can take it home on your last day.'

Moving on to the actual session

Around this point, you may wish to say something like 'As we're just beginning, I think it would be helpful if you could make a picture or tell me about your family. You can draw everyone in your family or use shapes to represent them or else you can tell me about them.'

Progressing through the first phase of the therapy

You may wish to introduce a general theme for the first few weeks to mobilise the therapy process. Themes that can be explored may relate directly to the reason the child was referred. Or you can discuss general themes such as 'You might like to tell me (or make a drawing) about the last time you were angry, sad, disappointed, hurt or confused', etc. As the therapy progresses, the child may begin to bring his own themes or spontaneously use the materials and toys.

Building a working alliance

Creating a safe therapeutic space

A child needs to feel that the therapeutic space is safe and reliable in order to be able to build a rapport. A sense of safety is created through ensuring that the session takes place at the agreed time and in the agreed place each week. If toys and/or art materials are to be made available, they should be put out just before each session. The room should be arranged in the same way each week.

To be able to trust the therapist, the child needs to experience her as being able to stay in her role and not get caught up in a real relationship. This means the therapist will always be thinking about what she is doing or saying and also about what she is thinking and feeling (e.g. 'I wonder why this is occurring to me now' or 'I wonder why I'm feeling a little on edge'). The therapist will not be responding too spontaneously in the moment but instead reflecting on whether or not to respond and, if so, how best to.

The therapist's capacity both to be present and engaged while also thinking and reflecting can be defined as a 'benign split': one part of the therapist is doing, observing or talking and the other part is thinking about this. (E.g. a child hands the therapist scissors and tape and asks her to hold them while he sketches a shape. As the therapist takes them from the child, she may be thinking, *Why has this child asked me to hold the scissors and tape? Does he need to control me? Or is it a sign of his trust? Is he going to ask me to use them? How do I feel about that? Will I agree to cut and stick if he asks me to? What am I feeling right now about it?*)

Having an internal space to reflect about the here and now is a key feature of being a therapist. Supervision provides an external space for the therapist to think with another. As the therapist grows in experience, the reflective frame of mind will become more natural and the external space of supervision will become internalised.

The language of therapy

Working as a therapist requires that we build a vocabulary. The language we use needs to be simple and direct. We need to be speaking from a position that does not expect a particular outcome or seek to elicit a specific response. Instead, we use language to create an atmosphere of safety, to convey containment, to regulate the relationship, to identify and name feelings and to help a child feel known and accepted. We work towards evolving a child-friendly way of communicating that is simple and easily understood.

Containment

A safe relationship can help the child feel contained and can lead to his feeling more securely attached. Children referred for therapy may be inhibited and withdrawn or impulsive and unable to focus or concentrate for long. Whatever their initial presentation, there will be underlying anxieties. The first session, and the first phase of work in general, may be anxiety-provoking for the child and also for the therapist for a number of reasons.

To contain the initial anxiety it may be useful to acknowledge the differences between therapy and everyday experiences. Examples of the kinds of observations the therapist may make are given below:

- 'Perhaps it's hard to think of what to say or do here. You're probably used to teachers telling you what to do.'
- 'Maybe you find it puzzling or frustrating that I won't answer your questions about me. I'm not answering because this time is for you. I'm interested in what's important *to you*.'
- 'Here *you* can decide what you want to do: what you want to make a picture about or what you want to play with. This isn't like your classroom where you have instructions to follow.'

With older children, the therapist may talk about the experience of therapy:

- 'Maybe you were expecting me to ask questions. I'm more interested in what you choose to talk about.' If there is little response, the therapist might then add, 'Perhaps you can say something about what you thought seeing a therapist would be like.' Or 'Perhaps you can say something about why you think the school suggested you see me.'

Practical guidelines

The following questions and statements can facilitate a non-threatening but genuine conversation in the first session:

- Is there anything you'd like to tell me about yourself?
- What's happened at home or school this week that you liked?
- What's happened at home or school this week that you've found difficult?
- You don't know me and you probably aren't familiar with this room – how does it feel to be here?
- It can be hard, can't it, to know what to do or say if no one is giving you instructions.

Conclusion

The first session with a young client can be an exciting but also an anxiety-provoking experience for both client and therapist. Our role is to make the child feel that he's entered a non-threatening, *very different* space, probably quite unlike anything he's experienced before. Without being overly reassuring, we can allay some of his anxieties by encouraging him to talk about the awkwardness he's feeling and empathising with it, while directing him to think about how the time can be used productively. In our anxiety to 'do the right thing', we can easily overlook the fact that therapy is to a large extent about building a powerful relationship between two human beings that is unlike any other, both using tools that are specific to it – analytical frameworks, reflecting on transference and counter-transference – and also those that are part of normal social interaction, such as humour, warmth and understanding.

Study questions

You might find it helpful to think about some or all of the vignettes below and especially about what might be behind the child's actions.

Vignette 1

Sally (7) is reticent about using any of the materials herself. She suggests that you draw a picture and she will colour it in. *What would you say?*

Vignette 2

Muhammad (11) says he wants to play a game: you are the teacher and he is the student. He wants you to tell him off and give him a detention. *What would you say?*

Vignette 3

Meena (9) decides that the two of you will play doctor and patient. She wants to examine you and says she'll look into your eyes and mouth. *What would you say?*

Vignette 4

Imran (6) wants to play being a baby, to sit on your lap and be fed by you. *What would you say?*

Vignette 5

Hakim (13) sits sullenly, avoiding eye contact and won't respond to you. *What would you say?*

Sample responses

Vignette 1

'I wonder if you're a little shy about making a picture of your own in this first session of ours. It would be helpful if you did, so I can get to know a bit about you. Don't worry about your drawing: there's no right or wrong way to make pictures here. It's not an art lesson.'

Vignette 2

'I think it's interesting that you want to play a game that has me being the teacher who tells you off and punishes you. I wonder what you're trying to tell me by suggesting a game like this. Maybe you're trying to work out how I'm going to react to you if you do something you think you shouldn't.'

Vignette 3

'Maybe you want to look inside me to figure out who I am because you don't really trust me yet. You can't look in my mouth but we can pretend this doll is me. What do you think you might see if you looked inside?'

Or 'You can't look into my mouth. But I think you're trying to tell me something. Maybe you think *I* want to look right inside of *you*. Sometimes children are worried about what's inside. Is it good? Is it bad? How good? How bad? Let's pretend we're looking together into this doll. What do you see inside?'

Vignette 4

'You may be curious to see whether I'm going to be a mum to you in here and whether I'll look after you. We all have a baby self; sometimes it feels like our baby self didn't get enough feeding and didn't feel cared for enough. In here you can express your baby side by using the doll and feeding it or asking me to feed it.' You may want to add, 'Perhaps we can explore together what you're feeling right now, maybe even why you're feeling that you want me to feed you.'

Vignette 5

'I think you're having a hard time being in this room. I suspect you don't know what's supposed to happen and how you're supposed to behave. You're probably wondering why I don't tell you what you should be doing. Therapy is about giving you the space to express things that you can't talk about with other people. It can be hard to get used to this, especially in the first session. Maybe you can say what you're feeling right now.' If there is no response, you might continue, 'I'm going to write down some of the feelings or thoughts that young people often have in the first session. Perhaps you can let me know what you're feeling by circling some of the phrases that apply to you. It might make it easier to talk.' (You can write down words such as 'feeling hopeless', 'angry about being here', 'worried about the future', 'don't care about my life', 'why should talking help?', 'don't fit in anywhere', 'don't like school', 'don't want to be here', 'feeling embarrassed', 'wish I could go now', 'can't trust anyone', etc.)

Chapter 15

Working with difference

Akin Ojumu

Introduction

Working in a school puts the therapist into contact with young people from diverse backgrounds, bringing a wide range of different experiences to the sessions. Obvious differences will be apparent, such as gender, age, ethnicity and sexuality. Differences in ways of thinking, personal belief systems, values and social identities will be less visible. The task of thinking about and working with these differences, using them to inform rather than hinder the work, is a vital aspect of the therapist's role.

Given that the therapy experience is dependent on the relationship between therapist and client, it is important to think carefully about how the relationship is affected by the differences between the two people in the room. For a young person, meeting a school therapist for the first time will stir up a number of conscious and unconscious anxieties and feelings. Working effectively with our clients means that we need to think about the possible preconceptions they have about us and our role. This is especially important in view of the often striking differences between client and school therapist. Monitoring how a young person makes sense of those differences and the way he perceives us is very helpful as we seek to understand how he relates to the external world.

The beginning of a therapeutic relationship is a time when the new client experiences a range of anxieties. Questions he might be asking himself include 'Why am I here? Have I done something wrong? What is therapy all about?' As has been noted, it is our job to contain and explore these anxieties, which goes some way towards establishing a working alliance with the client. For example, this involves being aware of the impact our appearance will have on a young person. Because of our age and role, we are figures of authority within the school. That being so, the child's initial attitude could be influenced by previous experiences with other adults within the school, as well as by associations with adult figures from his family and beyond. The student is likely to feel a sense of inequality about the relationship he is embarking on and might use an array of defences, including arriving late to sessions or not arriving at all, to protect himself from uncomfortable feelings of inferiority.

We can also think about what our client's expectations and anxieties about the differences between the two of us might be prior to the first meeting. Are we younger or older than expected? Male or female? Black or white? Is our accent strange, indicating a different social class or country of origin? Of course, on one level these are understandable concerns for the young person to have when thinking about whether and how well they will be understood by a school therapist. But these concerns can also represent ambivalent feelings about the therapy process as represented by the school therapist.

There is potential for disappointment or optimism as the client surveys the school therapist for the first time. For example, a white client might be underwhelmed at being allocated a black school therapist, thinking that he has been given someone who is not as skilled as a white professional. A primary school pupil could feel that the female school therapist is just another maternal figure similar to his mother and/or the largely female teaching staff at his school. As the relationship develops, it can be useful to raise these issues sensitively with the client, depending on the age and reflective qualities he displays. It can be illuminating to look for clues about his opinion of you and whether he feels hopeful or discouraged about the idea of establishing a connection with someone who seems quite different from himself. Similarly the school therapist will have her own anxieties and preconceptions about working with certain types of clients based on a range of experiences. These will have to be worked through in supervision and personal therapy if they are not going to interfere with the work.

Cultural differences

We are trained to think about the deeper meanings of what our clients say and how they behave in therapy sessions. With that in mind, how much importance should we give to their cultural background, especially when it suggests they might have attitudes and beliefs that appear unfamiliar to us?

We might, for instance, take on a client who comes from a cultural background in which therapy or therapeutic help is considered alien or intrusive, an attitude that initially could affect our efforts to engage with him. We must be careful not to make assumptions about the child until we have actually seen how he reacts to us during a session. Not to do so means we run the risk of making a judgement based on stereotypes.

Regardless of his background a young person may, at some level, welcome the opportunity to talk about his feelings, but have serious doubts over whether this is something he can manage successfully. Many students, faced with the prospect of developing a relationship with a school therapist, talking openly about themselves and exposing their vulnerabilities can inspire a variety of defences. The idea of therapy may seem at odds with how a young person perceives his cultural norms. But on the other hand – depending on how the referral has come about – an adolescent trying to assert an identity outside his family may be attracted to therapy if it seems to conflict with 'traditional' values. In such cases we must be careful not to collude with our clients.

We can speculate endlessly on the impact of an individual's cultural heritage but what we are principally trying to do as therapists is explore the feelings and thoughts that are important for that particular child. That does not mean we set aside cultural differences, but we must try to learn what our client makes of them and how they have been internalised. There are many aspects of our clients' lives that we do not know about and can only guess at, but since their experience of themselves will have been influenced by their cultural environment we should think about what the meaning might be for *them*. Our *phantasies*, which can be illuminating, should be primarily based on our experience of the young person in the therapy room.

Depending on the type of school and age of child we are working with, there may be an opportunity to meet with parents/carers as well as communicate with school staff to gain more specific biographical information about our clients.

Aiming to support and challenge our clients when necessary requires having a level of confidence to deal with cultural differences. Where do we place ourselves if a boy in early adolescence expresses offensive views about homosexuality or a girl in late adolescence talks about her difficulties with strict, traditional parents? While we mustn't collude with our clients and indeed can choose to challenge our client's views, it is necessary first to think about the levels of meaning behind what he is saying. Is his homophobia a sign of confused thinking about his own sexuality? Perhaps the voicing of this strong belief is a conscious or unconscious attempt to tease us out of role and get us to express a 'personal' opinion. And is the girl seeking an ally against her parents because her complex relationship with them is being affected by more than a clash of cultural beliefs? Perhaps she is conveying mixed feelings about the delicate process of establishing her own adult identity distinct from her family and their attendant values, while remaining informed by her upbringing and grateful for their parental care and concern.

These are sensitive situations and it is easy to feel somewhat deskilled when dealing with clients and situations that move far beyond our personal experience. But we should not underestimate our ability to get a sense of a client or situation by thinking carefully about the feelings aroused in us in the *counter-transference*. Obviously it is often hard to monitor our feelings sufficiently at the moment of trying to understand the underlying communication from our client. In supervision there is the chance to reflect on what has happened in a particular session and analyse the dynamics in the relationship. If we are feeling at a loss and unable to think clearly with a particular client, it can be an accurate reflection of what the client is actually feeling rather than the sense that something has got lost in translation due to cultural differences.

As therapy increasingly becomes an integral part of schools, there are greater attempts to tailor therapeutic provision to individuals or groups within the institution. For example, art and drama therapists can reach young people with creative work that is outside the expertise of a school therapist who may favour a purely verbal approach. Or an inner-city school with a substantial Somalian population might see considerable advantage in employing a school therapist from the same background. As well as bringing a greater understanding of cultural mores and language (which can be especially useful if meeting with parents and guardians), such provision signifies to pupils and parents that the school has thought sensitively about all the students for which they are responsible. However, it is easy to idealise the capabilities of the school therapist in this situation and expect spectacular results, even though the school therapist in question might not feel she has a particular affinity with those clients, and vice versa.

So far the focus of this chapter has been mainly on the experience of a white school therapist working in a multicultural school environment. But there are also challenges for school therapists from other cultural backgrounds. For example, if you are of a recognisable cultural background that is distinct from the majority of students in a school, fewer assumptions might be made about you. However, the differentness you represent is likely to provoke all sorts of conscious and unconscious fantasies about where you are from and how well you can relate to different people. You might share the same cultural background as a group within the school who have a 'good' reputation for hard work and discipline and the staff and pupils have a positive transference to you for those reasons. Or you might share the same background as a group who have a 'bad' reputation for ill-discipline and low attainment, resulting in a *negative transference*. You can find yourself the subject of powerful projections in such instances and it is important to think carefully about how you are viewed in the school and what the parameters of your role as a school therapist in reality are.

Race

The discussion of cultural identities above leads into the more specific area of race and how it affects the dynamics in a therapy relationship. This is an issue that has increasingly become a feature in recent psychoanalytic literature as more careful thought is being given to how racism, which is still so pervasive in society, affects the conscious and unconscious power dynamics in our work.

It has already been noted that a school therapist is not able to put herself into someone else's shoes to the extent that she can directly relate to that person's everyday experiences. We can, though, use our *counter-transference* and other experiences to develop our understanding. But for as long as racism continues to be such a powerful force in contemporary society, affecting how people see themselves and others, race will have particular resonance in therapy.

There is already a power disparity between therapist and client, mainly due to differences in age and authority within the school. But race adds another dimension. How does a white middle-class school therapist relate to a black teenager living in a council estate? Imagine that the teenager has had unfortunate experiences with authority figures (e.g. being stopped and searched by the police) that have made him suspicious and angry in similar situations. It is not difficult to see how such a teenager would have a *negative transference* to a white middle-class therapist, replaying the dynamics of previous unsatisfactory relationships or being influenced by attitudes within wider society. If possible, we should bring these issues into the open, enquiring whether our client feels that we are unable to understand them, wondering out loud if there is something unspoken in the room that could be affecting the relationship.

The power dynamics can be altered when the situation is reversed. Perhaps a white client suspects that he is getting an inferior or not 'good enough' school therapist when he starts working with a black professional. This can be couched in the notion that black school therapists are primarily effective when working specifically with black clients. It is a situation that, because it is relatively unusual, might seem especially strange to the client. Again, it can be useful to bring this issue out into the open. While it is a sensitive area, you can help counter *resistance* by suggesting that you are thinking with an open mind about the complexities of the relationship.

Race can be an issue whenever there is an obvious racial difference between school therapist and client. Seeing a school therapist from a different background could be the first time the child has been involved in a close relationship with someone from that particular racial background. But even when there has been prior contact with people from other racial groups, clients will still have powerful projections stemming from prejudices developed over time from family and peers as well as society at large.

Social identity

A client will go to see a school therapist with various preconceptions about what the experience will entail. These preconceptions vary widely and we should not forget that for some of the children referred to us, seeing a school therapist can seem like a daunting task. However, there will be clients who will be better prepared to use their therapy sessions. They will be more comfortable using reflective or creative thinking about themselves. Some clients will welcome the opportunity offered by therapy sessions while others may find it hard to think at all in the sessions, partly due to therapy being a new and challenging situation.

But there are some young people who will find it particularly difficult to make use of their sessions because they come from a social or family background where they are not used to talking about emotional issues in detail or perhaps at all. Furthermore they may experience a therapy referral as a judgement on their ability to cope with the school environment. They may come from a family in which there is a history of feeling that they have been badly served at school. This can result in family members having low expectations of the resources that schools make available. A school therapist will come across clients from a range of social backgrounds, but working with a young person from a relatively deprived background can involve particular complexities. An example is given below.

Clare is a ten-year-old girl from a family who rely on welfare benefits and are known to social services. She has recently been finding her schoolwork difficult and her teacher is concerned about her low self-esteem and lack of enthusiasm in class. Clare already feels inferior compared to her peers, and sees the prospect of therapy as another example of 'not being good enough'. This sense of herself may well be exacerbated by coming from a home where there are money problems and frequent dealings with authority figures (social workers, health workers, etc.) whose involvement is perceived as persecutory and as a signal that the family are finding it hard to cope.

Of course there are probably opportunities for Clare's emotional learning to develop with the appropriate input, but the pressures that surround her family make it more difficult to create a reflective environment where difficult subjects can be talked about in a safe way.

This example also brings to life the reality that children have different external resources to draw upon. If a child has grown up in an environment in which reflective thought is fostered and normalised, he can bring that way of thinking into the therapy room with greater confidence. This is not to say that all middle-class children will be articulate and analytical and that the reverse is true of children from more deprived backgrounds; but the pressure of social deprivation on emotional development can be significant. While we must be wary of making early assumptions about young people based on how they present themselves, these external signs can be useful.

If we are working with a child who does feel ill at ease during sessions for reasons discussed above, we can think about ways to help him feel more comfortable. Monitoring our language to ensure we are talking in a way that is easily understood is vital as we attempt to convey sensitive observations and interpretations in a way that can be digested by the client. Does our client understand what we are saying? If a young person is continually asking the school therapist to repeat words or phrases, perhaps he is making a conscious or unconscious communication about the apparent gulf between the two of them, showing how difficult it is to be understood by someone who is so different.

Some adolescents have a developed capacity for hearing and taking in what a school therapist has to say. They will even challenge us at times, although we need to be aware of when this is evidence of their *defences* being utilised rather than of self-confidence. Alternatively, some young people who have less experience of interacting closely with middle-class professionals will not feel able to challenge their therapist verbally, preferring non-verbal ways of acting out.

Family

Working in a school setting (especially with younger children) provides the opportunity to meet parents or carers. This can be useful for gaining extra insights into the child and gathering additional biographical information. If such a meeting does take place, it can also serve to highlight the multiplicity of family situations our clients may have come from. Thinking about the contemporary family unit means holding in mind the potential of a number of different arrangements. In addition to the traditional nuclear family set-up of mother, father and children, cultural and demographic changes have radically altered our conception of what a family looks like. As well as stepfamilies, some children may be living with same-sex parents or with relatives.

A large number of children do not live with both their biological parents. In most cases, the single parent is usually the mother. There is now less stigma attached to single-parent families than in the past along with a general acceptance that children can thrive in all sorts of families. Many single-parent families involve an arrangement in which the child lives with one parent and regularly sees the non-resident parent. In such cases there is less sense of their being an absent parent, although the child can still feel bereft, guilty and angry about the parental separation. When there is erratic contact or none at all from the non-resident parent, these feelings will be exacerbated, along with a sense of having been abandoned or not being worthy of parental care.

If the separation was particularly stressful for the family, feelings of abandonment and upset may recur when other relationships (including therapy) finish or when the child enters a period of transition, such as the move from primary to secondary school. As he goes through adolescence he may again experience feelings of loss; at this time of rapid physical and sexual development, when peer influence becomes ever more important, the absence of the same-sex parent can be particularly affecting as he looks for a parental role model.

Although psychoanalytic literature has traditionally focused on the nuclear family model, there are many other models. As families break up, many children gain half or stepsiblings and step-parents. Such developments can impact how a child is seen or sees himself in a family as is illustrated in the example below.

> Wayne is a 13-year-old boy who lived with his mother after his parents separated while he was in primary school. His mother has recently remarried and has a three-year-old daughter with her new husband. Wayne has seen his family change a number of times, moving from a nuclear family to single-parent model and finally to an enlarged family with a stepfather and half-sister. His sense of importance within that family has changed from being the focal point of his mother to competing with a new sibling and adjusting to a new parental figure. Within his new family he may be feeling alienated from the biological family unit represented by the other three. How does he place himself in this new family?

For many children whose parents have separated, and then formed new partnerships and had more children, there is an uncomfortable adjustment to make and powerful ambivalent feelings about the new additions to the family. These dynamics are even more complex if a child's father or mother has children with a number of different partners, potentially leading to a variety of parental pairings within one child's extensive family.

The focus so far has been on children living with their male or female parents (especially mothers), but that is not always the case. It is still relatively uncommon for the father to be the primary carer in a family, but when this happens through death, illness or separation we should be prepared to explore the considerable feelings of loss and anger that are provoked in the child. We have also been discussing heterosexual couples, but there are an increasing number of same-sex parents who obviously do not mirror the traditional family template. In these circumstances there can be greater flexibility for parents to take up parenting roles that are not so clearly defined by their gender, but there is still prejudice about such families and there can be opportunity for a child to believe there is a 'missing' parent in the family.

The concept of family composition changes across different cultures. For example, in many cultures it is accepted practice that children will live with other relatives such as an aunt or grandparent for extended periods while the biological parents are living abroad. While not unusual, we should be aware of possible ramifications for the child separated from his parents. What is important is the sense the child makes of this situation, which depends on various factors. Where are the biological parents? How long is the separation going to last? How has the separation been explained to the child? What is the nature of the attachment to the biological parents? How old are the replacement carers? What kind of attachment does the child have to them? And does the child believe they are likely to stay fit and healthy as the child grows up?

The reasons behind the separation are important, and children experience the knowledge that their parents cannot look after them in different ways. There is a significant distinction, for instance, between a child whose parents are working abroad and one whose parents are unable to leave a war-torn foreign country. Another type of separation is provoked by adolescents who fall out with their parents and move in with other relatives or friends.

Separations can be a frustrating or unsettling period for a young person. This will be mediated when there is a sense, even if distant at times, that there are parental figures who are able to provide consistent caring. 'Looked after' children living in care or with foster parents have often experienced chaotic early lives. Without the opportunity to form good attachments with parental figures, they may develop strong defences to insulate themselves from painful and difficult feelings. This can make it difficult to commit to the therapy relationship.

Gender

One of the most immediately apparent differences between school therapist and client is gender. Working in schools differs from private practice as the client has less, if any, say in choosing the gender of his school therapist. In rare examples cultural considerations can be the reason behind a preference for a same-sex school therapist–client relationship, but matching clients by gender is mainly dictated by the therapeutic resources available within the school. Whatever their gender, though, male and female school therapists are liable to be subject to preconceptions and *projections* about their gender that are inescapable.

In a primary school where the teaching staff is predominately female, a male school therapist can be highly valued, especially for work with boys. He is seen as having something extra to offer by the staff and there can be a sense of relief that a man with a greater innate understanding of boys is around. There is also the hope that a sensitive male school therapist can role model a reflective way of acting, while offering something different from the *maternal transference* children feel towards female members of staff. Of course this leads to high expectations being placed on the male school therapist, especially in his work with boys. There is an assumption that boys, especially those who have irregular or no contact with their own fathers, will automatically have a *positive transference* to a male school therapist. While this can in fact be the case, building an intimate relationship with a new man can lead to feelings of regret, anger and *resistance* as well as hope and greater openness.

In secondary schools where young people are more likely to face issues about their changing bodies, sexuality and relationships, the gender issue will seem more important, as sessions can cover material that causes the client awkwardness or embarrassment. The gender disparity in teaching and non-teaching staff is not as great as in primary schools, but in both primary and secondary schools there will be a substantial number of boys referred to therapy who then see a female school therapist. Given that the presenting problems for boys often include areas that are seen as stereotypically male, such as physical aggression and anger, a female school therapist often has to deal with the assumption from clients, parents and staff that she is less well equipped to deal with adolescent boys. Similarly a male school therapist can feel deskilled when presented with an adolescent girl who presents with an eating disorder, which is commonly associated with female clients.

Is there any way our gender is useful in providing additional insight into our clients? Obviously our life as a man or woman will have conditioned us in many ways and we have probably given a lot of thought to the importance of gender in our lives. A female school therapist will not be able to rely on memories of male adolescence, but as school therapists we don't have to be able to relate to the specific details of our client's life and compare them against ours. Indeed too much empathy of that kind can get in the way of listening to the client. We are seeking to understand his motivations and ways of thinking on a deeper level and for that we need to look at the client closely as an individual.

There are certainly instances when seeing a school therapist of the same gender is useful in engaging with some young people but for others, escaping the powerful *transferences* and *projections* that are associated with seeing a school therapist of the same gender can be liberating.

Age

Working with young people means we have to consider the age disparity between us and our clients. Regardless of how old we actually are or look, we shouldn't forget how much older we must seem in their eyes. A school therapist working with young people is not a peer. In fact, the differences in outlook and experience because of the age gap are considerable.

No matter how old the young person and how young the therapist, we are unlikely to be familiar with some aspects of how they live their life and the influences and pressures they deal with on a daily basis. Cultural references and colloquial language, particularly when spoken by an adolescent, will be unknown to us and will pose potential barriers to understanding to add to the others.

Conclusion

For younger clients, especially primary school children, the concept of emotional literacy and the idea of using the therapy sessions as a space to explore their inner worlds can be a difficult one to comprehend. We should consider the variety of ways in which we can work with them in both verbal and non-verbal ways (such as playing or drawing) as the latter can be less threatening, not to say more comfortable for them. Again it is important to adopt our response to individual needs. For example, a Year 7 child could find drawing a family tree a useful exercise for communicating personal information and feeling his way into the therapy process, while a Year 5 child, although still in primary school might be more confident in expressing himself verbally from the outset.

As children grow older, the way in which they see adults will change. An adolescent is more likely consciously and unconsciously to challenge the authority of the school therapist and boundaries of time and space. A younger child familiar with the more intimate environment of his primary school might appear more amenable to accepting the authority and boundaries imposed by a school therapist. But we need to bear in mind that when dealing with clients who have experienced difficult attachments and endings, the start of a therapy relationship can stir up conflicting emotions even for young children.

Study questions

The vignettes below explore some of the themes highlighted in this chapter.

Vignette 1

Muhammad is a 15-year-old boy who has been referred because he has angry outbursts in school. There are concerns about how he is coping with academic demands as his GCSEs approach. During a session he says that it is 'hopeless talking to me because you just can't understand what my life is like'. *What would you say?*

Vignette 2

Mark is 12-year-old who lives with his mother and two siblings on a troubled council estate in a socially deprived area. Recently he has occasionally started truanting, which has impacted on his academic work and behaviour. During a session he says one problem about coming to our sessions is that he can't really understand what I'm saying because of my 'posh accent'. *What would you say?*

Vignette 3

Lisa is a 10-year-old girl who has been referred following concerns about how she is coping with her parents' acrimonious separation. During the first session she says that she is surprised to see me today as she was expecting to talk to a woman. *What would you say?*

Sample responses

Vignette 1

'I can really feel your frustration about how things are when you use the word "hopeless". It gives me a sense of how you might feel at times. Perhaps you are wondering if I will be able to really listen to and understand where you are coming from. It is true there are some obvious differences between us and I can't know what it is like to be a boy like you. I might not have personal experience of the things you are going through and I realise that living around here can be difficult at times. But together we can talk about the things that are on your mind and I hope I can come to understand what you are really like.'

Vignette 2

'It's true that my accent sounds a bit different to yours. And that seems to be making you wonder about how useful coming to see me really is. You may be thinking that my background is very different to yours and that I can't possibly know about what you are like and the place where you live. It's completely understandable to think these things. I *don't* know what it is like to live on your estate, but I do realise that it can be difficult at times. It's always a bit strange when you meet someone new and you have to get to know them – especially in a situation like this. Perhaps you are not sure yet if I will be a good person to talk to and you're not sure how comfortable you feel with the idea of talking to someone like me, but that is entirely natural.'

Vignette 3

'Maybe it feels somewhat unusual to be talking to a man, especially as I've noticed that there are mostly female teachers in the school. I suppose this could be quite a new experience for you and it's something we can talk about. This might feel like something quite new for you and everyone finds it strange at first getting used to new things. Obviously I don't know what it is like to be a girl like you but I do know that it can be good to have someone to talk to when you are growing up for all sorts of reasons. I'm interested in getting to know you better and finding out what is important to you.'

Chapter 16

Managing the therapeutic frame

Reva Klein

A primary task of any therapy is to establish and manage what is termed 'the therapeutic frame'. This is made up of all the elements of therapy that provide containment and contribute to making the therapy feel safe. This includes practical aspects, such as ensuring that

- the therapy takes place at the same time and place every week and each session runs for the same length of time (usually 50–60 minutes for older children and young people and 30–45 minutes for younger children);
- the same toys and materials are made available for every session;
- a folder is brought to the session in which to keep any artwork made by the child. This folder is stored in a safe space in the school in between sessions e.g. a locked cupboard on a deputy head's office;
- confidentiality is not broken.

Therapists' role in the frame

The frame also refers to how we as therapists present ourselves and how we function in our role. Staying in role means that the therapist refrains from interacting with the child in a way that is more social than therapeutic. It helps to keep the following points in mind:

- Aim to be as relaxed as possible, keeping an open mind and conveying an interest in knowing all parts of the child.
- Try to be consistent in what you say and do.
- Strive to be non-judgemental. This means avoiding making value judgements, such as saying to the child 'the session went well today' or that the picture they made 'is well drawn' or 'pretty'.
- Refrain from accepting gifts or cards.
- Look upon behaviour and any form of acting out as a communication that is not to be taken personally but is to be thought about.
- Speak in a way that helps the child feel understood. We might name feelings and ask questions that stay with the feelings. For example, we might say, 'It

sounds like you were very hurt when that happened. Can you tell me about another time you felt hurt? Who might have noticed how you felt? Who could have helped?' And then 'Is there a link between these two incidents? Do you think something similar happened in both your examples?'
- Contain behaviour that seems to be escalating or getting out of control by reminding the child of the rules he has agreed to abide by and make an observation or an interpretation about what is being expressed.
- Signal to the child that we are listening by reflecting back or saying what we are observing or confirming what we are hearing. For example, we might say, 'I think you're frustrated with your teacher' or 'you seem to feel that no one believes you' or 'perhaps coming to therapy feels like punishment'. Such stand-alone comments can work well if used discreetly when we want to confirm an important thought or feeling. For the child, hearing us reflect back like this can be containing.
- Name a child's defences sensitively: 'It seems you've got to be as tough as a super hero' or 'you can't let your guard down' or 'you don't need anybody but yourself'.
- Develop a child-friendly language so you can communicate as effectively as possible. For example, use short sentences, avoiding complex thought processes and difficult words. Be aware of how you use your voice and pay attention to tone, volume and rhythm of speech.
- Resist giving direct reassurance and instead name the feeling. You might say, 'that's very sad' or 'that sounds like your feelings were hurt' or 'that may have been hard to hear' or 'how brave of you' or 'that's just so discouraging'.
- Silently think about what the child is communicating and how you are feeling in the moment. For example, if you're feeling quite anxious because the child doesn't know what to do and seems to be embarrassed by this, you might say something like 'Perhaps when you don't know where to start it can feel a little uncomfortable.' Giving the child permission to go at his own pace can help as well. You might add, 'It's OK to just be. You don't have to do or say anything.'
- Learn to move between an observing role and an interactive one.

Becoming a containing presence

The child experiences the therapist as containing because whatever is expressed verbally or non-verbally in the therapy room is taken in by the therapist, contained in her mind and thought about rather than spontaneously reacted to. As therapists, we judge what thoughts (if any) we will feed back to the child. Thinking helps us to make sense of what is happening in the room that, in itself, enables the child to experience us as an understanding other. This involves processing complex and contradictory feelings and thoughts.

Working as a school therapist can be an uncomfortable experience for us at times. You will need to be able to tolerate having a range of painful, unsettling or disturbing responses to the material presented by the child. At various points you may feel confused, uncertain, awkward, pushed and pulled internally in different directions, invaded, anxious, angry, humiliated, unsure of what to do or say, sad, excluded, mocked, triumphed over, belittled and more. Hopefully, these difficult moments will be balanced by times when you feel you are attuned to the child: that you are able to follow in your mind what the child is trying to communicate and give consideration to what you want to say.

There will also be times when you will need to intervene if the therapeutic frame is being pushed against too forcefully. See the vignettes below for ideas on how to respond.

Managing the therapeutic frame: interventions aiming to limit or manage behaviour in the session

Exercises to support your learning

Explore your response to the idea of

- having to deal with a child who is acting out his anger against you or the room;
- maintaining boundaries when a child wants to leave the room;
- very long periods of silence, during which a child seems cut off;
- a child presenting with prolonged and inconsolable crying.

Containing anger

If a young child is throwing toys at the wall in a way that might damage him and it seems the behaviour is escalating, you may need to be directive in order to contain the situation. You might say:

> You're throwing those toys with force! I'm wondering if you're letting me know you're fed up. It seems you have a lot of anger today. I don't want the toys to get broken, so I'm asking you to stop now. There are other ways you can express what you are feeling. Why not make a picture to show your anger?

You could also suggest a safe alternative to throwing objects: 'You can tear up paper and throw it around if you want to let your anger out.'

With an older child or adolescent, it may be more challenging both to experience and to try to manage incidents of angry acting out. Calmly but firmly putting into words what you are observing and what you think is going on for the young person will offer some containment and may act as a reality check at a time when he feels overwhelmed by his feelings. You might say, 'There's a lot of anger inside you right now. Can we try to talk about what's causing you so much upset?' Or 'Kicking that wall may feel like a release but it could hurt you as well as damage the wall. Why don't you try to tell me or write down the words that are coming into your mind right now?'

Responding to the offer of a gift or card

When a child wants to give us something, it is important to reply with empathy. Our response will be in tune with what we know about the child, what we are feeling at the time and what we think the child is trying to convey to us in that particular moment. We will want to think about what the giving of a gift or a card symbolises for the child, whether it is made in the session or is brought to it.

Children may make a card or a painting or drawing for you before a break. We do not want to give the child the impression that we are taking the card for ourselves, even though this is what the child wants. At the same time, we want to avoid coming across as if we are rejecting the child's gift or in some way criticising him for making the gesture. The following are some possible ways of responding to the situation:

- 'Right now, it feels good to be here with me. You want to give me this card to let me know that.'
- 'Maybe you want to be sure I will remember you.'
- 'Perhaps it's hard to believe that I can hold you in mind over the holiday.'
- 'You seem proud of what you've made and want to give me something of value. Maybe this shows how much you value coming here.'
- 'Let's keep it in your folder with everything else you've made. When it comes time to take your folder home, you can decide then what to do with the card.'

Conclusion

By establishing and maintaining a therapeutic framework, we create a clearly demarcated container for the conscious and unconscious material brought to the sessions by the client. This frame, or container, offers the client an ongoing experience of a boundaried space that can, in time, be internalised. It is through this process that the client symbolically creates his own holding structure, unconsciously gathering together and making sense of what may previously have been experienced as a fragmented and chaotic inner world. As this chapter has conveyed, managing the therapeutic frame has a deeply felt internal parallel for the client; we do our clients valuable service if we can offer them this kind of experience.

Study questions

The vignettes provided below can be used for individual learning or discussed with peers.

Vignette 1

Charlie (12) is a quiet boy who has found the first couple of sessions very difficult to deal with. Referred after his mother died three months ago, he appears visibly uncomfortable in the sessions, speaking only when answering questions and then only in monosyllables. There is no eye contact and no discernible affect. He arrives at his third session late with a friend and says he'd like him to stay with him for the full session. *What would you say?*

Vignette 2

Tasha (9) is a volatile child who veers between manic defensiveness and occasional anger. Her home life is chaotic; her mother has had a succession of boyfriends staying over and there are a number of stepsiblings. You have struggled to find a way of containing her in the sessions. Today, after five minutes in the room, she smiles mockingly and says she has to go to the toilet 'real bad'. *What would you say?*

Vignette 3

Elijah is a seven-year-old whose mother has been emotionally unavailable to him since his earliest days and whose father has been absent for several years. He is seldom responsive and comes alive only in fantasy play, when he enacts violent scenes. Today he comes into the session and says that his father's coming home soon and that he's going to bring him lots of expensive presents. He paints a picture of a big smiling man standing next to a little boy and says he wants to give it to his dad when he returns. *What would you say?*

Vignette 4

Nathan (15), after a slow start, has been increasingly responsive to therapy over the four months he has been attending. Recently he has moved out of his flat to live with his grandmother because of constant rows with his mother and new stepfather. Today he comes into the room at first sullen and then furious, kicking the walls. After a minute or two, he dissolves into sobs interspersed with expletives about his mother. *What would you say?*

> ### Sample responses
>
> #### Vignette 1
>
> 'I know that you feel uncomfortable coming to our sessions and that you might feel better having your friend in here with you. But therapy is about the two of us working together in privacy. Sometimes it can be difficult to get used to this, but having another person with you, even a good friend, won't help you in any real way. Let's try to work together on our own and see if we can get over this awkwardness, shall we?'

Vignette 2

'Do you remember that we talked in the first session about things like leaving the room during a session and why it's important to go to the toilet before we start? I wonder if you're finding it difficult today to stay in the room. Often if there's something that's bothering us we can find it easier to walk away from it. Maybe there's something you would rather run away from right now instead of being in touch with difficult thoughts or feelings.'

Vignette 3

'I see you've painted a picture that shows you and your dad. You'll remember that we discussed how we'll keep all artwork that you make inside a folder which I'll keep safely in here. You'll be able to take it home at the end of the year. I can understand that you'd like to take it home with you but I think it would be better to think together about what it means for you to be seeing your dad after such a long time.'

Vignette 4

'You're very angry and upset and I can imagine that something painful has happened to make you so miserable. I know how hard it can be to put such strong feelings into words but it would help you feel better if you could, so that we could think together about what's going on.'

Chapter 17

Working with school staff

Angie Doran

Therapists working in educational settings are granted the privilege of being able to observe and relate to the school from a very particular and distinctive position, one that is both 'within' and 'without'. We are afforded glimpses of the organisation as it functions 'behind the scenes'. These 'snapshots' are both intentionally and unwittingly given to us by school staff, by parents or carers and by the pupils we work with. This means that we are implicitly trusted with often highly confidential information about the school, its complex issues and its day-to-day functioning. Of course each picture offered represents a subjective take but nonetheless will reflect aspects of the real situation even if the picture is somewhat distorted or skewed by individual experiences or biases. We often witness from the margins how the organisation functions, including the school's main anxieties, how it operates under pressure, how staff relate to each other, the institutional and personal defences triggered, and so on.

As therapists aiming to hold a neutral role, it is likely that we will, at the same time, choose to stay outside many formal and informal aspects of everyday school life. We will think very carefully about how we manage our relationships with staff, weighing up whether or not – or to what degree – we might develop personal or social relationships with them or even how much we are seen by pupils to be talking with staff. In order to develop confidential relationships with our clients, it is important that the children and young people we work with understand our role as being distinct and discrete. Clients should have an understanding that we have a professional role in the school and that our input is respected and valued by the school organisation. Staff and students alike can come to appreciate our 'out of the ordinary' role and the professional position we adopt as observers, working *alongside* rather than *from within* the system.

As emphasised in preceding chapters, earning the respect and trust of school colleagues will take some time and effort, particularly if they have had little experience of working with a therapist. We need to establish and maintain a position with clearly defined boundaries which stay in place under pressure yet allow for some flexibility when required. At the same time, we need to be warm and approachable so that we can be experienced as an ally and not as a 'psychological expert' who may be observing the school community from a somewhat lofty

– and potentially critically minded – position. At best, we are experienced as supportive and interested professionals, working on an equal footing, with the shared agenda of maintaining the school's commitment to doing the best it can for its pupils.

Working with the system

Starting work at a school means entering a unique system. All schools have in common the primary task of educating their students, but the organisational dynamics that evolve over time will be particular to each institution. Much as therapists need to balance operating from both within and on the edges of the school organisation, we also need to strike a balance between being proactive and being responsive. If you are taking over from another therapist or taking up a role in an existing therapeutic team, some understanding of the therapist's position and of what can be offered will already have been established. However, if you are setting up a new service in a school, you will need to take up your role and foster your professional profile within a system in which there is no historic precedent to draw on and possibly no understanding, or very little, of what a school therapist is and what the role entails.

As described in earlier chapters, in such instances, it will take time for school staff to understand the significance and importance of maintaining the boundaries of space, time and confidentiality that are central to therapy. It is likely that these boundaries will be frequently tested. As a therapist – possibly a lone therapist and maybe the first the school has worked with – you will need to be able to resist being pulled out of role yet still manage to adapt when necessary.

Confidentiality

Confidentiality is one of the most sensitive aspects of work as a therapist and is particularly so in a school setting, where we work alongside teachers and other staff who themselves have a relationship with and an interest in our client. As therapists we must protect the confidentiality of the therapeutic relationship while being prepared to pass on information about students that is relevant or important for the school to know.

Providing some information to school staff about the progress of the therapy is a way of maintaining links and fostering a collaborative working relationship without breaking confidentiality. For example, you may wish to share

- information about the child's level of engagement; i.e. is the child receptive and able to engage or resistant to the process (you may also wish to offer your thoughts on why he is being either more resistant or more open to your work at a particular stage);
- the broad themes of your work together;
- when you'll be negotiating ending your work together;

- his attendance;
- that he's using your meetings fully and able to explore feelings and experiences in a useful way;
- that you've agreed to carry on your work together.

At least initially, staff may find it difficult to understand why aspects of our work remain confidential and there may be occasions when a teacher or support worker will enquire about details of a session. It is worthwhile being prepared to answer such enquiries in a way that is not going to be received as a rebuff but instead conveys a willingness on your part to respond positively to such signs of interest.

Although the one-to-one nature of therapeutic work should be protected as a matter of course, you may find that on occasion a three-way meeting with a client and member of staff can be useful.

> Take the example of Max, a very hard-to-reach teenager who was often truanting from school and experiencing a great deal of change in his life. When he was coming to the end of his work with his school-based therapist, it came to light that Max's learning support assistant (LSA) with whom he had a long-established relationship was leaving the school. The therapist had Max's agreement to invite his LSA to the final session for a three-way meeting. This gave Max an opportunity to witness two adults talking and thinking with him about his future, something of which he had had no previous experience. It also gave him the opportunity to experience simultaneously a good-enough ending with his LSA and therapist.

This short vignette highlights how every client–therapist relationship is unique and that what we undertake with one client might not be appropriate with another. A situation such as the one above illustrates how therapists need to be able to think about each client within the context of his particular circumstances, both past and present, and be prepared to respond creatively when called for. However, the client's best interests must always be the deciding factor. As a general guideline, trainee and experienced therapists alike use supervision to discuss all aspects of their work, especially instances when a shift away from standard practice is under consideration.

Arranging a meeting such as the one described with Max and his LSA should be planned only after discussion in supervision and then with the client's full agreement. At the start of any client meeting involving a third person, we need to ensure that the client and member of staff know that what is discussed in the meeting is to be kept confidential.

Once you've begun working with a client, day-to-day incidents may occur that test your ability to stay within the boundaries of your role while responding spontaneously and warmly to unexpected requests from staff. Ad hoc conversations that may be witnessed or overheard by other staff or children are to be avoided. In some cases it may be necessary to cut a conversation short because of such risks and to let the teacher know you can come by at break time, lunch or after school to pick up on it when you can talk more privately. When you meet the teacher later, it might be worth mentioning that speaking to each other in front of the client may arouse anxiety in him about what is being passed on. Even if the child is not present and the teacher asks how he is doing, it's important to suggest that you speak out of earshot of other pupils. This ensures that students do not witness what they imagine might be a breach in confidentiality or misconstrue what they hear. It also role-models adults respecting children's rights; just as we wouldn't talk about our relationship with another adult in front of others, so too must we protect the child's right to confidentiality.

It is useful to explain to staff at the outset why confidentiality is such an important feature of any therapeutic work, emphasising that it opens up a unique opportunity for the client to take risks and explore emotions or thoughts about his experiences that, in another setting or context, might feel far too exposing. At the same time, staff should be reassured that there are procedures in place to deal with the kinds of disclosures that need to be shared more widely, such as those instances when key school staff have to know about events in a child's life as part of their duty of care.

Disclosures

Every school will have a formal procedure outlining how issues relating to child protection or what can be called 'safeguarding children' are to be dealt with. All school therapists are required to familiarise themselves with their school's related policies and processes and to attend any child protection training on offer. If, during a session, a client discloses information about himself or his family that you have serious concerns about, it is vital to think very carefully about how to handle it. There are complex issues to be worked through relating to your client's trust in you and confidentiality. It goes without saying that there are certain kinds of disclosures that you will need to act upon immediately, informing your client in the session that he's told you something you will need to talk through with a senior school staff member. Here is an example of what you might say: 'It must have taken courage to tell me that. I think we need to explore this very carefully. Before we go any further, I need to tell you that I want to discuss this in confidence with the Head of Pastoral Care. How do you feel about that?'

If the disclosure doesn't necessitate immediate action, it is highly advisable – if not essential – to consult on how best to proceed. Most school therapists will have ensured that they can contact their supervisor between supervision sessions if a matter of urgency arises. In addition, many will make it a priority to develop a close working relationship with a school staff member with whom they can discuss sensitive matters and know that confidentiality will be respected. This may or may not be a designated child protection officer. It could, for example, be a senior teacher involved in pastoral care or a deputy or even the Head. Disclosures need to be worked with as delicately as possible so that the therapeutic bond is not ruptured irreparably. As well, serious disclosures call on the therapist and school staff to manage highly charged material that will inevitably trigger anxieties that could ripple through the system. This can result in a crisis-management style reaction that should be avoided if at all possible, for such a response can cause the child and his family to pull away and refuse to engage. Sustaining a client's trust through the period directly following a disclosure will take great skill, thoughtfulness and a capacity to tolerate uncertainty and anxiety. Working closely with selected school staff is essential.

Helping staff to see improvements

Teachers come into contact with a large number of students every day and their relationships with them will vary. Some teachers consider the pastoral aspect of their work to be very important, while others see their role as concentrating solely on the academic achievements of their students. An important aspect of your role as a school therapist will be to help school staff broaden and deepen the picture they have of the students you are working with. So in addition to thinking about the student's approach to learning, you will want to help staff consider the young person's relational, behavioural and emotional development as well.

In the longer term, the school therapist can help staff accept that change is incremental and that even seemingly small improvements in their pupils can be significant, potentially impacting on many areas of their lives. For example, an increase in the capacity to tolerate feeling anxious can help a student to feel more settled in himself and therefore better equipped to take small risks, perhaps for the first time being able to initiate conversation or to to engage with others in a meaningful way.

For the purpose of tracking incremental changes, making detailed notes of the first few sessions with a client can be very useful. Looking back on these notes near the end of therapy will help you identify small but important shifts. The more specific and detailed you can be in describing to staff the changes you have noticed, the more the child will come to life for them.

Once changes are brought to the staff member's attention, they may come to realise that some of these developments are being translated into the child's experiences in the classroom and playground. For avoidant clients, even managing to attend sessions can be seen as an improvement; for a child lacking in self-esteem, a more confident bearing can be considered a change; for a disruptive child, coming to the sessions calmly will be a sign of progress. At the end of your work, you can remind the member of staff you've been liaising with of the details of the initial referral. She may well be struck by the difference in how she perceived this child at the beginning of the therapy and how she experiences him now.

Report writing and the use of reports

Head teachers appreciate monitoring systems being set in place by school therapists. As written referrals may be sketchy, it can be useful to provide a report about six weeks into the work setting out reasons for the referral and the therapeutic aims. Interim reports might be requested when multi-agency meetings are convened on a student you are working with. If you cannot attend in person and present your report yourself, you can ensure a copy is made available at the meeting so that you make a contribution to the discussion on behalf of the client.

At the end of your work with each client, a final report can be prepared that looks back on the therapeutic aims and captures key areas of progress. How the school uses these reports will vary. Whatever their function, you will be providing information that will help school staff form a fuller picture of the pupil and will be of use if the student is referred on to other services. It is advisable to label your report 'Confidential' to alert staff to the fact that these reports should be shared strictly on a 'need to know' basis.

There are different ways of approaching report writing. The first sample below uses specific headings under which initial observations and outcomes are grouped together. This kind of structure ensures a comprehensive overview, but it can be rather time consuming to fill in the details. It is included here as a way of illustrating the different parts of a child's life that can be thought about when writing a report and may be positively impacted by a therapeutic intervention.

The first example is an End of Therapy Report written about work with a primary school child called Amy (not her real name). This child had witnessed domestic violence and her sister had been sexually abused by an uncle. As the report will be held in Amy's school file, it may be read by her parents or another professional or teacher at any time during Amy's school years. For this reason, particular aspects of her history are not written up explicitly in the sample report below.

END OF THERAPY REPORT

CONFIDENTIAL

School: London Town Primary School
Pupil: Amy Smith
Age: 8
Date of first session: 15 September
Date of last session: 12 July
Total number offered: 32
Total number attended: 29
Name of therapist: Jane Jones
Date of this report: 15 July

Family context

Amy lives with her mother and an older sister (15). She has no contact with her father, who moved away four years ago. Mother is keen for

Amy to be offered therapy and made time to come for an initial meeting with me. I was told by mother that the family is somewhat isolated as there are no relatives living close by and mother works long hours. There were serious difficulties in the family during Amy's early childhood, which will have affected all family members. (NOTE: Either the school SENCo or head teacher should be contacted for further information.) Mother also came for a final review meeting.

Reasons for the referral

Amy was referred for therapy because she is very unsettled at school. At the initial meeting with Amy's mother, I was told that Amy is often upset when dropped off at school in the morning. Amy was described by both her mother and her teacher as frequently displaying aggressive behaviour towards other children, often unintentionally, possibly because she is easily intimidated or frightened and often misinterprets social cues. Her peer relationships are impacted by this and she has few friends. Her teacher said that Amy usually finds it difficult to work in groups and to concentrate in general. As a result she is falling behind in her learning.

Identifying areas to work on

Learning The teacher who referred Amy was concerned about her lack of academic progress as described above. My aim was to offer Amy non-directive therapy to gauge how well she could manage her own expressive play and to get a sense of her capacity to sustain a 'storyline' or create a coherent narrative. I also hoped that Amy would be able to express and process some of her early experiences through free play so that her anxiety would decrease and she would be more able to take things in, concentrate for longer periods and be more open to learning in general.

Behaviour Her teacher described Amy as finding it hard to concentrate during lessons, often fidgeting, day dreaming or shutting down. She also observed an uninhibited and chaotic quality in Amy's play and in her art making. Engaging in group tasks presents particular challenges. Amy seems to freeze and cannot participate due to excessive anxiety and fear of things going wrong. An aim of the therapy was to give Amy the chance to express her anxieties symbolically through play and, through either hearing me reflect on them or being able to reflect herself, be less overwhelmed or dominated by unmanageable or unnamed feelings.

Relationships Amy seems to find it hard to trust her teacher. She often reacts aggressively when the teacher is trying to help, seemingly feeling criticised rather than supported. As described above, she finds collaborative exercises with fellow pupils particularly difficult. It was hoped that offering Amy the opportunity to experience a different kind of relationship (the therapist–client alliance) within a very boundaried and predictable safe setting might leave Amy feeling more secure and emotionally robust so that she could take more risks in her everyday relationships and find it easier to trust both adults and children.

Emotional well-being I observed Amy's confusion and uncertainty at the beginning of our work together. She literally seemed not to know her own mind, struggling, for example, with basic decisions about what resources to use. She had a very limited range of emotional expression with a general sense of chaos and confusion prevailing. I hoped to help her recognise some of the feelings underneath the chaos and confusion by naming them and enabling her to express them more openly.

Outcomes

Learning Over the course of our work together, there have been improvements in Amy's language skills, capacity for thinking and general dexterity. She has used the sessions extremely well, making good use of the resources. Telling stories out loud as she played or used the art materials gave her the opportunity to listen to herself talk (i.e. to start to give words to her experience and to begin to make sense of her world) and then, over time, to engage in conversation with me. This has contributed to an improvement in her vocabulary, in her capacity to use full sentences and in her ability to speak more clearly. Her teacher has commented on her improved confidence in class. Amy is now more able to accept her teacher's input and even to ask for support at times. She can speak more clearly and is much easier to understand. Her written work is less chaotic and she is able to focus on it for longer periods. She seems to take greater interest in her learning, particularly in her reading and writing.

Behaviour Amy is beginning to behave in a more age-appropriate way. When I first met her, she oscillated between expressing herself in ways that were either significantly older or much younger than her actual age. Her presentation has changed significantly and her mother has commented that she is 'much more like an eight-year-old now'. Her teacher has also noticed an increase in Amy's social confidence. She makes eye contact now and can hold it, she comes across as more relaxed and less wary and seems to have more faith in the possibility of good experiences resulting from social engagement.

Relationships Amy is very close to her mother but her early experiences mean that this attachment is often experienced by Amy as less secure than it might really be. The experience of therapy has given Amy an opportunity to explore a different kind of relationship with an adult, one that has taken place in a carefully boundaried and managed structure where the unpredictable does not feature and where the adult can offer a reliable degree of safety.

Forming a relationship with me has shown Amy that relationships can have different qualities. She has had an opportunity to experience reciprocity, trust and empathy and to take risks without repercussions. These are all valuable experiences for a child, especially one who has had complex and unpredictable family relationships in the past.

Emotional well-being Amy originally presented as highly suggestible, confused and chaotic. She was at times uninhibited in her behaviour and language and could express powerful and markedly contradictory feelings about the same event. At the start of our work Amy showed herself to be a child often overwhelmed by anxieties, with very little sense of her own mind or, indeed, of time. As well, she seemed to lack the capacity to read social cues or even, perhaps, to be aware of them. She appeared to be carrying unarticulated and unprocessed distress relating to her early childhood experiences. Throughout our time together, she revisited her anxieties in her play and her artwork and also worked through some of her losses. She has begun to understand her feelings and to make more sense of her experiences as a result of her therapy.

Conclusion In spite of her initial wariness, Amy proved to be receptive to therapy. In the first phase of our work, the ways in which she related to me and how she used the materials revealed her internal chaos and some of her key anxieties. As time progressed, she was more able to organise and structure her play. Her sense of time improved and she seemed more aware of the ending of each session. She was also able to talk more directly to me rather than solely through the dolls or made-up characters. Together, we have been able to build narratives and stories that carry symbolic meaning relating to her past, allowing her to process it and to get a better sense of her place in the world. She has begun to understand how healthy and secure relationships work and, as a result, is more willing to take risks with her peers. She now has three or four core friendships at school. Her mother noted that she is rarely tearful now when dropped off in the morning and seems more able to relax both at home and at school.

Below is an example of a final report for Sade, a secondary school pupil in Year 8. As will be clear, the information recorded about the reason for the referral and the therapeutic aims came primarily from conversations with Sade herself and not from a teacher or her parents.

END OF THERAPY REPORT

CONFIDENTIAL

School: London Town Secondary School
Pupil: Sade Ali
Age: 13
Date of first session: 19 September
Date of last session: 14 July
Total number offered: 32
Total number attended: 29
Name of therapist: Jane Jones
Date of this report: 18 July

Reason for the referral

Sade was originally referred as the school noted that she was bright but underachieving. In particular, Sade's literacy levels have not improved during her time at secondary school and her Head of Year is concerned. She was also described as having friendship difficulties at school.

Family context

In the first phase of our work together I learned that Sade has undergone significant changes within her family during the last few years, during which time her mother remarried and her younger sister was born. She lives with mother, stepfather and half-sister, who is just over a year old.

Therapeutic aims

Sade finds some friendships difficult to manage and this can interfere with her experience of school. Some members of school staff are also worried about Sade's relationship with food; there is a concern that she may not be eating properly. My feeling when I first met Sade was that she has a 'closed' quality and some difficulty in 'taking things in'. Initially she came across as suspicious of what was on offer and seems to find it difficult to anticipate her needs being met either through the therapy or in more general terms. Sade's description of her peer relationships conveyed a difficulty in feeling empathy towards her peers and a certain rigidity in her behaviour. She can also have quite fixed expectations of herself and others. In terms of her school work, Sade recognised that she is falling behind and does genuinely seem concerned about this.

Therapeutic aims we identified included the following:

- Providing Sade with the opportunity to describe her relationships at home and at school in more detail so that the difficulties she was having could be made sense of and the underlying feelings clarified.
- Identifying how some of her difficulties might link to changes both at home and at school (the primary to secondary school transfer was not an easy one for Sade as it coincided with the birth of her half-sister).
- Thinking about changes she could make in how she interacts with others so that she gets more out of her relationships.
- Clarifying how she manages her anxieties (including how this might relate to her relationship with food).

- Thinking about her learning and how she might better achieve her potential.

Therapeutic outcomes

Sade was able to attend her sessions on time throughout, without being reminded by a teacher, and came on her own. This in itself is a sign of her willingness to engage and to address some of the emotional blocks to her learning. She was talkative from the start. However, in the first phase of our work she showed very little feeling, even when describing what one would expect to be emotionally resonant experiences (e.g. her mother's new partner moving into the home, the birth of her half-sister, her best friend from primary school going to a different secondary school).

When I first started seeing Sade, she described her life as something of an uphill struggle and seemed to feel little hope that things could get better, especially with her relationships. However, as the sessions progressed Sade was able to get in touch with her feelings and to take the risk of describing very personal experiences, which were bound to expose her vulnerabilities. This in itself was a sign of real progress. She has been able to own her feelings of envy and anger while also identifying the areas of her life in which she finds pleasure and feels supported. I have the sense that she is less intensely preoccupied with aggrieved feelings now and is somewhat more receptive to new ways of thinking.

Sade talked about her relationship with food and described how she often missed lunch rather than having to decide where to sit in the school cafeteria and negotiate what could be a socially awkward experience for her. After discussing it, she was able to arrange to go to lunch with a classmate, which broke through her initial resistance.

Sade's relationship with her mother was revealed as a difficult and complex one. At present, understandably, her mother is preoccupied with the new baby. Sade has expressed her powerful feelings about this relationship and we have explored this in depth, as well as her relationship with her grandparents and stepfather. Sade also talked about her birth father, who now lives in another country, and was able to acknowledge the depth of her feelings around losing contact with him.

The combined experiences of transferring to secondary school without her best friend, having to cope with mother turning her attention to a new baby and losing touch with her birth father all contribute to Sade's difficulties in trusting that important relationships will, in fact, last and are worth investing in. However, being able to talk more openly about her home situation and about feelings she used to think she had to keep covered up has helped Sade to let down her guard and take more risks. She is also more accepting of rather painful realities such as relationships changing or being lost altogether over time.

In the last phase of our work, Sade has talked in very positive terms about several friendships, including a new one, that she finds affirming and this has led to some discussion of how she understands her identity and her place in her peer group. She talks more readily now of experiences that show an improved sense of self-confidence and more emotional resilience.

During the time that I have worked with Sade I have witnessed her personal development progressing. Until fairly recently, she seemed unwilling to leave aspects of childhood behind and resisted fully taking on all the challenges of adolescence. However, she is now more able to see the gains in growing up and has fewer unresolved feelings about losing her place in her mother's eyes as 'the baby of the family'. Sade now comes across as having more self-worth and speaks with an optimism that she found hard to believe in when I first started working with her.

Sade took an active role in deciding when our sessions would stop and we have given careful thought to ending our work together. She has expressed her sadness about finishing her therapy as well as acknowledging the impact of other endings she has experienced, most notably in leaving primary school and in the loss of contact with her father.

Recommendations

Sade says that she has found her experience of therapy useful and knows that the service continues to be made available at the school. She may choose to return to it at some time in the future. Given her receptivity to the therapy process and the progress she has made during our work together, I believe that she would be able to make good use of it again in future.

At the time of the referral, concerns were expressed by the school around Sade not fulfilling her academic potential. It was not possible to get direct feedback from teachers on whether progress had been made in this area. However, Sade now has more confidence in her positive qualities and therefore may be willing to face up to her

> need for additional support. Sade may be open to having a conversation with her Head of Year about ways in which she could approach her 'catch-up learning' and how the school could help her with her this.

Conclusion

Working with school staff will differ from setting to setting and from teacher to teacher. In the primary school context, there are often teachers who will be willing to observe the child referred, give feedback as required to the school therapist and monitor the pupil's progress in his emotional, social and classroom learning. These same teachers may also understand the parameters of the work and have realistic expectations of what can and cannot be fed back by the therapist within the bounds of confidentiality. However, there will also be circumstances and situations that seem to mitigate against direct collaboration between therapist and teacher. Whether partnership working is helped or hindered by the school ethos, by personal or institutional defences or by the sheer pressures of time, school therapists are most effective when they can find a way of working with school staff even if it is restricted to written communications. As this chapter has highlighted, preparing a report at the beginning of therapy and again at the end not only contributes towards building an evidence base for the school-based therapy service but also signifies a wish to communicate. By passing on to teachers important pieces of information, clarifying progress made and identifying areas that could benefit from further input, we demonstrate that we are including school staff in our work while also respecting client confidentiality.

Study questions

Explore your feelings about working alongside school staff by answering the following questions:

- What anxieties or expectations do you have about collecting a child from the classroom?
- How might you deal with a last-minute change of timetable that means you won't see your client?
- What do you think are the possible difficulties of working alongside teaching staff?

You may wish to reflect on, or discuss with peers, some or all of the vignettes provided below.

Vignette 1

Under-resourcing is increasingly impacting on schools and pressures on staff are mounting, exacerbated by expanding class sizes and the demands of meeting set targets. Your request to see a student on his own in the same place and at a fixed time each week may appear unreasonable to a teacher who feels her resources are stretched to the limit by having to work with 30 children of differing abilities in a cramped classroom. She may feel that she's often expected to respond to organisational changes or alterations to timetables with very little notice or consultation. In the example following, the school therapist needs to convey that she understands the teacher's position and that she is being consistent, rather than unthinkingly rigid, about how she works.

Since Jodie's mum recently left the family, Jodie has been getting into a lot of trouble at school. While she has been coming regularly to sessions with you for eight weeks, recently she has asked to bring a friend. You arrive at the classroom to pick Jodie up for her meeting and the teacher says, 'Jodie would really like to bring a friend with her to your session today. Can she bring one or two? It would be a real help to me – I don't have a classroom assistant to support me this afternoon.' *What would you say?*

Vignette 2

Sometimes a child will decide that he doesn't want to attend his session and may enlist the support of the class teacher in achieving this outcome. In the moment, the school therapist may experience this as a direct challenge to the value of her work. However, it will be more helpful if the school therapist can convey to the teacher that a child's ambivalence about attending is manageable and can be thought about.

You arrive at the door and the teacher says to you, 'Niazul says he doesn't want to come any more – he says he'd rather stay in his lesson.' *What would you say?*

Vignette 3

An emphasis on targets and attainment can mean that teachers find it hard to see how the school therapist's work contributes to their students' academic learning and success at school.

You go to collect Michelle and the class teacher says to you, 'She's missing too much schoolwork by coming to see you. She was having trouble keeping up before but now she's really falling behind.' *What would you say?*

Vignette 4

If a teaching assistant or learning mentor has had a disrupted morning with a pupil, she may think it helpful to come into the student's session with him. She may believe that she can give the school therapist an accurate picture of the pupil's real presentation and that the school therapist will support her in rebuking him for his bad behaviour.

You are waiting for Terry, a Year 10 student who can be very aggressive in class and frequently gets into physical fights in the playground. The LSA brings him to the session and sits down. 'Terry's had a dreadful morning – haven't you, Terry? He's been completely unmanageable and was in a fight. He threw a chair across the classroom and swore at me. Can you do something? We really need to sort this out now.' *What would you say?*

Vignette 5

Occasionally a teacher may ask the school therapist directly if she can support a child with his schoolwork in their session.

Ben has been referred because the school suspects he has ADHD and his restlessness means he doesn't get much work done in class. You arrive to collect Ben and his teacher says, 'Ben's bringing his maths book with him – he's been chatting all morning and hasn't done a stroke of work. Can you help him get this done?' *What would you say?*

Vignette 6

Tests and class activities can occur unexpectedly and the school therapist may need to respond spontaneously to changes in session arrangements. Each time this occurs, school therapists need to work out whether flexibility or consistency will be most helpful.

You go to collect a student from class and the teacher says, 'Sorry, Destiny can't come to her session with you today, we're preparing for an exam she'll be doing this time next week.' *What would you say?*

> ### Sample responses
>
> #### Vignette 1
>
> 'I'm sorry you're not getting enough support today. It must be difficult without a classroom assistant. However, much as I'd like to help, I can't. I offer individual appointments to children and they can't bring friends or classmates to their sessions. From time to time they might want to but this is usually because they are finding it hard to focus on what's going on for them. It wouldn't help Jodie in the longer term if she could bring a friend when she wanted to, so I am going to take her on her own as usual.'

Vignette 2

'I'm aware that Niazul finds it hard to come with me but once he is in the room, he usually manages very well. It would be great if you could support him in continuing his sessions with me. I'd really like to be able to see him as planned today. Once we're in the session, we can talk about his mixed feelings about attending.'

Vignette 3

'I understand that it can be difficult to see the work Michelle does in therapy as contributing to her learning. However, if she and I can use some of our time to think about what's on her mind and what makes engaging with school so difficult for her, it might help Michelle to feel more settled. In the longer term, this should improve her ability to concentrate. Why don't I pop by at lunchtime and we can talk about this again in more detail?'

Vignette 4

'Thanks for coming along with Terry. It sounds as if it's been a difficult morning for both of you. It's time for his meeting with me now – if he and I can talk about what happened we might be able to understand better what's been going on for him. I hear what you're suggesting; you think the three of us meeting together might help. Terry and I can talk about this and decide on the best way forward. I'll email you at the end of the day or you can come back after school and we can have a brief conversation then. I'll be here until 5 p.m.'

Vignette 5

'Focusing on his work this morning seems to have been more difficult than usual for Ben. We don't do academic work in our meetings, but perhaps our session will give him a chance to talk about what in particular has unsettled him today.'

Vignette 6

'Thanks for letting me know about the exam. Perhaps Destiny can come for some of her session with me today – she's expecting to meet with me as she usually does at this time. It'll also give her a chance to prepare for the session she'll miss next week because of the exam.'

Chapter 18

The ending process

Lyn French

The importance of working through endings

Endings punctuate the developmental pathway from pre-infancy through adulthood. For instance, the birth of a child marks the end of a nine-month period characterised by the total absence of separation between mother and the baby. The unique experience of carrying an infant has to be given up by the mother while the baby is required to relinquish the luxury of all its needs being met without his or her engagement. From that point on, each developmental gain is accompanied by a loss. The end of breast- or bottle-feeding occurs in synchronisation with the beginning of more independent feeding. The baby's growing sense of autonomy and self-agency inevitably sees out a period of full dependency and therefore the end of a particular form of intimacy with the mother.

In psychoanalytic terms, the ways in which both the baby and the mother negotiate endings along with the separations and losses that are a part of everyday life are inextricably linked to the nature and quality of their attachment. Babies with a secure attachment pattern will feel safe enough to express anger, anxiety, fear and even hatred as well as love and gratitude towards their mother or primary care giver. For her part the mother, in turn, can accept and validate these expressions and thus provide the baby with an authentic or 'true self' experience in the move towards individuation and independence. The maternal figure's capacity for emotional receptivity will determine if and how the infant experiences a secure attachment. Mothers who have not had many opportunities themselves to develop their internal resources may struggle to provide their infant with a 'good enough' relationship experience. As a result, their babies could develop avoidant, ambivalent or disordered attachments.

Mourning losses and acknowledging achievements are both central to working through endings. But because endings unconsciously evoke fantasies of dying and of death, it can make acknowledging an approaching ending something to be avoided, resisted, denied or only partially faced. Endings in general have much in common with coming to terms with the loss of a loved one. Missed opportunities, regrets, guilt over real or perceived conflicts, anxiety about how we will manage without the lost object as well as feeling powerless to change the situation are just some of the emotions or states of mind that can threaten to take over. In addition, the unimaginable thought of our own inevitable death will be acutely present, consciously or unconsciously, fuelling a sometimes urgent wish to play down endings, diminishing their significance or avoiding them altogether. Ending work with children or adolescents who have suffered a family bereavement will stir up complex and often confusing feelings that they may well want to repress. They might experience intense feelings of irrational guilt for the role they imagine they played in the death of their parent or sibling, reflecting the hostile or destructive feelings all of us will have towards those we love. When death occurs, self-recrimination and a need for self-punishment can come to the fore. Or the loss might feel so great that any reference to the subject could feel unbearable.

Children who have lost touch with a parent because of divorce or separation will also have strong feelings about endings. But even those with no personal experience of significant loss will find endings potent. It is part of the therapist's role to bear in mind her client's personal history and to be able to imagine what it might bring up. Although the feelings, fantasies and mental states generated by endings may be more or less common to all of us, the particular weight, tone and texture of the experience will be determined by our own unique histories.

Current endings will inevitably echo backwards in time, bringing up conscious and unconscious memories of forgotten, repressed or remembered endings. This means endings that are worked through in the present can go some way towards completing mourning processes related to earlier losses. Not all the loose ends can be drawn together and tied up. Endings can never be fully resolved; instead, we come to terms with the loss in the external world whether it is the loss of a particular form of intimacy (as in the mother–baby relationship), a person, a home, a possession, an opportunity or a cherished ideal. Recognising loss and the impact of any form of ending, acknowledging the attendant feelings and experiencing the resulting pain but surviving it strengthens our emotional muscle, leaving us with evidence of our capacity to learn from our past and to move on, however challenging that might turn out to be.

Thinking about the meaning of endings

Each of us will have our own history of endings as well as conscious and unconscious associations to what endings mean. It can be useful to look back over significant endings and identify what we went through at the time, noting recurring patterns in how we deal with endings. To facilitate this process, we can ask ourselves questions such as the following:

- How were endings managed in my childhood?
- How do I respond to endings now?
- Which endings have been hardest for me and why?
- What defences have I used to avoid or deny the pain?
- What do I feel most uncomfortable about when I think about working with endings in my role as a therapist?

In a similar way, we think about each ending with a client within the context of his personal history. Questions that can aid our thinking include the following:

- What are we, as therapists, trying to achieve by working through endings?
- What opportunities do we provide clients with when we process our ending with them?
- What might the client be defending against in the final stages of the therapy?
- What form might the defences take?
- What can the therapist do to prepare for the ending?
- What can the therapist say that will support the ending process?
- What are our own expectations about how an ending might unfold?

Some thoughts about endings relating to these questions are provided below.

What are we, as therapists, trying to achieve by working through endings?

As therapists, our intention is to enable the client to use his current ending with us as an opening for accessing his feelings about earlier losses and, if possible, bringing the residual feelings and thoughts into consciousness. Direct discussion about the current ending can lead to resurrecting memories of earlier losses both in the conscious mind and the unconscious. These felt memories, whether or not they are spoken about, are symbolic representations of more primitive losses or endings, many of which occurred in infancy, such as losing the breast. By creating a context for the *experience* of endings to come to the fore, we are making it possible for the client to progress his mourning on various levels, including the unconscious. When a client reveals his feelings around the loss of the therapist, he is, at the same time, symbolically expressing previously unarticulated feelings from the recent and distant past. The commonly identified fear of being unable to cope without his therapist can, for example, be understood at one and the same time as a reality-based 'here and now' anxiety triggered by the ending of therapy and as a representation of the child's fear of being unable to manage without the reassuring and supportive presence of his mother. Sometimes it is too difficult to focus on the loss or separation that causes the most pain. Instead, the conversation can stay focused on the end of the therapeutic relationship or be referred to non-verbally and be symbolically worked on through art-making or play – making it possible to identify feelings that would otherwise overwhelm the client.

Genuine sorrow over what is lost for ever (the breast, the mother's undivided attention, the favourite teacher, etc.) can be safely felt in therapy. As well, it is important not to lose sight of the gains that accompany loss. Every developmental milestone and each phase of the life cycle brings both. Gains may include increased independence or self-agency, skill acquisition or mastery, greater emotional resilience, deeper self-knowledge, empathy for others, gratitude for what has been, new possibilities for the future, and so on. In the therapy setting, progress can be acknowledged and small but significant gains can be emphasised. These might include less resistance to attending sessions, freed-up play or more open self-expression, a willingness to feel vulnerable, taking more risks, and so on. Importantly, gratitude can be expressed for the opportunity to engage in a meaningful relationship that can be seen to have value despite its time-limited nature.

What opportunities do we provide clients with when we process our ending with them?

As noted above, working through endings provides clients with the opportunity to re-experience the potent feelings they may have had at an earlier stage of their lives, including the period around weaning and their first consciousness of absences.

The client has the chance to articulate or symbolically express what can feel like socially unacceptable feelings, such as anger or frustration, in response to endings. For example, he may re-experience what can be felt as the humiliation of being powerless in the face of rejection or in some way left behind by an important figure. We will all have very strong feelings towards those whom we feel have abandoned us, even those who have left us by dying. Hatred – even murderous rage – is there to be acknowledged but this does not cancel out the love that may also be felt. The fantasy of being replaced by new love objects can also leave residual anger and jealousy that the client needs to process either consciously or unconsciously.

On the other end of the loss spectrum, the client may feel relief at being freed from what might have been experienced as a kind of pressure to maintain a relationship. This pressure can be linked with the need to tolerate the difficult feelings that arise in any significant relationship. Forming an attachment entails being dependent on another over whom we have no real control. We can never force the loved object (or the therapist) to make available everything that is desired or to give us what we wish for precisely when we want it. Neither can we prevent that person from having other, exclusive relationships of equal value (e.g. parents may have other children or stepchildren and a partner; therapists see other clients). Therefore, hatred, frustration, envy, jealousy and disappointment have to be tolerated along with the good feelings, and it can be a relief, at least in the short term, to leave this behind.

Due to particular aspects of their own history, some clients may have experienced the therapist as being too dependent on them for their sense of professional worth or for evidence of their capacity for empathy and reparation. Again, at the end of therapy, such clients may feel released from the burden of feeling responsible for meeting their therapist's needs.

As has been discussed throughout the previous chapters, all responses to the therapy and to the therapist will be heavily coloured by the transference. Therapists who are experienced in using the client to meet their needs could, for example, be representing a parent figure or even an older sibling who may have placed the client in this position. Ideally, working through the ending will include an exploration of feelings and impressions of this kind.

Helping the client to construct a more coherent internal narrative of his own history can result in an increased sense of containment and inner security. This can be achieved through reviewing the most important experiences in the client's life as discussed over the course of the therapy. Identifying the different themes explored and revisiting how the client felt at various stages of the work also serves to bring together what may have been experienced previously as fragments of a whole. It is useful to weave into these conversations why therapy was initially offered, what fantasies the client had about why he was referred, what things were like for him at home and at school when he began the sessions and what has changed, as well as what has remained the same.

Gaining a deeper and more compassionate understanding of the wider context to one's story is also useful for the client and can put things in better perspective. All this goes a long way towards leaving the client with a more integrated sense of self.

What might the client be defending against in the final stages of the therapy?

In addition to defending against a wide range of painful feelings associated with past losses and with the ending of therapy itself, clients may want to repress or deny the more uncomfortable feelings that are bound to come up towards their therapist. For example, a client who is ready to leave therapy might be unconsciously reminded of an aspect of his relationship with his mother. Perhaps he feels that every step taken away from her and into the wider world leaves her feeling rejected, abandoned and somehow demoted or depleted, possibly to be replaced by other adults who can offer something different, such as teachers or even therapists. Such a client might want to avoid feelings of guilt and protect the therapist from feeling left behind. He might try to keep the focus firmly fixed on thanking the therapist and unconsciously trying to reassure her of her continued worth. This could include excessive proclamations such as 'I'll miss you so much!' and behaviour that is designed to placate or please.

Clients might also wish to defend against more sadistic feelings. For example, there might be a desire to hurt the therapist because the client has been hurt by significant others who have left in the past. This could be expressed by openly denying that anything of value has been experienced or by symbolically attacking the room or the therapist so that there is nothing good left to miss. Some clients might make the therapist feel deskilled by scornfully or indifferently dismissing what has been achieved as retribution for the times the client has felt this particular kind of humiliation.

The thought that the sessions are coming to an end might bring up feelings rooted in panic and anxiety around separations. Adults as well as children can be unconsciously reminded of their infant selves and feel overcome by anticipatory dread or a temporary lack of trust in their internal resources, seriously doubting that they will be up to the task of surviving the loss and coping independently.

What form might the defences take?

Clients might want to avoid any reference to the ending and instead employ omnipotent thinking or behaviour to convince themselves that they are in control. This includes being adamant that only *they* will decide whether or not the sessions will come to an end. Additionally – or alternatively – they might talk about it in an inauthentic way that is very far removed from any real feeling or meaningful discussion. This can be understood as a form of intellectualization or avoidance.

It is common for children to want to focus on the good feelings and deny any anger, disappointment, hurt or fear of abandonment. They might want to make a goodbye card or a thank-you card or a present that would keep at a distance any feelings of dependency, loss or fear of separation. They might also express the wish to have a party to mark the ending and even ask to bring friends.

Some children who find the ending particularly painful will act out (without necessarily having any conscious knowledge that they are doing so). They might, for example, want to miss school on the last day of the session so that they can avoid having to acknowledge an ending or saying goodbye.

What can the therapist do to prepare for the ending?

The therapist can draw together what she has observed and all that she knows about her client, creating a whole picture in mind. This includes thinking back on the original reasons for the referral, remembering the salient points from the client's personal history, reflecting on how the client first came across, identifying big and small changes and being aware of the dominant feelings generated during the beginning, middle and ending phases of the therapy. Being present to the whole experience, if only in mind, gives the client a sense of himself as being recognised 'in the round'. All aspects of his identity will have been represented in some form or another in the therapeutic encounter. Hopefully he will have experienced accumulated moments of being truly seen; that is, those times when his mental states and feelings have been identified, accepted and validated even in non-verbal forms. This can help the client to feel in touch with a more authentic self and can contribute to feeling more at one with himself and with the world.

On a practical note, preparing for the ending provides the therapist with ready material to refer to should she need to prompt the client to identify the kinds of progress he has made. Often this progress will be in the realm of increased personal awareness, changes in the way he relates to the therapist and a more open or freed-up form of expression.

We can help our younger clients by introducing a calendar in the last phase of the work. Usually, the calendar will summarise the number of sessions already completed and give the dates of the final six sessions to come, clearly emphasising the last date.

What can the therapist say that will support the ending process?

Some of the kinds of observations or suggestions therapists may make during the ending phase are provided below:

- 'We won't be meeting again after our last session on [date]. However, both of us will be taking away memories of our work together that we will have for ever. Maybe you can describe a particular time that you'll remember.'
- 'Saying goodbye for the last time can bring up mixed feelings. Some people may feel disappointed or angry about the ending. At the same time, they may feel proud about what they've achieved by coming to their weekly sessions. Perhaps you can say what you're feeling about our ending.'
- 'In our everyday life, it is common to give presents or have a party as a way of saying goodbye. However, here we don't have parties and children don't receive cards or gifts. Instead, we have the chance to talk together about how it's been for you. For example, you may want to tell me what you've enjoyed about coming here or something you've learned or what you might miss.'
- 'Painful or difficult feelings come up for everyone when it's time to say goodbye. I think you're letting me know that you feel angry at me for making the decision to stop. Maybe if it was up to you, you might continue for longer.'
- 'Often when we are approaching an ending, we are reminded of other times when we've said goodbye. Perhaps you still remember people whom you don't see any more.'
- 'It's common to want to stay with what we're familiar and comfortable with. For example, many Year 6 pupils wish they could be in nursery all over again so that they could stay children and be looked after for a longer time. Do you remember feeling that way?'
- 'Endings can remind all of us of death. We know that people have to die just as everything in nature dies. Maybe you've had an experience of death. Perhaps a pet has died or a relative or even a friend. Or you may know someone who has gone through this. Perhaps you can tell me about it.'

What are our own expectations about how an ending might unfold?

As therapists, we may consciously or unconsciously want to orchestrate what we perceive to be a good enough ending. This may be driven by the desire to make up for childhood endings that left us with unresolved feelings or endings that we have not managed well in our own lives. We may be tempted to 'guide' our client towards what we would define as a good enough ending. However, each client will need to use us and the sessions in his own unique way for his own internal growth. It is important to allow a child to do what he needs to do, which may include throwing out his folder or leaving it behind, being angry or destructive or silently rejecting. Our role is not to make this experience better for him but to identify the feelings and acknowledge their intensity.

Conclusion

Side-stepping, avoiding or trying to skim over endings, and the inevitable pain that being in touch with loss brings up, is at odds with reality and creates a false picture of an artificial and idealised world. As this chapter has illustrated, acknowledging (even non-verbally or symbolically) that loss is part and parcel of everyday life and that strong feelings will be stirred up – including grief, anger, hate, guilt, remorse, anxiety, dread and so on – communicates authenticity. We all know that such feelings may be difficult to bear but at least they signify something *real*. Hate – one of the hardest feelings we can admit to having, especially about our loved ones – is implicit in loss. For example, it's possible to hate someone because we feel – rationally or irrationally – that, by leaving, she has in some way abandoned us and forced us to experience hard-to-bear, infantalising feelings linked to dependency. The feelings of hate and hostility generated both towards the person who is gone and towards those who remain can, in turn, trigger fear and anxiety linked to one's own potential destructiveness – as well as guilt. As discussed above, such feelings might not be addressed explicitly or openly with a child in therapy but they may come to the surface in their play or art-making and will be thought about by the therapist in the presence of the child.

This chapter has shown how a 'good enough' ending can be role-modelled by acknowledging with the client that there will always be regret, sad feelings and even anger around endings, but at the same time there can also be a sense of achievement and an acceptance that it is time to move on. A worked-through ending can equip the client to more readily and less painfully move on in future. The example of primary/secondary school transfer is a good one to note. Many children wish they could stay on at primary school as it represents the known and the familiar, as well as their childhood years when they were intimately looked after. However, moving on is necessary and although it brings losses, it also offers new opportunities. By the end of their first year at secondary school, the majority of Year 7 pupils feel more or less settled and even stimulated by the possibilities opening up for them.

All of us will be affected by how the people around us relate to loss. As a society, we need to be able to talk about our losses openly and process them rather than passing over them in silence.

Study questions

Ending therapy is a potent time for both the therapist and the client. Questions that can help us process our own experience of ending work with a client include the following:

- What had I hoped to offer this client? Did my intentions change over time?
- Was I able to offer this client a 'good enough' experience? If not, what do I think prevented the work from evolving in a more meaningful way?
- What feelings come up when I think about ending with this particular client?
- What does the ending bring up for me personally?

Coming up with responses to the children's comments in the vignettes described below will help you to develop your own language to talk about endings. Suggested replies are provided.

Vignette 1

Sade, a Year 4 girl, saw her calendar on the table when she came into the room. She looked quickly at it and then put it back in her folder. She seemed a little restless and agitated as she looked through the box of coloured paper. 'I know!' she said with some relief as she reached for the pink paper, 'I'm going to make a card for my best friend. You find the glue!' she instructed the therapist and then asked, 'Where did you put the scissors?' *What would you say?*

Vignette 2

Janice, a Year 6 girl, fiddled with her hair as her therapist showed her the calendar listing the remaining dates. Without looking at the calendar and in a tone of voice that was trying to convey indifference but came across as anxious, she asked, 'Are you going to be in this school next year?' Then she pleaded, 'Can we have our own party on the last day? I can bring some biscuits if you get cakes and drinks. We can play games too!' *What would you say?*

Vignette 3

Reggie, a Year 10 boy, looked awkward and embarrassed when the therapist mentioned they had six sessions left and would be finishing at the end of the summer term. 'Do I have to come for all six? Why can't I finish now?' he asked. He didn't look at the therapist as he spoke but clicked a ballpoint pen open and shut. He seemed both bored and also a little anxious. *What would you say?*

Vignette 4

It was the first session after the May half term break. Aran, a Year 7 boy, sat quietly as his therapist showed him his calendar and pointed out the number of sessions left. He said, 'Why are we stopping? How come I can't see you next year?' His tone of voice and facial expression conveyed anxiety and fear. The therapist knew that Aran lived alone with his father; his mother had left the family two years before. Then he asked, 'Who will you see next? Please tell me. I need to know! Please!' *What would you say?*

Sample responses

Vignette 1

The therapist says, 'The scissors are right here' and then adds, 'I wonder why you're thinking about your best friend just now? Maybe it's because you'll have to say goodbye to me soon, and it helps to remember who will still be around for you.'

Or 'Perhaps seeing the calendar made you realize that our time together will finish soon. Sometimes it can be difficult to think about endings – we'd rather keep our mind on good things like the friendships we enjoy.'

Vignette 2

'I can see you're interested in our ending and in what's going to happen after we stop meeting together. It's not easy to think about, is it? Maybe having a party would be a way of staying away from upsetting feelings.'

Or 'Endings can bring up feelings that most of us find quite uncomfortable. It's natural to want to focus on having a goodbye party rather that thinking about the more difficult feelings. Here, we can find our own way of acknowledging the good things as well as talking about the more painful side of saying goodbye.'

Or 'Maybe you want to have a special ending to our time together by bringing in cakes and gifts. We can make it special in other ways. For example, we can make something together that represents our time together.'

Vignette 3

'Maybe it feels difficult to focus on finishing our work together. It might seem easier to stop today so that you don't have to think or feel anything about the ending. How have you said goodbye to other people?'

Or 'Sometimes we can feel a little worried about finishing something because we've got used to it; it's become part of our life. Perhaps knowing we have only six sessions left reminds you that nothing stays the same.'

Vignette 4

'It seems hard for you to believe that you will be able to manage on your own when we stop seeing each other.'

Or 'I wonder if stopping the sessions with me is reminding you of when your mother moved out? Perhaps you're letting me know how difficult it is not to know where she is now or who she might be seeing.'

Or 'Maybe it's hard to believe that an ending can leave you with good memories to take away. Perhaps it's difficult to trust that you can manage on your own and that you will be alright.'

Part IV

Monitoring and evaluation

Chapter 19

Writing case notes

Stefania Putzu-Williams

This chapter looks at the use of note writing as a reflective tool that aids the therapeutic process. Every school or organisation will have its own guidelines on recording information as part of record keeping. While there are different approaches to how records are kept, they are not all included in this chapter. Instead, the focus is on the ways in which writing detailed case notes can mobilise creative thinking, enabling us to make links that were difficult to arrive at in the session and enriching our own self-understanding.

Trainee therapists usually try to build time for note writing into their working day. It is common practice for trainees to book two hours for each client seen: one for the appointment itself and the other to write it up. Established therapists recognise the value in writing notes but often will not have time set aside to write full accounts of all sessions. Once you are more experienced, it becomes easier to identify what is important in each session and to write more succinct notes.

There are a number of functions that writing notes simultaneously fulfils:

- An on-going record is kept on the client both for the therapist to refer back to and in case the organisation or the school asks for an account of the client. (Notes are useful as a reference for report writing.)
- The therapist can more easily spot recurring emotional content and narrative themes.
- Over time, the therapist can better understand the transference relationship through tracking how the client responds to her at particular points within the session.
- Through mapping transference responses, the therapist can more readily identify key anxieties and defences.
- The therapist has documented material to take to supervision.

Just as importantly, note writing supports thinking and analytic processes. Writing about clinical work seldom amounts to detailing facts about the client and his life story, although recording as much as we can about his history is important. Instead, we focus on capturing the essence of the session and what we think the client was trying to get across. In addition, we often record what feelings we're left with at the end of the session.

The context that will have shaped the client's inner world is to be found in the concrete information we gather, such as whether or not the client's parents are still together or have remained in contact; if he has siblings, where he falls in the birth order; what the significant events are that have occurred in his family, and so on. When writing notes after the session, the therapist will find herself making links between what the client has told her about his past and how she experiences him in the session and vice versa. The thinking that takes place around the client, both during note writing and then in supervision, is an integral component of the therapeutic process.

We often gain personal insight through noting what our reactions are to the client's feelings and presentation. We can increase our self-awareness through reflecting on what each client brings up for us.

More detailed written notes will usually include the following:

- brief summary of the content of the session (main themes)
- significant verbal/non-verbal exchanges
- emotional responses
- evidence of shifts in the client
- evidence of shifts in your response to the client
- points of resistance
- defensive manoeuvres.

Using notes in supervision

The school therapist may choose to dedicate a whole supervision session to one client or perhaps two, especially when clients are new. This helps to create a shared picture in mind of the client. The presentation will include the material outlined below.

The content of the session

- Client's history, the risk assessment, the student's appearance.
- Young person's account of problem/life situation – is the narrative coherent?
- School, work, significant activities, interests: how the young person spends time and energy.
- Relationships with significant people, family, friends, neighbourhood.
- Identity, self-concept, feelings and attitudes about self.
- Values, beliefs, hopes, fears, fantasies, religion, strengths, aspirations, goals, vision of future – attitudes regarding sex differences, gender roles.
- Interventions and techniques that you used. What was the intent of the intervention? What might you have done instead?

The process of the session

The process refers to the thoughts, fantasies and feelings the therapist experiences during the actual session:

- How the session starts and finishes.
- The boundaries that were held or pushed by you or the client.
- Transference and counter-transference feelings and fantasies (note your internal processes: What was happening within you? What emotions and/or bodily experiences were you aware of during the session?).
- Did the session trigger any of your own material? Who was the client for you?

To aid your thinking about the process, you may want to ask yourself the following:

- How does the young person make me feel?
- What did the young person say and do to lead to my feeling the way I do?
- What does the young person want from me and what sort of feeling is he trying to arouse in me to get it?
- What was happening within the young person? What is alive and what is expressed non-verbally at a particular moment?

During the session, therapists try to listen for the following:

- Changes in tone, timbre or intonation of voice, which may indicate an emotion that is being seen or felt differently.
- Aspects of content that you cannot actually follow or understand and that perhaps the client cannot either, or something he says that arouses confusion.
- Encoded statements about other people or situations that at some level may be about the young person himself; e.g. 'It really upset me to see the little dog all alone.' Reformulating this back to him might be, 'Seeing the little dog gave you a sense of desolation and abandonment. Something about loneliness seems to cause you anxiety.'
- Indirect or disguised communication. In other words, things the client tells you about other people may be about you and/or the therapy relationship.

Assessment and reformulation

Some therapists choose to include a summary assessment or reformulation in their presentation to their supervisor. This can be shaped by asking yourself the following questions:

- How do you account for and explain the present problem?
- What are the recurring patterns, strands, themes and/or connections that are emerging?

- What is the young person's state of mind?
- What is the state of his internal object relations (accounting for developmental difficulties/deficits, internal conflicts, defence system)?
- What are internal and external factors contributing to his state of mind?
- What would you give as a clinical description of this client (you might note here resilience, underlying strengths, capacity for sublimation, mastery and progressive development or potential for growth and development; ability to control negative feelings and impulses, ability to tolerate and contain anxiety)?

It can help to make notes of what you want to think about in supervision. For example, some therapists write down a list of questions to take to their supervisor to prompt joint reflection. Because thinking on the spot in a session is not always easy, the combination of note writing and supervision can be used to help you think about what you might have said in any given moment. In addition, taking time to write down possible responses to particular circumstances and to refine one's language so that it is in tune with the child or young person can be very helpful in the long run.

Composing a summary of the client to keep for ease of reference

It is common for therapists to write up a summary of their client for their supervisor to keep so that they have essential information to hand to refer back to in supervision sessions. Often the therapist will give the supervisor a copy of this summary as well as a copy of whatever material has been written up in advance for presentation that day. The summary will usually include the following.

Personal data:

- First name only, gender, age/life stage, ethnicity.
- Your first impressions of his physical appearance.

Context:

- Referral, how the student came to see you.
- Setting.
- Pre-contact information. What you knew about the student before you first met. How you used this information. Any existing relationship or previous contact with you or with the service and possible implications.

Presenting problem and contract:

- Summary of the presenting problems.
- Your initial assessment.

- Duration of problem, including precipitating factors. Why now?
- Current conflicts or issues.
- Contract: frequency, length and number of sessions. Initial plan/hypothesis.

Questions for supervision:

- Key question(s) or issues you want to discuss in supervision.

Problem definition:

- Construct a picture of the client's view of his current situation.
- How would the client like things to be? What would it be like for the student without the complaint/problem?

Preparing to present:

- What did the client pose as a problem or present as an issue that was difficult for you?
- Do you have any doubts or questions about your work with a particular child or adolescent?
- What theories come to mind?
- What interventions worked well?
- What did not work well?
- Read through your records/notes. What stands out?
- What would like to learn? What would you like to focus on?

Receiving feedback in supervision

Monitoring your own reactions in supervision enhances your self-awareness as well as providing information on your client. As therapists, we all have our own material that needs to be processed and reworked. However, if you have an unusually powerful reaction to something the supervisor says, it may suggest that you are experiencing your supervisor's feedback in a way that your client would. This is called 'parallel process' and is described in a little more detail below. Your own material may still be triggered, but in addition your response could hold important information about your client. It can be useful to ask yourself the following questions:

- What feelings were aroused in you during your supervision? (E.g. did you experience feedback as criticism? Did you feel yourself becoming defensive?)
- Could you paraphrase and repeat to your supervisor what you heard? Could you describe the impact it had on you in the session? Could you take in positive feedback?

- Do you feel locked into a childlike state with your supervisor? If so, how would you rather be?
- Does your supervisor remind you of anyone? Do you remind her of anyone? (E.g. what is the transference and counter-transference telling you?)
- Unconscious parallel process: could you be bringing to supervision unrecognised and unexpressed emotions from the session with the client? Identifying this will help the work with your client.
- Challenge and support: are you getting what you need from supervision? If not, can you explore this with your supervisor?
- Do you regularly review with your supervisor the work you have undertaken?

Conclusion

Although time-consuming, writing notes as thoroughly as possible helps us in myriad ways. It will enable you to get the most out of the relationship with your clients and supervisor. Not only does it support our clinical work, it also provides a container for what can be very difficult material. If we put the session down on paper, we can more easily 'file it away' so that we do not risk being overwhelmed by the content of our sessions. It can also bring theory to life in our minds and usefully prompt us to reread texts or find new references. And it greatly aids our self-reflection, enabling us to learn more about ourselves and how we function in relationships.

Chapter 20

Identifying the impact of therapy services in schools

Lyn French

Increasingly, emphasis is being placed on those working in the field of psychological therapies to create a stronger evidence base for their practice. Traditionally therapists have adopted a more informal approach, using the ending phase of the work as an opportunity to look back with their client on changes that were initially hoped for, to reflect on progress that has been made (whether or not it matches original aims), to gauge the extent of the progress and to identify what might be returned to at a later stage perhaps with another therapist. In the school setting, therapists have evolved their own practices. As discussed in Chapter 18 ('The Ending Process'), most therapists use the last few sessions or the final appointment to revisit milestones in the therapy and, in general, to review the work with their client both to create a more joined-up narrative and to evaluate outcomes. Whether or not – and if so, how – feedback is given to the school can vary considerably. For example, some therapists will write a concluding report summarising their original aims and evaluating their outcomes, while others might give verbal feedback at pastoral-care meetings and some will wish to keep the sessions client-focused, giving no feedback to the school to fully protect confidentiality. Therapists will be guided by the school ethos, their own training and the head teacher or the leadership team's preferences.

As budgets in the educational sector become ever tighter and are more closely monitored, interest is increasingly being shown in assessing the impact of all additional or extended services offered. This can be viewed as a welcome opportunity for school therapists to use reports to enhance the profile of their service, clarify what it can and cannot offer and emphasise the benefits to be gained from therapeutic input. Reports can also raise awareness of key psychoanalytic themes such as those related to attachment patterns and child development, which may be of interest to teachers while also serving to promote the value of such professional knowledge. For example, some therapists may choose to contextualise their client's presentation by translating what the school might describe as 'clingy behaviour' into 'shows signs of an insecure or anxious attachment expressed as clinging-on behaviour'. If reasons for this have been discovered by the therapist, they may be included here, such as 'This seems to be linked to her mother's regular absences due to having to go abroad for months at a time to care for an elderly parent.'

Reports can also reframe the way pupils are seen and appeal to a teacher's natural empathy. For example, a pupil who comes across as being wilfully disobedient, unnecessarily challenging or acting out in some way may be going through a difficult experience at home of which the school is unaware. A change as seemingly low key as a grandparent moving away can represent a significant loss if the child had a strong relationship with this relative and was used to seeing him or her regularly. Other events that the school might not know about could include the birth of a new half-sibling, mother's partner moving in, the death of a close relative, a sibling falling seriously ill, a parent sinking into a serious depression or developing an addiction, and so on. Such emotionally impactful family events are bound to have an effect and school staff can be more accepting of difficult behaviour if they understand the context for it. Including a sensitively worded reference to changes at home in a beginning therapy report can easily and helpfully fulfil this function.

In the busy world of school life, the therapist may not manage to schedule pre- and post-therapy meetings or have the time to dedicate to the kind of careful thinking that reports require if they are to provide useful information for staff while also respecting client confidentiality.

This chapter includes examples of how evidence-gathering might be approached, bearing in mind that every therapist needs to decide for herself what priority to give it and how best to go about it. Our intention here is to offer some ideas and sample structures that can be used as they are presented, adapted or modified, held in mind but not used as a paper document or simply viewed as a starting point for thinking about creating an evidence base for therapy work in schools.

The primary school setting

As discussed in previous chapters, therapists working in the primary school setting may use a formal assessment tool that provides a structure for gathering information from the parents, the teachers and the child before and after the block of therapy is delivered. The most common in the UK is the Strengths and Difficulties Questionnaire (Goodman et al. 1998).

Therapists can adapt such questionnaires to create their own forms, which can be completed pre- and post-therapy. Generally, the forms try to capture the main characteristics of a child including his approach to classroom learning and relationships with peers as well as with adults, while also recording key aspects of the child's behaviour. Areas to comment on might be grouped together in categories relating to different parts of the child's life.

An example of the kind of questionnaire that could be used as an assessment tool is included below. This questionnaire is designed to assist school therapists in gathering information about their clients during the first phase of therapy and in evaluating their input during the last phase of the work. At the start of therapy, a questionnaire for school staff such as the one to follow might be completed by the therapist over a course of short meetings or during one longer, initial conversation with the class teacher. Alternatively, it can be emailed to the teacher or a paper copy can be left for completion, preferably by a fixed date agreed in advance.

This questionnaire can also be used as a guiding document or adapted by the therapist to gather feedback from the child's parents during a first meeting. All the relevant information passed on by teachers and parents can then be summarised and written up in the form of a beginning therapy report to be given to the school. The therapist may wish to formulate aims or a therapeutic focus based on what is revealed in the questionnaire for inclusion in this report, ensuring that the hoped-for outcomes itemised are specific enough and can be accurately assessed.

At the end of the work with the child or young person, this process is repeated so that the class teacher and, whenever possible, the parents can give their views on any progress they think the child has made whether or not it relates to the original reason for the referral or to the aims formulated by the therapist at the start. The therapist may have to take quite an active role, coaching them to identify small but significant changes. For example, often only highly visible improvements are looked for, with less obvious but equally important changes missed. The therapist needs to enable the teacher and the parents to focus their attention on noticing the more nuanced shifts in attitude, mood and/or behaviour. When gathering feedback from a teacher or parent at the end of a piece of work, for example, the therapist might need to invite them to go away and closely observe the child, bearing in mind specific questions such as the following:

> Can the child now listen more closely or concentrate for longer periods? Can he take in critical feedback without reacting defensively? Do you have an example of this? Can he tolerate getting things wrong some of the time? Can he learn from his mistakes most of the time? Is the child less likely to get tearful when left out of playground games? Can he be more assertive about asking to be included? Is he more confident now? How does this show? Can he express a wider range of emotions? What have you noticed? Is he easier to be around? If so, in what way?

And so on. The therapist will then return to these questions in a follow-up meeting to hear what they have discovered from their observations.

Whether or not a questionnaire such as the one reproduced below is used, the therapist may still suggest that the teacher and the parents look carefully for any discernible changes in the child's relationship to learning, interaction with peers, relationships with adults, mood states and levels of confidence. Information of this kind can be summarised in a final feedback report for the school at the end of the therapy, demonstrating how effective therapy can be and contributing to an evidence base. Observational exercises can also help the adults to hold the child in mind, in a meaningful and reality-based way. This may lead towards increased objectivity and foster a more positive and compassionate attitude towards the child, a helpful outcome in itself. In addition to drawing together the results of a period of observation, the original reasons for the referral and the resulting therapeutic focus, which may have been included in a beginning therapy report or summary, can be returned to and evaluated. All the feedback gathered, as well as the therapist's own observations of how the child has developed through the course of the work, including how he has managed the therapeutic relationship itself, can be summarised in an 'end of therapy' report.

CREATING A PROFILE OF THE PUPIL OR YOUNG PERSON: PRE- AND POST-THERAPY QUESTIONNAIRE TO BE USED WITH TEACHERS AND PARENTS/CARERS

Name of the pupil or young person + year group _____
Teacher/Parents/Carers providing the information for this form: _____
School therapist: _____
Date of completion of 'beginning therapy' profiling: _____
Date of completion of 'end of therapy' feedback: _____

1 Relationship to learning

1.1 How would you describe the kind of learner this pupil is? Please tick:

	PRE-THERAPY			POST-THERAPY		
This pupil is	NEVER	SOME-TIMES	ALWAYS	NEVER	SOME-TIMES	ALWAYS
Frustrated						
Distracted						
Anxious						
Curious						
Engaged						
Confident						
Tolerant of making mistakes + able to learn from them						
A consistently high achiever						
A consistently low achiever						
Unpredictable achiever						

Any comments/observations?

Pre-therapy: What improvements would you like to see?

End of therapy: What improvements have you observed?

Any further comments/observations?

1.2 What are the best learning conditions for this pupil? Please tick:

	PRE-THERAPY			POST-THERAPY		
This pupil learns best	NEVER	SOME-TIMES	ALWAYS	NEVER	SOME-TIMES	ALWAYS
In a group						
On his/her own						
With an adult						

Any comments/observations?

Pre-therapy: What improvements would you like to see?

End of therapy: What improvements have you observed?

Any further comments/observations?

1.3 How would you describe this pupil's ability to learn? Please tick:

	PRE-THERAPY			POST-THERAPY		
This pupil	NEVER	SOME-TIMES	ALWAYS	NEVER	SOME-TIMES	ALWAYS
Is able to take things in						
Pretends to know but doesn't						
Can be reflective and thoughtful						
Can tolerate others receiving praise						
Is stimulated by healthy competition						
Can function under pressure						

Remembers what she has learned and can make use of it						
Is a consistent learner						

Any comments/observations?

Pre-therapy: What improvements would you like to see?

End of therapy: What improvements have you observed?

Any further comments/observations?

2 Behaviour in the class

How would you describe this pupil's classroom behaviour? Please tick:

	PRE-THERAPY			POST-THERAPY		
This pupil	NEVER	SOME-TIMES	ALWAYS	NEVER	SOME-TIMES	ALWAYS
Is cooperative						
Is able to concentrate						
Stays seated						
Follows instructions						
Can tolerate not being chosen to give an answer						
Shares resources with others						
Helps others with their learning						
Seeks attention in a challenging way						

Any comments/observations?

Pre-therapy: What improvements would you like to see?

End of therapy: What improvements have you observed?

Any further comments/observations?

3 Behaviour in break time

How does this pupil behave at break time? Please tick:

	PRE-THERAPY			POST-THERAPY		
This pupil is	NEVER	SOME-TIMES	ALWAYS	NEVER	SOME-TIMES	ALWAYS
Competitive						
Aggressive						
Cooperative						
A leader						
A follower						
A team player						
An independent player						
Isolated and withdrawn						

Any comments/observations?

Pre-therapy: What improvements would you like to see?

End of therapy: What improvements have you observed?

Any further comments/ observations?

4 Peer relationships

How would you describe this pupil's peer relationships? Please tick:

	PRE-THERAPY			POST-THERAPY		
This pupil	NEVER	SOME-TIMES	ALWAYS	NEVER	SOME-TIMES	ALWAYS
Makes friends easily						

Has friends who are around the same age						
Keeps friends						
Is sensitive to the needs of others						
Wants to take control						
Easily feels controlled						
Fears losing friends and is easily manipulated						
Tends to manipulate friends to keep them						
Cries easily						
Comforts others						
Can be a victim						
Can be a bully						

Any comments/ observations?

Pre: Therapy: What improvements would you like to see?

End of therapy: What improvements have you observed?

Any further comments/observations?

5 Relationships with adults

How does this pupil interact with adults? Please tick:

	PRE-THERAPY			*POST-THERAPY*		
Around adults, this pupil is	NEVER	SOME-TIMES	ALWAYS	NEVER	SOME-TIMES	ALWAYS
Confident						
Comfortable						

Respectful						
Shy and/or self-conscious						
Ill at ease						
Anxious						
Afraid of being judged						
Over-eager to please						
Over-familiar						
Disrespectful						

Any comments/observations?

Pre-therapy: What improvements would you like to see?

End of therapy: What improvements have you observed?

Any further comments/observations?

Working in the secondary school setting

The processes outlined above may not be applicable in the secondary school context. As has been noted in previous chapters, it is often more difficult to schedule time to see teachers or other school staff in a big secondary school and it may not be appropriate to meet with parents of an adolescent. However, the themes covered in the sample questionnaire provided above can be used to guide thinking about the pupil or young person. The school therapist may even choose to find a way to go over some of the main questions included in direct conversation with the client in the first phase of their work together.

Or the therapist may use the first meeting, or even the first couple of sessions, to go through a pupil questionnaire such as the sample one reproduced below. A pupil questionnaire can be used as a framework for the initial meeting or first few sessions. It should be kept simple with the emphasis on providing opportunities for opening up conversation around key areas such as family and peer relationships in addition to gathering feedback on the pupil's own perception of his main concerns.

CONFIDENTIAL BEGINNING THERAPY QUESTIONNAIRE FOR PUPILS

What is this form?

All pupils go through this confidential questionnaire during their first meeting or first few sessions. It offers us the chance to think together about how support might help you. This form does not have your name on it and will not be shown to parents or teachers. It is for our use only. Brief answers to the questions will be written down. This is only so that we have a record of our conversation to return to if we choose. Near the end of our time together, we will go back to this questionnaire so that we can see how coming here has made a difference. I will keep your form in my own file, which I will have with me each week.

SCHOOL: _____ PUPIL'S INITIALS: _____
THERAPIST: _____ DATE: _____

PART I helps us to clarify why you are coming to see me

What do you think you need support with?
I need support with/ I'm worried about *(complete the sentence)*
_____

How bad is it?
Not too bad 1 2 3 4 5 6 7 8 9 **10 Very bad**

When you feel this way, how strong are the feelings or the thoughts?
Not very strong 1 2 3 4 5 6 7 8 9 **10 Very strong**

Why do you think the school wants you to see me?

How bad do you think school feels this is?
Not too bad 1 2 3 4 5 6 7 8 9 **10 Very bad**

The school asked me to see you because *(explain the main reasons for the referral)*

PART 2 gives us a sense of how you are feeling

Which of the following feeling states apply to you? *Select as many as you like:*

_____ **Low confidence**

I feel this some of the time 1 2 3 4 5 6 7 8 9 10 most of the time

When you feel this way, how strong are the feelings or the thoughts?
Not very strong 1 2 3 4 5 6 7 8 9 10 very strong

_____ **Feeling anxious**

I feel this some of the time 1 2 3 4 5 6 7 8 9 10 most of the time

When you feel this way, how strong are the feelings or the thoughts?
Not very strong 1 2 3 4 5 6 7 8 9 10 very strong

_____ **Feeling angry**

I feel this some of the time 1 2 3 4 5 6 7 8 9 10 most of the time

When you feel this way, how strong are the feelings or the thoughts?
Not very strong 1 2 3 4 5 6 7 8 9 10 very strong

_____ **Feeling down**

I feel this some of the time 1 2 3 4 5 6 7 8 9 10 most of the time

When you feel this way, how strong are the feelings or the thoughts?
Not very strong 1 2 3 4 5 6 7 8 9 10 very strong

_____ **Other feelings** *(please describe)*

I feel this some of the time 1 2 3 4 5 6 7 8 9 10 most of the time

When you feel this way, how strong are the feelings or the thoughts?
Not very strong 1 2 3 4 5 6 7 8 9 10 very strong

When you're having difficult feelings or thoughts, what do you do to feel better?

What do you like best about yourself? Name some of your strengths that we can build on.

PART 3 helps us think about how life is for you

Who is in your immediate family? Who is in your extended family or family network? *(E.g. aunts, uncles, cousins, grandparents, step-relations, important family friends.)*

Who lives at home with you?

What do you like best about your family?

Are any relationships in your family causing you concern or difficulty? Yes No

If family relationships are causing you concern or difficulty, how do you feel about it?
Not too bad 1 2 3 4 5 6 7 8 9 10 **Very bad**

Who do you like to spend time with (family, friends)? Or do you prefer to spend time on your own?

Are any relationships outside your family causing you concern or difficulty?

If outside relationships are causing you concern or difficulty, how do you feel about it?
Not too bad 1 2 3 4 5 6 7 8 9 10 **Very bad**

What is school like for you?

If school is not going well, how bad is it?
Not too bad 1 2 3 4 5 6 7 8 9 10 **Very bad**

Are there any classes that cause you particular concern?

If classes are causing you concern, how bad is it?
Not too bad 1 2 3 4 5 6 7 8 9 10 **Very bad**

PART 4 identifies what you most want to change

What stops you from getting the most out of school or your life?

What could we focus on together to help?

What would you most like to change by coming to see me?

Is there anything else you'd like to add?

PART 5 Conclusion

Did you know you were coming here today?

Have you seen someone like me before?

How did you feel about being offered this time?

Is there anything else you'd like to say about seeing me?

CONFIDENTIAL END OF THERAPY FOLLOW-UP QUESTIONNAIRE FOR PUPILS

The school wants to ensure that the service it provides to young people meets their needs. Now that we are nearing the end of our sessions, we are going to identify what has changed for you. The information you provide will only be used to form a picture of the reasons why young people would like support and how much they think their sessions have helped them.

SCHOOL: _____ PUPIL'S INITIALS: _____
THERAPIST: _____ DATE: _____

Reasons for coming

I was worried about *(complete the sentence)*

How worried are you now about this?
Not very worried 1 2 3 4 5 6 7 8 9 10 worried most of the time
How strong are these feelings or thoughts now?
Not very strong 1 2 3 4 5 6 7 8 9 10 very strong

I needed support with *(complete the sentence)*

How bad is it now? not too bad 1 2 3 4 5 6 7 8 9 10 very bad

How strong are these feelings or thoughts now?
Not very strong 1 2 3 4 5 6 7 8 9 10 very strong

The school thought this could help because *(complete the sentence)*
How bad is it now? not too bad 1 2 3 4 5 6 7 8 9 10 very bad

How strong are these feelings or thoughts now?

Not very strong 1 2 3 4 5 6 7 8 9 10 very strong

Which of the following feeling states applied to you when you first started coming?

____ **Low confidence**
Now, I feel this some of the time 1 2 3 4 5 6 7 8 9 10 most of the time

How strong are these feelings or thoughts now?
Not very strong 1 2 3 4 5 6 7 8 9 10 very strong

____ **Feeling anxious**
Now I feel this some of the time 1 2 3 4 5 6 7 8 9 10 most of the time

How strong are these feelings or thoughts now?
Not very strong 1 2 3 4 5 6 7 8 9 10 very strong

____ **Feeling angry**
Now I feel this some of the time 1 2 3 4 5 6 7 8 9 10 most of the time

How strong are these feelings or thoughts now?
Not very strong 1 2 3 4 5 6 7 8 9 10 very strong

____ **Feeling down**
Now I feel this some of the time 1 2 3 4 5 6 7 8 9 10 most of the time

How strong are these feelings or thoughts now?
Not very strong 1 2 3 4 5 6 7 8 9 10 very strong

_____ **Other feelings** (please describe)
Now I feel this some of the time 1 2 3 4 5 6 7 8 9 10 most of the time

How strong are these feelings or thoughts now?
Not very strong 1 2 3 4 5 6 7 8 9 10 very strong

Were any **relationships in your family** causing you concern or difficulty? YES/NO
If so, how do you feel about it now?
Not too bad 1 2 3 4 5 6 7 8 9 10 very bad

Were any **relationships outside your family** causing you concern or difficulty? YES/NO
If so, how do you feel about it now?
Not too bad 1 2 3 4 5 6 7 8 9 10 very bad

Was **school** causing difficulties? YES/NO If so, how do you feel about it now?
Not too bad 1 2 3 4 5 6 7 8 9 10 very bad

Were there any **classes** causing you particular concern? YES/NO If so, how do you feel about it now?
Not too bad 1 2 3 4 5 6 7 8 9 10 very bad

Describe any progress that has been made:

Is there any other feedback you'd like to give?

Using the sample 'Beginning Therapy Questionnaire'

Two examples of how the pupil's questionnaire provided above can be worked through in the first session or sessions are given below.

Example 1

In this example, the client, a Year 8 student, has been referred because of disruptive behaviour in class.

Therapist: Hello, I'm Jane. You must be Carl. Please, take a seat. As you probably know, I'm a school therapist here at London Town Academy.

	My role is to support pupils by helping them to make sense of their feelings and experiences, especially the more difficult or confusing ones. Whatever their age or background, most people can benefit from talking with someone like me. Before we get started, I'd like to clarify a few things with you. I want you to know that I won't be passing information on to the school about what we discuss here – our time together is confidential. However, the school might give me information about what's happening in your life either at home or in school if they feel it would help our work together. As this is an introductory session, I'm going to ask you some questions and we're going to fill in a questionnaire together. I'm going to be writing brief notes directly on the questionnaire so that you and I have a record of what we've discussed. Once we've finished with this, which might take us up to the end of our time today or even another session or two to complete, you'll be deciding what you want to talk about each week and I won't be asking you so many questions. Does this make sense so far?
Carl:	Yes.
Therapist:	This questionnaire will help us to clarify a focus for our work. We'll be able to bring it out and look at it again from time to time to keep us on track or to see if what we're doing here is helping. It's just for our use. I'll make sure we go back to it again near the end of our time together so we can identify what we've achieved. OK?
Carl:	Yes. Fine.
Therapist:	*(The therapist then starts working through the questionnaire with the pupil.)* The first part will help us to think through why you've been offered time with me. You probably know that your Head of Year suggested we meet – do you know why she thought it was a good idea?
Carl:	Because I keep talking back to teachers.
Therapist:	All teachers?
Carl:	Mostly science and PE *(pause)*. Well, sometimes other ones too.
Therapist:	There are always underlying reasons why we behave as we do. Often these reasons are linked to difficult feelings or experiences. I suggest this is a subject we return to. Hopefully, we'll be able to explore together what life is like for you both here in school and at home. To go back to the questionnaire, next to 'reasons for coming' shall I write down, 'Carl says he wants to work on understanding his relationships with his teachers'? [Note how the therapist re-phrases Carl's reason for attending so that it is framed less judgementally.]
Carl:	OK.
Therapist:	Your Head of Year told me that the teachers don't want you to have a bad experience of being at school. In fact, Mrs Jones hopes that by coming here, you'll be able to talk about why it might be hard to

	listen to teachers or to take their feedback. But that's not the only thing we can discuss. Do you think that there is anything else that might be helpful to work on?
Carl:	I don't know.
Therapist:	Anything you're worried or anxious about?
Carl:	I'm not sure.
Therapist:	Maybe things will come to light as you talk more about your life. Let's go on to the second part of the form. Perhaps you could start by telling me about your family.

At this point, the therapist will move on to questions relating to the pupil's life, beginning to explore family and peer relations as well as learning experiences. School therapists using a pupil questionnaire such as this one might choose to expand on the family network question, encouraging the client to make a family map or a picture representing the extended family, using a separate piece of paper and felt-tip pens, or whatever media the therapist provides (e.g. paints, modelling plasticine, clay, etc.). While the client is creating the family representation, the therapist will be closely observing, silently watching out for clues about the young person's unconscious reading of other family members and also how relationships across the extended family and, if applicable, step-parents and siblings, are experienced.

At the same time, the therapist may choose to open up conversations around what is being depicted on the map, inviting the client to talk about how relationships between family members and between generations are experienced, who is most important (branching into extended family to include aunts, uncles, cousins, etc.), who is closest to the client, whether or not both parents still live at home, and, if not, when the separation occurred, whether or not the absent parent is still seen, whether or not there are new partners and stepsiblings, and so forth. The therapist will follow the young person's lead throughout this exchange, choosing at every point along the way either to go forward or to close down the conversation gently with a containing comment such as 'Perhaps this is something we'll want to talk more about in sessions to come.' Throughout, the therapist will be observing the client's expressions and tracking her own feelings as well as noting to herself relevant details, such as how the map is laid out, whether it is created with confidence or self-consciousness, sketchily or with care, in an engaged way or indifferently, and so on. These observations may be written up in process notes at the end of the session.

Some questions might trigger uncomfortable feelings. For example, when asking a young person to describe something he is self-conscious or wary about, such as 'Are there any relationships in your family causing you difficulty?' he may give a two-word reply: 'My dad.' In this case, the therapist may ask 'Can you say more about that?' to encourage him to talk in more detail. Or the therapist might make a mental note of the client's wariness and choose not to go any further at this stage, knowing there will be ample opportunity to go back to this subject in subsequent sessions.

If the mapping exercise prompts an easy conversational flow, the therapist may choose to continue to expand on the themes under discussion, making space for significant family events to be disclosed and important stories to be told. During this process, the pupil questionnaire might be put to one side. The therapist may not write anything down on it at this point, as the mapping exercise will provide a useful record.

Moving through the questionnaire, when asking about whom the young person likes to spend time with, the therapist might need to be ready to broaden out the question to ask *how* the young person likes to spend time, asking about favourite activities, which could include listening to music, playing on the computer and anything else the therapist thinks might be relevant to the young person. This can be a sensitive way of approaching the question with clients who find it difficult to name family members or peers they really enjoy being with or who may not have any friends in or out of school and feel somewhat exposed by the question.

When talking about school-based experiences, the client may bring up classes that are particularly problematic or hard for him to manage. The therapist could use the unfolding conversation to role-model focusing on the nature and quality of the client's relationships and the ensuing feelings rather than the facts. For example, the young person could be encouraged to describe more specifically how he experiences the particular teacher he claims he is having a reaction to. Is the teacher, for example, coming across to the client as critical, demanding, unapproachable and with a tendency to single the client out unfairly? Or is the teacher seen as overlooking the client, never noticing that he is struggling, and often favouring other pupils? Perhaps the client feels he is the only one who can't follow the lesson. The therapist might then ask questions such as 'What's it like for you when it feels as if the rest of the class can keep up and you think you're the only one who can't?' You can also challenge distorted perceptions: 'When you think about it, is it really true that you are the *only* one?' Or 'When your teacher gets cross with you for falling behind, what do you imagine she is thinking? Is she really cross? Maybe your teacher is disappointed or frustrated because she knows you have the potential to do better.'

These examples serve to illustrate how the pupil's questionnaire can be used as a way of generating meaningful connections and building bridges between the therapist and client, thus ensuring that the conversational space is not left empty for too long. Therapists use their own judgement to determine how active they feel they need to be with each client. This will be based on closely tracking how the client is experiencing silences as they come up. Does a period of silence provide a valued opportunity for reflection or does it raise anxieties that are felt as too persecuting? Does the client have the capacity for sustaining the conversation? Or does he try to fill the space with nervous chatter? The first phase of the work will inevitably evoke the kinds of anxieties particular to new situations, which usually include feeling self-conscious, a little awkward or even quite exposed. The questionnaire can function as a safe structure that can scaffold what might otherwise be experienced as a terrifying void-like space.

For some young people, the questionnaire will provide an effective way of role-modelling how sessions can be used, especially for those who have little or no history of thinking about their experiences, stepping back and reflecting on their feelings, making links and working out why situations unfold as they do, trying to understand why certain feelings are always triggered in particular moments, and so on.

At the end of the session, the therapist might say:

> We're almost at the end of our time for today. As we haven't finished this questionnaire yet, we can return to it next week. I'm beginning to get a clearer picture of your life, which is very useful. Before we stop, I want to remind you that once we finish with this questionnaire, I won't be asking you so many questions. It will be up to you to decide what you want to focus on each week. As I said earlier, I won't be passing on to the school any specific information about what we talk about here. Of course, if something comes up that I feel we could use extra support with, then I will want to share it with the school. In that case, I'll discuss it with you first.

The therapist may then show the client his folder, adding,

> I have a folder here for you. If you choose to use the art materials, we'll keep what you make in the folder. I'm going to put your family map and questionnaire in here as well. Once it's finished, it will stay in here so that we can bring it out at any time. For example, if you find it hard to think about what to talk about, we can refer back to the questionnaire or to your family map and see what comes up. I should also note that it can take a little time to get used to our sessions. For that reason, I always suggest that young people come for five or six times before making their mind up about how they feel about seeing me. We've now reached the end of our time today. If you get out your school planner, you can put our appointment down for period 3 next Tuesday. Just make your own way here. I look forward to seeing you then.

If the questionnaire has been completed in the first session, then the therapist can conclude the session by saying:

> We're almost at the end of our time for today. We've finished the questionnaire, so I'm going to put it in the folder I have here for you. You can bring it out anytime you choose to and pick up on some of the subjects we've covered so far. Even if we don't go back to it, I'll make sure we look at it again in our last few sessions so we can gauge how much coming here has helped.

The therapist can continue along the lines indicated above, reminding the client that what is spoken about remains confidential before ending with confirmation of the time and day of the next booked appointment.

There will be instances when even the first session reveals at-risk behaviour or serious concerns about the child's mental state, home life or other safeguarding issues. For example, in response to the question 'When you're having difficult feelings or thoughts, what do you do to feel better?' a young person might say, 'I cut myself.' The therapist may have to contain a strong reaction to such a blunt statement, or indeed to any disclosure of this kind, and use the opening created to sensitively ask a few clarifying questions relating to how long it has been going on, how frequently it is happening, where it happens (at school, at home, both), who knows about it, what seems to prompt it, and so on. It can help if the therapist can respond to the communication in a containing way by conveying her understanding that cutting is a response to difficult and seemingly unbearable feelings that the physical pain distracts from or makes more real. The therapist will also need to tell the young person that she will be talking in confidence to the teacher in the school responsible for pupils' well-being and ask how this feels. It is most useful if the therapist can convey that the adults can come together and think about the client rather than getting the client into some form of trouble because of the disclosure. The therapist does not have to convey that some kind of 'crisis management' is called for or even of knowing exactly what needs to be done. Every situation is unique and needs to be thought through carefully with the relevant school staff and with the client. This can be discussed directly with the young person. The therapist will want to consult with her supervisor as well to try to understand what cutting means for this particular young person and what the unconscious triggers are.

Example 2

The client in this example was referred to the school counsellor because her father died. In this case, the therapist can start the session off in much the same way as described in the example above, introducing herself, explaining how the first session will be structured around the questionnaire, talking about confidentiality and then progressing as follows:

Therapist: The first part of this questionnaire will help us to think through why you've been offered time with me. You probably know that your Head of Year suggested we meet – do you know why he thought it was a good idea?

Makeda: Because my dad died last year?

Therapist: Yes, Mr Smith knows that a family death is a significant experience. It stirs up feelings and thoughts that might be painful, uncomfortable or just hard to understand or make sense of. We can use our time together to think about what your dad's death meant for you. We might also talk about what it was like before he died and what's changed. But there may be other things that you want to focus on. We don't have to talk only about your dad. What would you like me to put down as the reason or reasons you're coming here?

Makeda:	Because my dad died.
Therapist:	I'll write that in. [As the therapist is writing, she might say, 'A father's death is a big thing for any young person to go through. We'll have plenty of time over this term to go back to this. It's an important subject.']
Therapist:	Next, you can see that there is a list of feeling states to choose from, such as 'low confidence', 'anxious', 'angry' or 'low in mood' and a space if you want to add something else. What best describes what you'd like support with? You can tick as many as you'd like or name your own.
Makeda:	Feeling sad.
Therapist:	Feeling sad – yes, I can imagine that losing a dad can leave one feeling very sad. I'll write that here where it says 'other feelings'.
Makeda:	And alone.
Therapist:	Well, let's add that too. I'll write in 'sad and alone'. Can you say, on a scale of 1 to 10, how sad you feel? One is just a little sad and 10 is very, very sad?
Makeda:	I guess it would be 8 or 9, sometimes maybe more.
Therapist:	And what about 'alone'?
Makeda:	The same for 'alone'.
Therapist:	It sounds like it's been a difficult time for you. It can be very painful when a parent dies, no matter how old you are. I'll put '8 or 9' here. Hopefully, that will change as we work together. It takes time to come to terms with such a big loss. The next part looks at what your life is like. I don't know much about you yet. It could be helpful if you made a family map. There's no right or wrong way to do it. You can use circles for females and squares for males or make up your own shapes or even sketch in the people. What do you think?
Makeda:	I'd like to do that.
Therapist:	Please help yourself to paper. You can use coloured felt tips or a pencil. It's up to you.

From this point on, as in the first example above, the therapist will decide how to progress, attuning herself to the client and pacing the session accordingly. As this first meeting draws to a close, the therapist might want to check in with Makeda, asking her how it has felt talking about herself and her family.

Evaluating progress

When using a follow-up questionnaire, the original form is revisited. Looking back at what was recorded and focusing on the areas that are measurable will give both the therapist and the client a chance to think about what changes have taken place over the course of the work.

During these final sessions, you can help your client to identify general progress in addition to, or instead of, seeing if the original aims were met. For example, if a young person can't think of anything that has changed for the better, you might refer to what you have observed, saying:

> I've noticed you seem more confident here with me. You're more able to make eye contact, you can decide for yourself how you want to use your time with me and you seem more relaxed in the sessions. What did it feel like when you first came to see me? What does it feel like now?' [This can be expanded on:] And what about in general? You mentioned you can talk about what's on your mind here with me. What about with friends or at home? Do you feel comfortable speaking out in general? Can you give any specific examples?

With your client's agreement, you can include this kind of progress in a follow-up form.

The feedback you gather, along with your own observations, can be written up in an end of therapy report. Ideally, the report should present material that is useful while, at the same time, respecting your client's confidentiality. Knowing what to include, how to word it and what might be best left out requires some thought. It is recommended that trainees review this in their supervision.

Even when a referral from the school is very sketchy and there are no opportunities to talk to teachers or parents, the school therapist can make the most of her direct experience of her client. Striking first impressions based on how the client comes across, and on the therapist's own feelings and thoughts in response to the young person, can be written down afterwards. The therapist's initial notes could include observations such as the following:

> All I know is that Ola's father died in March last year. He seems very wary; comes across as anxious whenever his dad is referred to; does not seem used to thinking about himself; is finding it hard to open up; he even looks quite closed and detached; I can feel stuck when I'm with him – at a real loss for words (maybe this is how he feels? he may not have the language to describe the experience he's been through); hard to feel myself warming towards him; feel pushed away (perhaps he feels pushed away by his mother who must be going through her own grief process – sounds like it was a close family from what I've gathered so far).

And so on.

When the final phase of work is reached, the therapist may be able to reflect on some of the changes she has noticed and summarise them in a brief written description such as the following:

> Ola's father died last spring. When Ola started his sessions with me, he came across as wary and somewhat withholding. Thinking about himself was a new experience for him. As our work progressed, he was able to relax and to start to reflect on his loss. His communication style improved and he was

more fluent in general. He was increasingly able to make eye contact and hold it. There were moments when he let himself show what he was feeling, which was a considerable risk for him to take. He said he was able to talk to his mother and let her know what he's feeling. In my view, his anxiety decreased considerably as our sessions unfolded and, by the last phase of our work together, he was able to engage in a more meaningful way with me.

A snapshot summary such as the one outlined above can be written up along with the name of the teacher making the original referral, the number of sessions offered and the number attended. Even a document this brief can provide a record of a client's progress, illuminate the importance of grief work, identify positive changes and protect confidentiality. A carefully worded short report represents the first step in creating an evidence base for therapy services in schools.

Conclusion

The majority of therapists monitor their service as a matter of course, often shaping a therapeutic focus and recording their careful observations in the first phase and weaving evaluation into the last two or three sessions. As this chapter has illustrated, creating a more formal structure for this process does not have to be a time-consuming exercise. The sample questionnaires reproduced in this chapter can be used by school therapists as a handy reference to aid their thinking processes. As has been described, simply taking note of a few key observations at the start of work with each client that can be looked back on at the end of the work and written up in summary form can be a good place to start.

School therapists make an inestimable contribution to pupils' well-being, one that often goes unrecorded and may even be taken for granted. Writing up short reports can capture the nature of the therapeutic encounter while raising awareness of how therapy works. We've all been touched on many levels and in different ways by our work in schools. It is vital that the deeply human – and humbling – experience of engaging with a child or adolescent who is in some way struggling to articulate his pain or confusion does not go unnoticed and is given the value it deserves. Creating an evidence base for our service does not have to be seen as an empty, 'box-ticking' exercise or as a process that will distort our practice. Instead, school therapists can work towards structuring their feedback so that their professional integrity is preserved while at the same time the process is illuminated, progress is recorded and the client's confidentiality is respected.

Reference

Goodman, R., Meltzer, H. and Bailey, V. (1998) The Strengths and Difficulties Questionnaire: A Pilot Study on the Validity of the Self-Report Version. *European Child and Adolescent Psychiatry*, 7, 125–130.

Afterword

Lyn French and Reva Klein

One of the central themes running through this book is that therapists who are working in schools, especially those taking up a post or a trainee placement for the first time, face a complex task within a complicated setting. We have seen how everyone in the school community, including all school staff, parents and pupils will have mixed reactions to and conscious and unconscious assumptions about what the word 'therapy' signifies, what therapy services can and cannot offer and what it means to provide such services on the school site during curriculum time. As well, we have noted how vulnerable or at-risk children and adolescents stir up powerful primitive fantasies and anxieties that resonate for all of us on different levels and in different ways. For example, the teacher who as a secondary school pupil suffered unnoticed and in silence when her own mother died may consciously want her pupils with family bereavements to be helped but may unconsciously envy the support offered to them, as she was not given access to a therapist when she so acutely felt her own loss as an adolescent.

As therapists working in schools and supervising trainees, we believe that we can approach our work with more compassion and greater understanding if we learn to take up a position akin to that of the observer/participant. This book has attempted to illustrate how vital it is to be able to stand back and resist taking situations personally, such as those instances when teachers or parents cancel or do not show up for meetings, room bookings are changed, school staff idealise the service at the start only to lose interest when challenging pupils do not change quickly enough, and so on. By following the age-old adage of putting ourselves in their shoes, we can see how the known and hidden pressures schools and families face can easily result in varying forms of unconscious acting out. We, too, will inevitably act out, but our training and ongoing supervision provide us with the tools and internal resources to recognise our own role and that of others, to keep an open mind, hold onto the larger picture and go on thinking even in those moments when we can't help but feel disempowered, deskilled or undervalued, or when we catch ourselves taking up a role that we feel is in some way counter-productive.

The practitioners contributing to this book have a common interest in psychoanalytic and psychodynamic ideas. However, the goal was not to add to the rich collection of theoretical literature that already exists. Instead, a shared aim has been to present a kind of 'tool kit' combining descriptions of the practice of therapy with study guidelines or questions to support therapists beginning their work in schools and in delivering individual sessions to children and adolescents. This task was not undertaken lightly. Understandably, we were reluctant to suggest that what, in practice, is careful work uniquely shaped and defined by and with each client, can be reduced to a 'how to' manual. The comparison with learning a new language that was first alluded to in the introduction can be usefully returned to here. We all know that learning the basics of a foreign language can be aided with the use of workbooks and exercises. However, to truly speak it, one must get a feel for it and make it one's own. The same can be said for the language of therapy. We hope that what we have provided here will not only function as a useful reference book but also go some way towards containing some of the anxiety we can all feel in taking up a new role for the first time. Some of the most helpful supervision we have experienced has been in those instances when a supervisor has not only shared examples of her own practice but also had the courage to reveal what it is *really* like to try to work with a staff member, parent or child when their anxieties are triggered and acting out – theirs and ours – results. We hope we have achieved something similar here.

Finally, these chapters have been written by practitioners, most of whom have been, or are, involved in ongoing work in inner-city schools in London, England, as either psychotherapists, counsellors, art therapists or play therapists. All the examples provided come from real-life experiences of working in the school context. Although at times the material discussed may cover similar ground, different ways of articulating the same thing can deepen understanding, just as new perspectives can generate new insights. We hope the same applies to the chapters in this book and that the variations in style, tone and presentation do not get in the way of furthering understanding.

It is the authors' hope that the themes covered in the chapters will be relevant to professionals who are providing counselling, child psychotherapy and creative therapies in schools around the world, whether in inner-city, suburban or rural settings. If we have achieved our aim, the book will serve as an eminently useful resource that will be turned to again and again to help support trainees and newly qualified therapists as they acquire their own individual perceptions and language in their work.

Index

acting out *see* enactments
adolescents: challenges of 23, 157; meeting the needs of 68; responsive to structured approach 46–7; school-based therapy for *see* secondary school-based practice of therapy
Adult Attachment Interview 106
age 161
aggression 42–3 *see also* anger management/containment
ambivalence 13, 43, 63, 73, 153, 158–9, 184; attachment and the ambivalent child 42
anger management/containment 40, 105, 166
anxieties: anticipating parental anxieties 115–16; and the beginning of the therapeutic relationship 148, 152–3; containment of 148; and defences 19, 27, 109 *see also* defences; and disclosures 173–4; 'here and now' 109, 189; maternal 11; study questions 27; in taking up school-based therapy 1–3; of teachers 63–4; understanding core anxieties 109
appointment systems 72–3; appointment slips 139; timetables of therapy sessions 84
assessment process 99–112; and the boundaries of confidentiality 105–6; building on the referral information 124–5; family trees and 106–7, 108; first encounter 101–2, 107–10 *see also* first session of therapy; introducing the therapy 107–10; parents and 103–4; particular areas to cover 109–10; piecing together a picture of the client 100; primary school setting 102–4; profiling forms 125–6, 210–15; of risk 104–5;

secondary school setting 104; Strengths and Difficulties Questionnaire 125, 208; study questions 111–12; summary assessment in supervision presentation 203–4; taking histories 106–7
associations 2, 56–7, 58, 63, 188; cultural 53–4, 57
attachment: Adult Attachment Interview 106; categories of 106; insecure 37, 106, 207; patterns 2, 41–2, 55, 106, 187, 207; secure 106, 147, 187; and stories 44; in the therapeutic relationship 22
avoidance 41–2 *see also* resistance

beginning therapy questionnaires 216–19, 221–7
beginning therapy reports 208, 209
Bettelheim, Bruno 45
Bion, Wilfred R. 21, 22, 36
Brearley, Mike 8

carers *see* parents/carers
case notes 201–6; summary of the client 204–5; using notes in supervision 202–4
child-friendly language 2, 138, 145, 147, 157, 165
child protection 2, 76; disclosures 117, 173–4
children: adolescents *see* adolescents; attachment patterns 2, 41–2, 55, 106, 187, 207 *see also* attachment; the avoidant child 41–2; building a picture of the child 93, 100; the child who is open 22; disclosures 173–4; the disorganised child 42; drawings by 45–6; early experience *see* early experience; education history of 125; gaining trust of 23; impact of previous experiences of professionals 22; infants

see infants; informing the primary school child about the first session 73, 133–8; informing the secondary school client about the first session 138–9; missing therapy sessions 73, 142–3; observation of *see* observation; offering of therapy in schools to *see* primary school-based practice of therapy; school-based therapy; secondary school-based practice of therapy; perceptions of therapy 62–3, 64; the resistant or ambivalent child 42 *see also* resistance; school-based therapy with *see* school-based therapy; seeing ourselves through the child's eye 26; stories of 44–5; understanding of reason for therapy 21, 37, 144–5; understanding of role of therapist 62

Children's Appercention Test 46

classroom support workers 71, 132, 134, 138–9, 172

clay 20, 87

collusion 111, 154

communication *see also* language: generalising 39; interpretation *see* interpretation; non-verbal 39–40; normalising 39; questioning techniques 39; reflecting back 39; of the transference *see* transference

confidentiality 171–3; assessment and the boundaries of 105–6; and disclosures 117, 173–4; explaining confidentiality contract to children 145; explaining confidentiality to parents 117; and feedback 70, 105

consent, parental 71–2

containment: of anger 40, 166; of anxieties 148; of behaviour in the session 165, 166; being a containing presence 147–8, 165–6; of confidentiality *see* confidentiality; of disturbing thoughts 68; and the ending process 191; and the first session of therapy 147–8; through interpretation 165; lack of 38, 42; in managing self-destructive fantasies and behaviours 69; of naming emotions 58 *see also* naming emotions/feelings; symbolised by folders 88 *see also* folders; of the therapeutic relationship 147–8, 165–6 *see also* therapeutic relationship; therapist's capacity for 36, 165–6; therapist's thoughtful containing response 56; therapy room as symbolic container 79 *see also* therapy room

counselling room *see* therapy room

counter-transference: as a powerful tool 31–2, 155; and projective identification 14–17; study questions 34

culture: cultural associations 53–4, 57; cultural beliefs 64; school ethos 55, 60, 61, 72, 75, 131–2, 140, 207; therapeutic 79 *see also* therapeutic frame; working with cultural differences 153–5

Dale, Francis 39

defences: and anxieties 19, 27, 109; and the child who is open 22; denial 25–6; and early experience 11–12, 19; and the ending process 191–2; impact of children's previous experiences of professionals 22; naming defences 165; need for 19, 21, 27; and the need for patience 24–5; observation of defensive behaviour 43–4; projection *see* projection; seeing what is in front of us 21–2; splitting 13–14; study questions 27; against vulnerability 11; and working with trauma and grief 23–4, 228–9

denial 25–6 *see also* repression

disclosures 117, 173–4

Dockar-Drysdale, Barbara 38

drawings 45–6; kinetic family 46

early experience *see also* infants: and the formation of defences 11–12, 19; importance of 10–12; and the unconscious 9–12

education histories 125

ego 20; ideal 57; strength 110

emotional learning 54–5, 76, 157; emotional literacy 61, 161; integration with knowledge-based learning 57–8; naming emotions/feelings 58, 109, 147, 164–5, 177

emotional management 10, 11, 12

emotional receptivity 110, 187

enactments 26, 28–9, 69, 140, 143, 192, 230; and the transference 26, 28–9 *see also* transference

ending process 187–97; and client defences 191–2; and client opportunities 190–1; end of therapy follow-up questionnaire 219–21; end of therapy reports 175–83, 210; goals of working

through endings 189–90; importance of working through endings 187–8; meaning of endings 188–9; post-therapy questionnaires 210–15; study questions 194–7; and the therapist's expectations 193–4; therapist's preparation for 192; therapist's support in 193
envy 30, 58; of teachers 56, 64
evaluation: evaluating progress 227–9; identifying impact of school-based therapy 207–29; primary school setting 208–15; questionnaires *see* questionnaires; reports *see* reports; secondary school setting 215–27
evidence-based practice 3–4; identifying impact of school-based therapy 207–29; primary school setting 208–15; questionnaires *see* questionnaires; reports *see* reports; secondary school setting 215–27; teachers' focus on 64
expectation management 58, 74–5; parental 117–18

family life: importance of early experience 10–12; mother–infant relationship *see* mother–infant relationship; parents *see* parents/carers; separations and changing family composition 158–9, 188, 223; working with differences 157–9
family trees 106–7, 108
fantasies 22, 63, 64, 65, 68; managing self-destructive fantasies 69; revenge fantasies 69; triggering of 57; unconscious 2, 53, 57, 63, 64, 65
feedback: from the child 146, 219–21; and confidentiality 70, 105; end of therapy follow-up questionnaire 219–21; invitation for 146; to parents 115; from parents 209; in reports *see* reports; to the school 207; in supervision 205–6; to the therapist 62, 63, 146, 183, 205–6, 209, 219–21
first session of therapy 142–51; and the assessment process 101–2, 107–10; beginning therapy questionnaire used in 221–7; building a working alliance 147–8; and containment 147–8; how the child is collected or arrives at the therapy room 142–4; informing client about *see* informing the child/young person about the first session; introductions 144–6; and language 145, 147; practical approaches to 144–6,

148; preparing for 139–40; primary school setting 142–50; study questions 149–51; unconscious factors involved with a child coming on their own 142–3
folders 84, 88, 146, 164, 167, 194, 225
forgetting 9, 15, 24, 111, 142–3
Fraser Principle 71
Freud, Sigmund: defences 19; resistance 20

gender 159–60
generalising 39
genograms 106–7, 108
glitter 87
governors 61–2
grief 194; working with 23–4, 228–9
guilt 20, 30, 45, 69, 87, 187–8, 194

Harris, Martha 38
hatred 13, 187, 190
head teachers 3, 55, 60–1, 65, 67, 72, 76, 81, 83, 91, 114, 174
Holmes, Jeremy 37–8
hostility 42–3

idealisation 14; challenging idealised notions of therapy 58; ego ideal 57
infants: development of capacity to think 36; development of symbolic functioning 38–9; importance of early experience 10–12; mother–infant relationship *see* mother–infant relationship; projective identification 36; and the roots of defences 11–12, 19
inferiority feelings 152, 157
informing the child/young person about the first session 131–41; primary school setting 73, 133–8; secondary school setting 138–9; study questions 141
insecurity 11, 13, 40, 142 *see also* inferiority feelings; insecure attachment 37, 106, 207; maternal 11; and stories 44
inter-generational networks 54
internal world 2, 26, 29, 57, 106, 114–15; internal space 147 *see also* neutral space; potential space; therapeutic space
interpretation: containment through 165; observation and 36–48; reflecting back 39; sensitivity in 38–40

interruptions: preventing 82–3; during therapy sessions 83–4

Joseph, Betty 26

kinetic family drawings 46
Klein, Melanie 42–3
Koppitz, Elizabeth M. 45

language: child-friendly 2, 138, 145, 147, 157, 165; therapeutic 2, 116, 144, 147
learning: emotional 54–5, 57–8, 76, 157; integration of emotional and knowledge-based 57–8; our relationship to 53–4; and vulnerability 11–12

Main, Mary 106
materials 85–8; dealing with different materials 86–8; storage 84, 88; study questions 89
Meltzer, Donald 25
mentalisation 99, 110
monitoring *see* case notes; evaluation; reports
mother–infant relationship 10–11, 36; and aggression 42–3; and the development of capacity to think 36; and the importance of early experience 10–11; negotiation of separations and loss 187; solitary play in the presence of the mother 38; weaning 187
mourning 187, 188, 189

nameless dread 20–1, 43
naming emotions/feelings 58, 109, 147, 164–5, 177
negative transference 30–1, 114, 155, 156
neutral space 68–9
non-verbal communication 39–40
normalising 39

observation: of attachment patterns 41–2; of defensive behaviour 43–4; early observation and setting the tone for the therapy 37–8; and interpretation 36–48; looking for clues 44; seeing what is in front of us 21–2; self-observation *see* self-observation; of the transference 40–1
open questioning 39

paints 85, 87

parents/carers: and the assessment process 103–4; coping mechanisms 119; feedback from 209; feedback to 115; gathering information from 118–19; goal setting with 119; informing the child/young person about the first therapy session 134, 135; meeting and working with 72, 113–23, 157–8; parental consent 71–2; perceptions of their children's problems 118; projection by 115; resilience 119; teachers talking to 63; transference of 114–15; views of school-based therapy 65
passivity 43
patience 17, 24–5, 26
perception: and mind patterns 8–9; and self-deception 8
persecutory feelings 11
play: approach to activities and 46–7; making sense of spontaneous play 47; sand play 47; solitary play in the presence of the mother 38
play dough 85, 87, 88
potential space 36
power dynamics 155–6
pre-transference 109
primary school-based practice of therapy 60–6; advantages 61; assessment process 102–4; children's perception of 64; from the child's perspective 62–3; evaluating the impact of 208–15; first session of therapy 142–50; informing the child/young person about the first session 73, 133–8; limitations 61–2; multi-agency framework of 61; parents' and carers' views 65; profile 60–1; referrals 63, 92, 93, 95–6; study questions 66; teachers' attitudes and responses to 63–4; teachers' role 63
profiling forms 125–6, 210–15
projection 9, 19; being at receiving end of negative projection 58; and gender 160; by parents 115; and splitting 13–14; by teachers 58, 63–4; and transference 13–14 *see also* transference
projective identification 36; and counter-transference 14–17
psychoanalytic framework of therapy 7–18; counter-transference *see* counter-transference; and the dangers of theory 7; defences *see* defences; importance of early experience 10–12;

interpretation *see* interpretation; the need of theory 7–8, 17; observing *see* observation; projection and transference 13–14 *see also* projection; transference; projective identification and counter-transference 14–17 *see also* counter-transference; from the psychodynamic perspective 8–13 *see also* psychodynamic therapy; relationship in the therapy room 12–13 *see also* therapeutic relationship; resistance in the therapy room 20–1 *see also* resistance; study questions 18; transference *see* transference; the unconscious 8–9 *see also* the unconscious

psychodynamic therapy 8–13, 54–5; approach to activities and play 46–7; and the challenges of adolescents 23; and the child who is open 22; counter-transference *see* counter-transference; gaining children's trust 23; and the importance of early experience 10–12; observing and interpreting 36–48 *see also* interpretation; observation; recognising defences, resistance and anxieties 19–27; in schools *see* school-based therapy; seeing ourselves through the child's eye 26; seeing what is in front of us 21–2; theoretical framework of *see* psychoanalytic framework of therapy; and the transference *see* transference; and the unconscious 8–13; use of relationship in the room 12–13 *see also* therapeutic relationship; working with trauma and grief 23–4, 228–9

questioning techniques 39
questionnaires: as assessment tools 208–10; beginning therapy 216–19, 221–7; end of therapy follow-up 219–21; pre- and post-therapy 210–15; Strengths and Difficulties Questionnaire 125, 208

race 155–6
receptivity 37, 54, 99, 126; emotional 110, 187
referral process 90–8; building a picture of the child 93; building on the referral information 124–5; and ensuring the therapy service is valued 95; general principles 90–1; guidelines 93; liaison and collaboration 92; meeting complex needs 94; primary school setting 63, 92, 93, 95–6; referral forms 95–8, 124–5; referral structures 91; and the school context 94; secondary school setting 71, 73–4, 92, 97–8; study questions 98; urgent referrals 73–4
reports 174–5, 207–8; beginning therapy reports 208, 209; end of therapy reports 175–83, 210; and evidence-based practice 4, 207–10
repression 20, 28–9, 44, 114, 188, 191
resilience 17, 26, 119, 189
resistance 20–1 *see also* defences; denial; repression; attachment and the resistant child 42; and the challenges of adolescents 23; denial 25–6; and gender 160; grief, trauma and 23–4; and the need for patience 24–5
resources: materials *see* materials; study questions 89; toys *see* toys
revenge 69, 143
review sessions 75
risk assessment 104–5
room allocation 56; effects on therapeutic relationship 56, 79; multi-use room 82; negotiation 80–2
The Royal Family 9

sand play 47
school-based therapy: and age 161 *see also* primary school-based practice of therapy; secondary school-based practice of therapy; anxieties in taking up 1–3; appointment systems 72–3; approach to activities and play 46–7; assessment process *see* assessment process; building a working alliance 147–8 *see also* therapeutic relationship; case notes *see* case notes; and the challenges of adolescents 23 *see also* adolescents; challenging idealised notions of therapy 58; children missing sessions 73, 142–3; child's understanding of reason for therapy 21, 37, 144–5; conscious and unconscious messages conveyed by a service 56–7; and cultural differences 153–5; disclosures and 117, 173–4; ending *see* ending process; establishing a service 55; expectation management 58, 74–5; and the family 157–9 *see also*

parents/carers; first session *see* first session of therapy; gaining children's trust 23; and gender 159–60; informing the child/young person about the first session 73, 131–41; and the integration of emotional and knowledge-based learning 57–8; managing self-destructive fantasies and behaviour 69; managing the therapeutic frame 82–4, 164–9 *see also* therapeutic frame; meetings with teachers and staff 124–30; observing and interpreting 36–48 *see also* interpretation; observation; parents/carers and *see* parents/carers; and power dynamics 155–6; in primary schools *see* primary school-based practice of therapy; progressing through first phase 146; promotion and nurturing of idea 55, 58, 95; and race 155–6; referral process *see* referral process; resistance in the therapy room 20–1 *see also* resistance; room *see* room allocation; therapy room; in secondary schools *see* secondary school-based practice of therapy; and social identity 156–7; supporting emotional learning and well-being 54–5; symbolic function of service of 53–9; teachers/staff and *see* teachers/staff; theoretical framework of *see* psychoanalytic framework of therapy; and the wider network 69, 92 *see also* Special Educational Needs Coordinators; working with difference 152–63; working with teachers and staff 58, 72, 124–30, 170–86; working with the system 171–86; working with trauma and grief 23–4, 228–9
school governors 61–2
school life: conscious and unconscious messages conveyed by a therapy service in 56–7; inter-generational networks 54; school ethos 55, 60, 61, 72, 75, 131–2, 140, 207; school's primary task 53; support of emotional learning and well-being 55; therapy and whole school development 67–8
school support workers 71, 132, 134, 138–9, 172
school teachers *see* teachers/staff
school therapists *see* therapists
secondary school-based practice of therapy 67–76; appointment systems 72–3, 139; assessment process 104; contact with parents 72; contact with teachers 72; evaluating the impact of 215–27; and the impact of the unconscious 68–9; informing the client about the first session 138–9; managing expectations 74–5; managing self-destructive fantasies or behaviour 69; meeting the needs of adolescents 68; parental consent 71–2; referrals 71, 73–4, 92, 97–8; review sessions 75; service context 70; service structure and management 70–1; study questions 76; waiting lists 74; and whole school development 67–8; and the wider network 69 *see also* Special Educational Needs Coordinators
security *see also* insecurity: maternal 11; secure attachment 106, 147, 187; and stories 44–5
self-deception 8, 9
self-destructive behaviour: management 69; risk assessment 104–5
self-esteem 11, 25, 45, 93, 110, 157, 174
self-observation 40; seeing ourselves through the child's eye 26; use of the counter-transference *see* counter-transference
self-reflection 110
SENCos *see* Special Educational Needs Coordinators
shame 20, 42, 115
slips of the tongue 44
social identity 156–7
Special Educational Needs Coordinators (SENCos) 70, 91, 99, 100, 124, 125, 126, 127, 132, 134, 138, 139
splitting 13–14
storage 84, 88
stories: children's 44–5; therapist's use of 39–40
Strengths and Difficulties Questionnaire 125, 208
suicide 69, 105
supervision: and disclosures 173; and the processing of our internal responses 58; as a provision of external space 147; receiving feedback in 205–6; use of case notes in 202–4
supply teachers 64, 144
support workers 71, 132, 134, 138–9, 172
symbolic functioning: conditions for evolution of 38–9; of the ending process

190; of a school-based therapy service 53–9; symbolic message of the room allocation 56; of therapy room 79

teachers/staff: anxieties 63–4; attitudes and responses to therapists and their service 56–7, 62, 63–4; and confidentiality of therapy 105, 171–3; envy of 56, 64; feedback to 105; head teachers *see* head teachers; helping them see improvements 174; informing the child/young person about the first therapy session 133–4, 135, 138–9; interruptions by 82–4; meeting with 124–30; positive attitudes to therapy 63; primary school 63–4, 91, 133–4; projection by 58, 63–4; referrals from *see* referral process; secondary school 72, 126, 138–9; SENCos *see* Special Educational Needs Coordinators; study questions on meetings with 127–30; study questions on working with 183–6; supply teachers 64, 144; talking to parents 63; therapy and the role of 63 *see also* referral process; working with 58, 72, 124–30, 170–86
teenagers *see* adolescents
theoretical framework of therapy *see* psychoanalytic framework of therapy
therapeutic frame: appointment systems 72–3; confidentiality *see* confidentiality; folders 84, 88, 146, 164, 167, 194, 225; gifts and cards 196–7; interventions to manage behaviour in the session 166; managing the frame 82–4, 164–9; materials *see* materials; preventing/dealing with interruptions 82–4; and responding to offers of gifts or cards 167, 196–7; the room *see* room allocation; therapy room; study questions on management of 167–9; therapists' role in 164–6; toys *see* toys
therapeutic language 2, 116, 144
therapeutic relationship: anxieties at start of 148, 152–3; assessing client's capacity to form therapeutic alliance 110; and confidentiality *see* confidentiality; containment in 147–8, 165–6; creating a safe therapeutic space 147, 148–9; effects of the room 56, 79; and the first session 147–8; and gender 159–60; impact of children's previous experiences of professionals 22; use of relationship in the room 12–13; vulnerability in 22, 37
therapeutic space: allowing children to test 21; creating a safe space 147, 148–9 *see also* therapeutic relationship; frame of *see* therapeutic frame; physical room *see* therapy room; unobtrusiveness in 38–9
therapeutic stance 36, 68, 74, 109, 136–7
therapists: anxieties 1–3; children's understanding of role of 62; collusion with the client 111, 154; containing role *see* containment; counter-transference *see* counter-transference; and the ending process *see* ending process; eschewing memory and desire 22; feedback *see* feedback; and gender 159–60; informing the child/young person about the first therapy session 134–5, 139; interpretation by *see* interpretation; interventions to manage behaviour in the session 166; managing expectations 58, 74–5, 117–18; managing self-destructive fantasies and behaviour 69; managing the therapeutic frame 82–4, 164–9; meeting and working with parents/carers 72, 113–23, 157–8; meetings with teachers and staff 124–30; negotiating space within the school 80–2 *see also* room allocation; and neutral space 68–9; observation by *see* observation; patience 17, 24–5, 26; promotion and nurturing of idea of therapy 55, 58, 95; receptiveness 37, 126; responding to offers of gifts or cards 167, 196–7; response of school community members to, according to personal associations 56–7; seeing themselves through the child's eye 26; self-observation *see* self-observation; sensitivity 38–40; stance 36, 68, 74, 109, 136–7; supervision *see* supervision; therapeutic relationship *see* therapeutic relationship; unobtrusiveness 39; working with teachers and staff 58, 72, 124–30, 170–86; working with the system 171–86; writing case notes 201–5
therapy: assessment for *see* assessment process; ending *see* ending process; evaluation *see* evaluation; evidence-based *see* evidence-based practice; first session *see* first session of therapy; monitoring *see* case notes;

reports; psychodynamic *see* psychodynamic therapy; referrals *see* referral process; school-based *see* school-based therapy; theoretical framework *see* psychoanalytic framework of therapy

therapy room: allocation *see* room allocation; effects on therapeutic relationship 56, 79; materials *see* materials; multi-use room 82; negotiating space within the school 80–2 *see also* room allocation; preventing/dealing with interruptions 82–4; resistance in 20–1 *see also* resistance; setting up the room 84–5; study questions 89; as a symbolic container 79; toys *see* toys; use of relationship in the room 12–13 *see also* therapeutic relationship

thinking: development of capacity to think 36; mentalisation 99, 110; morbid/suicidal 69, 105

Thomas, Madeleine 46

timetables of therapy sessions 84

toys 43, 85, 86, 87–8, 101, 117, 146, 147, 164; study questions 89; throwing of 33, 166

transference 28–31; and the ending process 190; and gender 160; negative 30–1, 114, 155, 156; observation of 40–1; of parents 114–15; and projection 13–14; shaped by way client is told about first meeting 139–40; study questions 33–5; understanding enactments 28–9

trauma, working with 23–4

trust 23

the unconscious: and early experience 9–12; impact in secondary schools of 68–9; psychodynamic perspective on 8–13; recognising unconscious dynamics in the room 12–13 *see also* counter-transference; transference; unconscious associations 2, 56–7, 58, 63, 188; unconscious envy 58; unconscious factors involved with a child coming on their own to therapy 142–3; unconscious fantasies 2, 53, 57, 63, 64, 65

urgent referrals 73–4

vulnerability: defences against 11; infantile 11–12; and learning 11–12; in the therapeutic relationship 22, 37

waiting lists 74

Winnicott, Donald W. 36, 38–9, 43–4, 47